PRAYERS
FOR MY BROTHERS
365 Devotionals for Men

TIM SHERRILL

WHAT PEOPLE ARE SAYING ABOUT THIS BOOK

In a world that constantly challenges men to find their purpose and their why, being grounded in the Word of God each day is a vital key to living up to their fullest potential as a person, regardless of age. This devotional will help you stand on the solid ground that the Word of God provides. Tim Sherrill offers a daily, biblical, and thought-provoking guide for you as husbands, fathers, and leaders. It will fuel your spiritual growth.

Here is a resource tool from God's Word that has been battle-tested to build your resiliency. If you have not discovered your "Why" and "Purpose," this devotional will set your compass to true north—to your creator.

-Katharina (Tina) Siemens
Author, historian, motivational speaker,
and owner of the West Texas Living Heritage Museum

As a pastor, I wrestle in prayer for men to walk with God. But no one wrestles harder for men than Tim Sherrill. I am always encouraged and challenged to deeper faithfulness when I am with Tim. Every morning for the past two years, I have had the privilege of reading his daily devotion, which you now hold in this book. Also, he lives every word he shares. Tim is the real deal and has consistently ministered to men in West Texas for many years. His messages are simple, straightforward, and clear, and men listen.

Tim is one of the first people I call when I have a prayer concern, so it is a great honor to endorse this book. It is a privilege to recommend this daily devotional from my dear friend. I believe that men who read this will hear a clear call to draw closer to Jesus. I am grateful that more men can now access these daily encouraging messages. It may well be the catalyst for that daily walk Tim, I, and many others wrestle for each morning.

Tommy Rosenblad
Pastor, First Baptist Church, Brownfield, TX

WHAT PEOPLE ARE SAYING ABOUT THIS BOOK

Tim Sherrill is not just my prayer warrior, but he's a great friend. These prayers and devotionals come morning by morning as he approaches the Throne to find mercy and grace for himself as well as for all of those God has placed in his path. I'm amazed that his daily messages align perfectly with my unspoken needs.

He makes sure his friends wake up to a fresh word from God to start their day. He often asks, "Are you okay?" Those three words force me to examine my heart before I answer. Tim has certainly found his calling, and everyone who reads these words will discover that God was thinking of them as he prayed and wrote them on Tim's heart—a man after God's own heart!

Dennis Adams
Pastor, Friendship Church, Lamesa, TX

I was so excited to hear of this project! Tim is the prayer warrior of prayer warriors. He is down-to-earth, straightforward, and tells it like it is. Tim teaches us through his prayers to love Jesus and to love people. He has prayed for me for years, and I am so grateful! I can always rely on him to have me covered in prayer no matter what. This devotional will draw you near the Father and near to the needs of others.

You'll relate to many of his life experiences. Some you will cry over, and some you will laugh at. But in all of them, you will see the grace of Jesus. I pray for your eyes to see and your ears to hear as you are led by this series of daily reflections on our most gracious and good Father.

Kalith Brown
Pastor

Tim is a dear friend to many. He is like a big brother to me, and he's a mighty prayer warrior for the kingdom. He has an enormous heart for people and for them to know the Lord more deeply. He particularly

WHAT PEOPLE ARE SAYING ABOUT THIS BOOK

desires the lost to come into a relationship with Jesus, their Savior. Tim uses this gift well in daily life and is now blessing others with this prayer devotional to guide us in honoring our big God with bold prayers of faith! This devotional will truly bless, challenge, and sharpen your faith and your prayer life. To God be the glory!

Stephanie McFadden
Touch of Grace Ministries

Tim's deep and devoted relationship with Jesus Christ and God the Father shines through every page of this devotional. For years, he has faithfully shared his heartfelt reflections and prayers with those in his circle, offering encouragement and spiritual insight. Now, through this book, his inspired words are available to bless a wider audience.

I've personally experienced the power of Tim's prayers and the guidance God has given him in every circumstance. My hope is that you, too, will be richly blessed by the wisdom and grace found within these pages.

Jeff Roper
Friend

THE LORD'S PRAYER

OUR FATHER,
WHICH ART IN HEAVEN,
HALLOWED BE THY NAME.
THY KINGDOM COME. THY WILL BE DONE,
IN EARTH, AS IT IS IN HEAVEN.
GIVE US THIS DAY OUR DAILY BREAD.
AND FORGIVE US OUR DEBTS,
AS WE FORGIVE OUR DEBTORS.
AND DO NOT LEAD US INTO TEMPTATION,
BUT DELIVER US FROM THE EVIL ONE.
FOR YOURS IS THE KINGDOM,
AND THE POWER, AND THE GLORY.
FOREVER. AMEN.

MATTHEW 6:9-13 NKJV

COPYRIGHT

Copyright © 2025 by **Tim Sherrill**
All rights reserved. No portion of this publication may be reproduced, stored in an electronic system, or transmitted in any form by any means, electronic, mechanical, photocopy, recording, or otherwise, without the author's prior permission, except with brief quotations used in literary reviews and specific non-commercial uses permitted by copyright law. For permission requests, please contact the publisher at info@harvestcreek.net.

The views expressed in this book are the author's and do not necessarily reflect those of the publisher.

Scriptures marked as "ESV" are taken from The ESV® Bible (The Holy Bible, English Standard Version®), © 2001 by Crossway, a publishing ministry of Good News Publishers. ESV Text Edition: 2025.

Scriptures marked as "MSG" are taken from The Message, Copyright © 1993, 2002, 2018 by Eugene H. Peterson.

Scriptures marked as "NIV are taken from the Holy Bible, New International Version®, NIV® Copyright ©1973, 1978, 1984, 2011 by Biblica, Inc.® Used by permission. All rights reserved worldwide.

Scripture references marked as "NKJV" are taken from the New King James Version®. Copyright © 1982 by Thomas Nelson. Used by permission. All rights reserved.

Scripture references marked as "NLT" are taken from the Holy Bible, New Living Translation, copyright © 1996, 2004, 2015 by Tyndale House Foundation. Used by permission of Tyndale House Publishers, Inc., Carol Stream, Illinois 60188. All rights reserved.

Cover and Interior Layout by 2025 Harvest Creek Publishing and Design, www.harvestcreek.net

Prayers for My Brothers—1st ed.

ISBN: 978-1-961641-43-3
Printed in the United States of America

DEDICATION

To Diane, my wife

The one who prays for me through all my struggles, and keeps me grounded in Jesus.

ACKNOWLEDGMENTS

To our Lord and Savior, who has allowed me to share a daily prayer with all of you, my brothers.

To my wife, Diane, who has never complained about my getting up early to send out prayer texts every morning, even while we are out of town on a quick getaway.

To all the men who have never complained about how early my texts come in the morning, and seem to be happy to receive them.

To my editor, Teresa, and her team, who understood my desires for this book and have been very professional and helpful in the process.

FOREWORD

It's typical for a Foreword to begin with someone introducing an author and stating their personal credentials to recommend "why" you should read a book. But the truth is, I am a regular guy who works to support his family, who lives life enjoying family and friends, and who strives to be Christ-like in my daily walk (with a great deal of stumbles and setbacks along the way). I'm not any more qualified than the next person you'll meet to pen a Foreword for an author. But I love God and His people, and I am growing in my love for all He created every day.

Tim and I first met while staffing a spiritual retreat for men. I couldn't help but notice that he was always praying for folks. He would listen to the men talk, regardless of whom they were speaking to, and when the chat seemed over, Tim would begin praying about the conversation's needs. Sometimes he would state that he wanted to pray, which was always met with a receptive "Yes."

At other times, he would simply start praying, which was met with folks bowing their heads and thanking him afterward. I felt Tim was a man looking to God for himself and for others, no matter how long he'd known them. Since then, Tim and I have worked at numerous spiritual retreats in various capacities. And I've seen how his passion for prayer is strong and heart-warming.

He was raised as a ranch-hand cowboy who took to rodeo life. A journey of poor decisions led him down a one-way street to emptiness and loneliness. When the Spirit of God caught his attention, Tim stopped traveling down that road, turned around, and started pursuing Jesus Christ. And it was with a passion and zeal—never forgetting where he had come from and always in appreciation for how Christ had set him free from his past.

FOREWORD

Throughout his life journey, Tim continues to grow in being a man of prayer. He will pray with anyone, anytime, and anywhere. He is unashamed to speak to God in prayer for those needing healing or blessings. In short, Tim is a man of God who almost constantly speaks with Christ and listens for his voice.

The book contains daily devotions that Tim originally distributed daily, even on holidays, to a couple of hundred of his personal acquaintances. The devotions are scriptures that the Lord brought to Tim's mind. Tim then offers brief reflections on the scripture's personal significance to provide context and food for thought. A brief prayer always follows his teaching.

These were not written by a theologian, biblical scholar, or pulpit pastor/preacher. These devotions are from an everyday, blue-collar cowboy and man of God who genuinely cares about the folks receiving them. The format is not necessarily the same for all devotions. They're not lengthy; most are fairly short. These teachings are like the thoughts that might come to mind as you watch the sunrise come up over a West Texas horizon or when seeing a thunderstorm roll over the countryside. They remind you of the majesty of the Creator Himself!

Tim is big on listening to God, and he tries his darndest to do what the Lord is moving him to do. Why should you read this book? Well, I'm not sure there's a good answer to that question. But here is why *I* read the daily devotions that Tim sends to me—because Tim loves the Lord and he loves me!

If you're looking for a teacher who is authentic and doesn't care about being perfect or using fancy language, Tim is the guy! His devotions are heartfelt, and he has walked through rain, fire, and sunshine! His teachings are from a man who will pray

FOREWORD

for you at the drop of a hat and continue to do so as long as you need or want.

Everyone wants to learn from genuine folks who are transparent and real. In my life, Tim is that person. His genuineness and love for the Lord are expressed through his prayers for everyone he meets. Be blessed as you read this book, and know that Tim is praying for every reader.

May God bless you and yours,
Greg Holt

Do not be afraid to face the new year! It has many promises for you. Trust God and everything will be fine!

JANUARY – DAILY DEVOTIONAL #1

Therefore, if anyone is in Christ, the new creation has come: The old has gone, the new is here!

2 CORINTHIANS 5:17 NIV

REFLECTIONS:

When you accept Jesus as your Lord and Savior, you are forgiven and made new. So, when the enemy comes and tries to trip you up or throws your past in your face, remember you left that at the feet of Jesus, and no one can make you pick it back up or hold it against you. You are a blood-bought child of the King, forgiven and restored to who he made you to be. Continue to press on towards Jesus, allowing him to use you in mighty ways.

REQUESTS:

Lord, just as we are made new in Christ—and the old is gone, and your mercies are made new each morning—Lord, may the New Year be truly new in you. May the old from last year be gone, and may you bless these men and their families with all that they need to walk in your peace and presence as you make all things new. Lord, may there be more victories than struggles for them in the New Year.

Lord, we love you and thank you for answering our prayers.
In Jesus' name. AMEN

JANUARY – DAILY DEVOTIONAL #2

. . . you who call yourselves citizens of the holy city and claim to rely on the God of Israel—the LORD Almighty is his name: I foretold the former things long ago, my mouth announced them and I made them known; then suddenly I acted, and they came to pass. For I knew how stubborn you were . . . Therefore, I told you these things long ago; before they happened, I announced them to you so that you could not say, 'My images brought them about; my wooden image and metal god ordained them.' You have heard these things; look at them all. Will you not admit them? **"From now on I will tell you of new things, of hidden things unknown to you...."**

ISAIAH 48:2-6 NIV

REFLECTIONS:

Looking back at the accomplishments I thought I had achieved on my own, I now realize how God's hand was all over them. During my worst mistakes, I didn't talk my way out of trouble; God provided the way out. From the home I live in to the truck I drive, I didn't earn them, and I don't deserve them. Just as all coaches say there is no "I" in "team," there is certainly no "I" in "God."

REQUESTS:

Lord, may we yield more of ourselves to your will. Like a river, if we try to fight the current, that usually means we are trying to do what we want. Help us see the flow of your will. We may still stumble and fall, but we will be headed in the right direction when we stand up. Bless these men today with forgiveness and godly achievements.

Lord, we love you and thank you for answering our prayers.
In Jesus' name. AMEN

JANUARY – DAILY DEVOTIONAL #3

Finally, brothers and sisters, rejoice! Strive for full restoration, encourage one another, be of one mind, live in peace. And the God of love and peace will be with you.

2 CORINTHIANS 13:11 NIV

REFLECTIONS:

God is the God of restoration. He sent his son to the cross so that we could have a relationship with him through the shedding of the blood of Jesus. So, if you have a friend or a family member you have become distant from or you have separated yourself from them, begin to pray, asking God to restore the relationship and to show you what you need to do to make things right.

Remember, the prodigal son had to get up and walk back home. The crazy thing is, God restored the father-son relationship before he ever made it to the house. Maybe restoration comes when we begin walking towards it and not tiptoeing around the problem.

REQUESTS:

Lord, every family and every church has those who do not see eye to eye. As the sun rises on a new day, I ask you to begin to restore relationships in families and in our churches. Lord, may you never leave our side. This year, Lord, may we be more aware and attentive to your presence and peace all around us.

Lord, we love you and thank you for answering our prayers.
In Jesus' name. AMEN

JANUARY - DAILY DEVOTIONAL #4

"As the Father has loved me, so have I loved you. Now remain in my love. If you keep my commands, you will remain in my love, just as I have kept my Father's commands and remain in his love. I have told you this so that my joy may be in you and that your joy may be complete. My command is this: Love each other as I have loved you. Greater love has no one than this: to lay down one's life for one's friends. You are my friends if you do what I command. I no longer call you servants, because a servant does not know his master's business. Instead, I have called you friends, for everything that I learned from my Father I have made known to you. You did not choose me, but I chose you and appointed you so that you might go and bear fruit—fruit that will last—and so that whatever you ask in my name the Father will give you. This is my command: Love each other. . . . "

JOHN 15:9-17 NIV

REFLECTIONS:

You may not have been called to be a missionary overseas, but you are called to be in the mission field. Stop and consider the places that are a mission field: your workplace, where you shop, where you go out to eat, or the primary place—your very own neighborhood. So go love someone today, however the Lord leads you.

REQUESTS:

Lord, today as we go through our duties of the day, may we see those that we see every day the way you see them. Instead of a head nod or just a smile as we pass by, help us see them as a friend in need and love them as you do us. Lord, bless each one of these men today with your love and peace.

Lord, we love you and thank you for answering our prayers.
In Jesus' name. AMEN

JANUARY – DAILY DEVOTIONAL #5

"When you enter the land of Canaan, which I am giving you as your possession, and I put a spreading mold in a house in that land, the owner of the house must go and tell the priest, 'I have seen something that looks like a defiling mold in my house.'. . ."

LEVITICUS 14:34-35 NIV

REFLECTIONS:

God is saying to us today, "I have brought you to salvation through the death and resurrection of my Son, Jesus." So, if you see sin in your heart, you must come to the High Priest, Jesus, and confess it, and be forgiven. Yes, when you asked Jesus to come into your heart, he gave you a new heart. You were forgiven of all your sins.

However, confessing your sins daily keeps us in a steady, constant relationship with him. If you let sin go unconfessed, eventually, you will be further away from the Lord than you've ever been. Still, he is faithful and just, and will restore you when you confess those sins.

REQUESTS:

Lord, give us eyes to see the sin in our hearts that is keeping us from fully and completely walking with you in peace. Lord, bless each of these men and their families as they go about their day, whether in fellowship with others or worshiping you. May your words come to mind; build them up in their faith in you.

Lord, we love you and thank you for answering our prayers. In Jesus' name. AMEN

JANUARY – DAILY DEVOTIONAL #6

For we are to God the pleasing aroma of Christ among those who are being saved and those who are perishing. To the one we are an aroma that brings death; to the other, an aroma that brings life. And who is equal to such a task? Unlike so many, we do not peddle the word of God for profit. On the contrary, in Christ we speak before God with sincerity, as those sent from God.

2 CORINTHIANS 2:15-17 NIV

REFLECTIONS:

Whether you're in the pulpit, witnessing on the street, or in your prayer room by yourself, handle the Word of God as life or death. So many people use the Word of God as a feel-good sermon or witness. They think, *give to the church and God will prosper you, no matter how you live.* I'm sure you've seen this repeatedly. But one day, those who handle God's Word in such a way will be held accountable for the blood on their hands.

So, go out and share the love of Jesus. Share how he has changed you from being who you once were to who you are now—a new creation with Jesus in your heart.

REQUESTS:

Lord, may we always speak the truth of your Word—it's either life or death. Lord, bless these men and their families with your peace and presence throughout their homes. Lord, may we always seek to be more like Jesus in our daily walk with you.

Lord, we love you and thank you for answering our prayers.
In Jesus' name. AMEN

JANUARY – DAILY DEVOTIONAL #7

Therefore, I urge you, brothers and sisters, in view of God's mercy, to offer your bodies as a living sacrifice, holy and pleasing to God—this is your true and proper worship. Do not conform to the pattern of this world, but be transformed by the renewing of your mind. Then you will be able to test and approve what God's will is—his good, pleasing, and perfect will.

ROMANS 12:1-2 NIV

REFLECTIONS:

How do you do that? Well, for me, it means beginning each day with prayer and acknowledging that I cannot do anything without the Lord leading me. I try to be prepared for him to use me by reading the Word and seeking his wisdom and his will.

The most important thing to do is to learn to listen, and I'm not very good at that. To learn to listen—not just hear—but to *listen carefully*, one must grasp every word. The words must move you. For instance, in football, you may have a pass thrown to you, but if you don't grasp it or catch it, you're not going anywhere.

REQUESTS:

Lord, give us ears to hear and eyes to see your will. But also give us a heart to grasp what we are hearing and seeing, so we may be changed and used for your perfect will. Bless these men and their families with your goodness.

Lord, we love you and thank you for answering our prayers.
In Jesus' name. AMEN

JANUARY – DAILY DEVOTIONAL #8

The Spirit of the Lord GOD is upon me, because the LORD has anointed me to bring good news to the poor; he has sent me to bind up the brokenhearted, to proclaim liberty to the captives, and the opening of the prison to those who are bound; to proclaim the year of the LORD's favor, and the day of vengeance of our God; to comfort all who mourn . . . to give them a beautiful headdress instead of ashes, the oil of gladness instead of mourning . . ..

ISAIAH 61:1-3a ESV

REFLECTIONS:

If you have ever wondered about your purpose as a Christian, here it is: You, sir, can reach people others can't. You may never stand up in a church behind the pulpit and preach, but your pulpit is in your neighborhood, your job, or it could even be your local grocery store.

We think it's all up to the preachers or pastors to do that job. Well, that's a bold-faced lie from the enemy. You are a child of the Most High God and a joint heir to the King, so tell somebody! Be a part of the adoption process for the kingdom of God.

REQUESTS:

Lord, today let us cross paths with at least one person we can pray with and tell of your goodness. Bless these men and their families with warmth. Fill their homes with your peace and your presence.

Lord, we love you and thank you for answering our prayers.
In Jesus' name. AMEN

JANUARY - DAILY DEVOTIONAL #9

Carry each other's burdens, and in this way you will fulfill the law of Christ. If anyone thinks they are something when they are not, they deceive themselves. Each one should test their own actions. Then they can take pride in themselves alone, without comparing themselves to someone else, for each one should carry their own load.

GALATIANS 6:2-5 NIV

REFLECTIONS:

The next time you look at someone who is standing on the corner with a "Need Help" sign, don't think you are better than them. I know some are scam artists. But here's the problem: What burdens in life brought them to that point? Did anyone try to help carry their burden, or did everyone think they were too good to help?

REQUESTS:

Lord, give us eyes to see people and love people right where they are, just the way you do. Thank you for those who have helped us and continue to support us through our burdens. Bless these men with your presence and peace, filling their homes with your glory. Bring healing to everyone in their homes who may be sick.

Lord, we love you and thank you for answering our prayers.
In Jesus' name. AMEN

JANUARY – DAILY DEVOTIONAL #10

Then the LORD said to Moses, "Go to Pharaoh and say to him, 'This is what the LORD, the God of the Hebrews, says: "Let my people go, so that they may worship me."

EXODUS 9:1 NIV

REFLECTIONS:

In the book of Exodus, from chapters seven to ten, God told Pharaoh, "Let my people go," so they could go and worship. In this passage today, I believe God is saying, "My people, let the world go, and come walk and fellowship with me."

This isn't just about those who are lost; it's more about you and me. Have we truly given the Lord our desires in exchange for what he desires for us?

REQUESTS:

Lord, we ask you to help us day by day to seek more and more of your desire for our lives. We pray for the wisdom to know the difference between your desires for us and our desires. Please give us your wisdom as we serve you. Watch over these men and their families; heal those who are sick. Fill their homes with your peace and presence.

Lord, we love you and thank you for answering our prayers.
In Jesus' name. AMEN

JANUARY – DAILY DEVOTIONAL #11

"... If anyone is ashamed of me and my words in this adulterous and sinful generation, the Son of Man will be ashamed of them when he comes in his Father's glory with the holy angels."

MARK 8:38 NIV

Therefore, there is now no condemnation for those who are in Christ Jesus, because through Christ Jesus the law of the Spirit who gives life has set you free from the law of sin and death. . . . What, then, shall we say in response to these things? If God is for us, who can be against us?

ROMANS 8:1-2; 31 NIV

REFLECTIONS:

The world may frown at your past, but you, sir, are a child of the King of kings, bought with the blood of Jesus. So if the Father isn't ashamed of you and your past, then you, as a child of the King, do not need to be embarrassed.

REQUESTS:

Lord bless these men with the confidence that comes with being your children. Not with an arrogant confidence, but with one that says, "Yes, I have a past, but let me tell you about my Jesus!" Lord, bless these men and their families with peace and fill their homes with your presence, bringing them all that they need.

Lord, we love you and thank you for answering our prayers.
In Jesus' name. AMEN

JANUARY – DAILY DEVOTIONAL #12

Now faith is confidence in what we hope for and assurance about what we do not see.

HEBREWS 11:1 NIV

REFLECTIONS:

Have you ever been asked how confident you are in your ability to do something? For example, taking an exam at school, or winning a game you're about to play? We show confidence when we get into our car without hesitation or doubt. So, here's the real question: Does the world see our confidence and trust in the Lord?

REQUESTS:

Lord, may the way we carry ourselves and walk through our day show the confidence we have in you. You are more faithful than anyone this world has known. Bless these men with your presence and peace. Lord, may your light shine through them.

Lord, we love you and thank you for answering our prayers. In Jesus' name. AMEN

JANUARY – DAILY DEVOTIONAL #13

Do not be misled: "Bad company corrupts good character." Come back to your senses as you ought, and stop sinning; for there are some who are ignorant of God—I say this to your shame.

1 CORINTHIANS 15:33-34 NIV

REFLECTIONS:

Years ago, when I first read this scripture, I took a deep look at my friends. I realized that it's not just about friends. Our jobs and churches can also corrupt our morals. Are you associating with people who corrupt your godly convictions? Are you influencing their lives for the better? Or are they negatively influencing yours?

REQUESTS:

Lord, may you guide us away from those who influence us to have poor character. May we own up to our mistakes, and may we show the character of Christ in our lives. Lord, I ask you to continue to bless these men with your peace and presence, wherever they go.

Lord, we love you and thank you for answering our prayers. In Jesus' name. AMEN

JANUARY – DAILY DEVOTIONAL #14

What is more, I consider everything a loss because of the surpassing worth of knowing Christ Jesus my Lord, for whose sake I have lost all things. I consider them garbage, that I may gain Christ and be found in him, not having a righteousness of my own that comes from the law, but that which is through faith in Christ . . . I want to know Christ—yes, to know the power of his resurrection and participation in his sufferings, becoming like him in his death, and so, somehow, attaining to the resurrection from the dead. Not that I have already obtained all this, . . . but I press on to take hold of that for which Christ Jesus took hold of me. . . . Forgetting what is behind and straining toward what is ahead, I press on toward the goal to win the prize for which God has called me heavenward in Christ Jesus.

PHILIPPIANS 3:8-14 NIV

REFLECTIONS:

What is it to gain the whole world and lose my soul? No matter what your house looks like or the car you own (or maybe you don't have either), your mindset should be: "Money or gold, I do not have to share. But what I have to share is Jesus, the one who provides all that I need."

REQUESTS:

Lord, you know each of these men's situations, so I ask you to help each of them with all that they need. Bless them beyond measure, filling their homes with your peace and presence, and guiding them to all that you have for them.

Lord, we love you and thank you for answering our prayers.
In Jesus' name. AMEN

JANUARY – DAILY DEVOTIONAL #15

And now, Israel, what does the LORD your God ask of you but to fear the LORD your God, to walk in obedience to him, to love him, to serve the LORD your God with all your heart and with all your soul, and to observe the LORD's commands and decrees that I am giving you today for your own good?

DEUTERONOMY 10:12-13 NIV

REFLECTIONS:

Are you starting your day seeking Jesus, the one who directs our steps in the way we should go? Or are you worried about what has to be done and hoping he comes with you?

You may not understand it, but you'll get more accomplished if you start your day focused on him who gave you breath today.

REQUESTS:

Lord, bless these men with eyes to see you and ears to hear you. May they walk in your peace as you direct their steps through the day, for today may be the only one they have left. Why not spend it with you? Lord, fill their homes with your presence and peace.

Lord, we love you and thank you for answering our prayers.
In Jesus' name. AMEN

JANUARY – DAILY DEVOTIONAL #16

"But if you can do anything, take pity on us and help us." "'If you can'?" said Jesus. "Everything is possible for one who believes." Immediately the boy's father exclaimed, "I do believe; help me overcome my unbelief!"

MARK 9:22B-24 NIV

"But if You can do anything, have compassion on us and help us." Jesus said to him, "If you can believe, all things *are* possible to him who believes." Immediately the father of the child cried out and said with tears, "Lord, I believe; help my unbelief!"

MARK 9:22B-24 NKJV

REFLECTIONS:

Have you ever said, "Lord, I don't know if you can, but if you can, would you?" I've prayed that prayer many times. And I'm reminded each time that all things are possible with Jesus. But, ultimately, it's his will that must be done.

REQUESTS:

Lord, just as this man said, "Help us with our unbelief," may there be no doubt in us that you can change any situation for our good, according to your will. Help us see your goodness when what we think you should do for us isn't what happens. Bless these men with your peace and presence in their homes and their jobs!

Lord, we love you and thank you for answering our prayers.
In Jesus' name. AMEN

JANUARY – DAILY DEVOTIONAL #17

. . . I am not writing you a new command but one we have had from the beginning. I ask that we love one another. And this is love: that we walk in obedience to his commands . . . I say this because many deceivers, who do not acknowledge Jesus Christ as coming in the flesh, have gone out into the world. Any such person is the deceiver and the antichrist. Watch out that you do not lose what we have worked for, but that you may be rewarded fully. Anyone who runs ahead and does not continue in the teaching of Christ does not have God; whoever continues in the teaching has both the Father and the Son. If anyone comes to you and does not bring this teaching, do not take them into your house or welcome them. Anyone who welcomes them shares in their wicked work.

2 JOHN 1:5B-11 NIV

REFLECTIONS:

Jesus died on the cross and rose again so we could have eternal life, but also a relationship with him and the Father. It's so important that we walk with them, allowing the Father and the Son to guide us in the way we should go. So don't let an unbeliever lead you ahead of his will, interrupting your relationship with the Father and the Son.

REQUESTS:

Lord, bless these men with a deep desire to be in your presence daily. When they stumble, I know you are faithful and just, to pick them up and dust them off so they can keep walking with you. Lord, surround these men with like-minded brothers, so they can continue in your teaching together.

Lord, we love you and thank you for answering our prayers.
In Jesus' name. AMEN

JANUARY – DAILY DEVOTIONAL #18

Then he returned to his disciples and found them sleeping. "Simon," he said to Peter, "are you asleep? Couldn't you keep watch for one hour? Watch and pray so that you will not fall into temptation. The spirit is willing, but the flesh is weak." Once more he went away and prayed the same thing. When he came back, he again found them sleeping, because their eyes were heavy. They did not know what to say to him. Returning the third time, he said to them, "Are you still sleeping and resting? Enough! The hour has come. Look, the Son of Man is delivered into the hands of sinners. Rise! Let us go! Here comes my betrayer!"

MARK 14:37-42 NIV

REFLECTIONS:

Will Jesus find you asleep when he comes back to take us home to Glory? You may think he won't return in your lifetime. And you may believe this: "I've got my insurance papers through the Cross Insurance Company, so I'm good."

Jesus went to the cross for a relationship with you—to walk with you daily, moment by moment—not to sit and watch you waste the life you've been blessed with. So, wake up and seek him, hear him, and follow him.

REQUESTS:

Lord, bless us with eyes to see and ears to hear you so we may grow in you as we seek you. Guide us in the way we should go. Bless these men today with your peace and presence all around them. May they know they are standing on holy ground.

Lord, we love you and thank you for answering our prayers.
In Jesus' name. AMEN

JANUARY – DAILY DEVOTIONAL #19

Remember this: Whoever sows sparingly will also reap sparingly, and whoever sows generously will also reap generously. Each of you should give what you have decided in your heart to give, not reluctantly or under compulsion, for God loves a cheerful giver. And God is able to bless you abundantly, so that in all things at all times, having all that you need, you will abound in every good work. As it is written: "They have freely scattered their gifts to the poor; their righteousness endures forever."

2 CORINTHIANS 9:6-9 NIV

REFLECTIONS:

This affects both the spiritual and physical aspects of life. If you work sparingly, you get paid sparingly, and if you share Jesus sparingly, you save lives sparingly. We don't work for blessings, but when you work hard, blessings come. So get to work!

REQUESTS:

Lord, bless all of us with a drive to seek where we can be used in your kingdom to share the gospel of Jesus Christ. May we have willing hearts to do the work you have prepared for us to do. Bless these men with eyes to see and ears to hear from you.

Lord, we love you and thank you for answering our prayers.
In Jesus' name. AMEN

JANUARY – DAILY DEVOTIONAL #20

... sorrowful, yet always rejoicing; poor, yet making many rich; having nothing, and yet possessing everything.

2 CORINTHIANS 6:10 NIV

REFLECTIONS:

This scripture teaches us why we can say, "Riches and gold I do not have, but what I have brings eternal life." If you have Jesus in your heart, you are a child of the King!

REQUESTS:

Lord, I ask you to open our eyes to see what it truly means to be a kingdom child, bought and paid for by the blood of Jesus. Lord, I ask you to fill these men's homes with your presence and peace, protecting them from all harm.

Lord, we love you and thank you for answering our prayers.
In Jesus' name. AMEN

JANUARY – DAILY DEVOTIONAL #21

For though we live in the world, we do not wage war as the world does. The weapons we fight with are not the weapons of the world. On the contrary, they have divine power to demolish strongholds. We demolish arguments and every pretension that sets itself up against the knowledge of God, and we take captive every thought to make it obedient to Christ.

2 CORINTHIANS 10:3-5 NIV

REFLECTIONS:

We have this power only on our knees in prayer. Sometimes you may not be able to get on your knees physically. But being on your knees before God the Father may simply mean coming with a humble heart.

REQUESTS:

Lord, we do come with humble hearts, asking that your power breaks down every stronghold coming against these men and their families. May you cover their homes with the blood of Jesus, protecting them from the one who comes to kill, steal, and destroy. Lord, we love you and thank you that we are more than conquerors in Jesus. May your peace and presence lead us through this day.

Lord, we love you and thank you for answering our prayers.
In Jesus' name. AMEN

JANUARY – DAILY DEVOTIONAL #22

In other words, it is not the children by physical descent who are God's children, but it is the children of the promise who are regarded as Abraham's offspring.

ROMANS 9:8 NIV

REFLECTIONS:

The depth of this statement is far more than our minds can comprehend. Basically, it means this: It doesn't matter whether your physical dad is rich, poor, or somewhere in the middle. You can only be a Child of God through Jesus, our Lord. Abraham's earthly dad was an idol worshiper, but Abraham's Father was God.

REQUESTS:

Lord, may this truth get into the depths of our hearts, helping us look beyond our physical selves and dig deeper into who we are in Christ Jesus. Lord, we claim every part of Abraham's blessing. We thank you that we are children of the promise and counted as Abraham's offspring. May we become men of faith, just as he was.

Lord, we love you and thank you for answering our prayers.
In Jesus' name. AMEN

JANUARY – DAILY DEVOTIONAL #23

For Christ did not enter a sanctuary made with human hands that was only a copy of the true one; he entered heaven itself, now to appear for us in God's presence.

HEBREWS 9:24 NIV

REFLECTIONS:

Have you ever wondered what it's going to be like to be in God's presence in the middle of his sanctuary? Do you have a yearning to be in his holy presence?

REQUESTS:

Lord, I ask you to give us a heart to persevere after your presence in our homes and everywhere we go. I know we can't see you with our eyes until we get to heaven, but give our hearts eyes to see you. Lord, bless each of these men with a yearning to be in your presence constantly.

Lord, we love you and thank you for answering our prayers. In Jesus' name. AMEN

JANUARY – DAILY DEVOTIONAL #24

Consider it pure joy, my brothers and sisters, whenever you face trials of many kinds, because you know that the testing of your faith produces perseverance. Let perseverance finish its work so that you may be mature and complete, not lacking anything.

JAMES 1:2-4 NIV

REFLECTIONS:

As we approach our trials, always remember Jesus is with us to help us and to lean on so we may grow in faith and in wisdom. May his good work be completed in us.

REQUESTS:

Lord, teach us in our pain and struggles that we can still find joy in the fact that we are going to get through our situation. Even if it does seem like it, you are with us. Lord, even in our weakness and fears, may you be glorified. Bless each one of these men with your presence and your goodness.

Lord, we love you and thank you for answering our prayers.
In Jesus' name. AMEN

JANUARY – DAILY DEVOTIONAL #25

Don't grumble against one another, brothers and sisters, or you will be judged. The Judge is standing at the door! Brothers and sisters, as an example of patience in the face of suffering, take the prophets who spoke in the name of the Lord. As you know, we count as blessed those who have persevered. You have heard of Job's perseverance and have seen what the Lord finally brought about. The Lord is full of compassion and mercy.

JAMES 5:9-11 NIV

REFLECTIONS:

Persevering after the things of this world only leaves us empty and wandering around like a lost puppy. Yet, persevering towards Jesus even through rough waters brings heavenly blessings beyond what our minds can fathom.

REQUESTS:

Lord, may our eyes stay focused on the goal we are persevering towards, which is to be in your presence. We desire to walk in your love no matter what, so on the day we pass from this world, we are in your presence in heaven.

Lord, we love you and thank you for answering our prayers.
In Jesus' name. AMEN

JANUARY - DAILY DEVOTIONAL #26

The LORD is my shepherd, I lack nothing. He makes me lie down in green pastures, he leads me beside quiet waters, he refreshes my soul. He guides me along the right paths for his name's sake. Even though I walk through the darkest valley, I will fear no evil, for you are with me; your rod and your staff, they comfort me.

PSALM 23:1-4 NIV

REFLECTIONS:

I believe that as we stay focused and in the will of God, we will all walk out these verses from Psalm 23.

REQUESTS:

Lord, I ask you to protect these men from the attacks of the enemy. Thank you for your anointing, which we pray will be prevalent in their lives. Let others' lives be touched and changed as a result. Lord, fill each home with your peace and presence, blessing each family beyond measure.

Lord, we love you and thank you for answering our prayers. In Jesus' name. AMEN

JANUARY – DAILY DEVOTIONAL #27

Moses answered, "What if they do not believe me or listen to me and say, 'The LORD did not appear to you'?" Then the Lord said to him, "What is that in your hand?" "A staff," he replied. The LORD said, "Throw it on the ground." Moses threw it on the ground and it became a snake, and he ran from it. Then the LORD said to him, "Reach out your hand and take it by the tail." So Moses reached out and took hold of the snake, and it turned back into a staff in his hand. "This," said the LORD, "is so that they may believe that the LORD, the God of their fathers—the God of Abraham, the God of Isaac and the God of Jacob—has appeared to you."

EXODUS 4:1-5 NIV

REFLECTIONS:

Have you ever wondered what it is going to take for the person you have been witnessing to for days, months, or even years to come to know Jesus? Or better yet, what is it going to take for you to believe God with every part of your being for their salvation?

REQUESTS:

Lord, today we lift up those who have yet to come to know Jesus as their Lord and Savior. I ask you, whatever it takes, bring them to Christ. Also, help us completely trust you as we go where you're calling us. Help us turn it all over to you. Lord, bless these men and their families with your peace and presence in their homes.

Lord, we love you and thank you for answering our prayers.
In Jesus' name. AMEN

JANUARY – DAILY DEVOTIONAL #28

". . . But about the resurrection of the dead—have you not read what God said to you, 'I am the God of Abraham, the God of Isaac, and the God of Jacob'? He is not the God of the dead but of the living."

MATTHEW 22:31-32 NIV

REFLECTIONS:

This Scripture is still growing to include the names of all who come to God. Can you truly read it as "I am the God of [Add Your Name]?" I read it as, "I am the GOD of Timothy."

REQUESTS:

Lord, give these men confidence in their relationship with you to say, "Yes, he is my God, and I am his child—bought and paid for by the blood of Jesus!" Bless these men and their families with your peace and presence in their homes.

Lord, we love you and thank you for answering our prayers.
In Jesus' name. AMEN

JANUARY – DAILY DEVOTIONAL #29

"... Therefore go and make disciples of all nations, baptizing them in the name of the Father and of the Son and of the Holy Spirit, and teaching them to obey everything I have commanded you. And surely I am with you always, to the very end of the age."

MATTHEW 28:19-20 NIV

REFLECTIONS:

Have you ever thought about sharing your faith with someone in the grocery store? Or maybe witnessing to the person you stop to help or the person who stops to help you? More often than not, many encounters are divine appointments, both for them and for us.

REQUESTS:

Lord, every time we leave our homes, give us eyes to see and ears to hear you so that we do not miss a divine opportunity to witness to someone about Jesus. Lord, fill these men's homes with your peace and presence.

Lord, we love you and thank you for answering our prayers.
In Jesus' name. AMEN

JANUARY – DAILY DEVOTIONAL #30

But if I say, "I will not mention his word or speak anymore in his name," his word is in my heart like a fire, a fire shut up in my bones. I am weary of holding it in; indeed, I cannot. I hear many whispering, "Terror on every side! Denounce him! Let's denounce him!" All my friends are waiting for me to slip, saying, "Perhaps he will be deceived; then we will prevail over him and take our revenge on him." But the LORD is with me like a mighty warrior; so my persecutors will stumble and not prevail. They will fail and be thoroughly disgraced; their dishonor will never be forgotten.

JEREMIAH 20:9-11 NIV

REFLECTIONS:

No matter what you're facing, let the fire of God that's within you come out and watch your enemies flee. Stand on the foundation of the Word and let your Jesus shine.

REQUESTS:

Lord, let us not hold back with the fire that's within us. May your anointing not fall on deaf ears, but let it fall on hearts that you have prepared to hear and receive your forgiveness. Let these changed hearts live a life persevering after Jesus until the day they are called home. Lord, may each of us pour out Jesus to those you send our way through your divine appointments.

Lord, we love you and thank you for answering our prayers.
In Jesus' name. AMEN

JANUARY – DAILY DEVOTIONAL #31

I write these things . . . so that you may know that you have eternal life. This is the confidence we have in approaching God: that if we ask anything according to his will, he hears us. And if we know that he hears us—whatever we ask—we know that we have what we asked of him. If you see any brother or sister commit a sin that does not lead to death, you should pray and God will give them life. . . . We know that anyone born of God does not continue to sin; the One who was born of God keeps them safe, and the evil one cannot harm them. We know that we are children of God, and that the whole world is under the control of the evil one. . . . And we are in him who is true by being in his Son Jesus Christ. He is the true God and eternal life. Dear children, keep yourselves from idols.

1 JOHN 5:13-16, 18-21 NIV

REFLECTIONS:

This passage gives us hope and confidence. If we are in Christ and he is in us, we are taken care of and our prayers are answered according to his will. But if we look at how the passage ends, it's saying that if you receive all this from your father, then keep yourself from idols. Anything that interrupts your confidence or takes precedence over spending time with the Lord is probably an idol.

REQUESTS:

Lord, show us what our idols are. It's too easy for us to say, "I didn't do that" or "I don't even like that." So Lord, give us eyes to see what interrupts or takes precedence over time with you. Bless these men with a heart that chases after you and your will for them and their families. Blanket them with your peace and fill their homes with your presence.

Lord, we love you and thank you for answering our prayers.
In Jesus' name. AMEN

God is the only one who makes the valley of trouble a door of hope.

Catherine Marshall

FEBRUARY - DAILY DEVOTIONAL #1

Blessed is the one who trusts in the LORD, who does not look to the proud, to those who turn aside to false gods. Many, LORD my God, are the wonders you have done, the things you planned for us. None can compare with you; were I to speak and tell of your deeds, they would be too many to declare.

PSALM 40:4-5 NIV

REFLECTIONS:

When the sun rises in the morning, we should be joyful. The Lord has given us another day, not to speak of ourselves, but to tell of his glorious riches and to share the love of Jesus.

REQUESTS:

Lord, I ask you to bless these men and their families, no matter what their struggles are. Bless them with your peace and fill their homes with your presence. Bless them, Lord, with all they need. Fill their hearts with your overwhelming joy.

Lord, we love you and thank you for answering our prayers.
In Jesus' name. AMEN

FEBRUARY - DAILY DEVOTIONAL #2

Again I looked and saw all the oppression that was taking place under the sun: I saw the tears of the oppressed—and they have no comforter; power was on the side of their oppressors—and they have no comforter. And I declared that the dead, who had already died, are happier than the living, who are still alive. But better than both is the one who has never been born, who has not seen the evil that is done under the sun. And I saw that all toil and all achievement spring from one person's envy of another. This too is meaningless, a chasing after the wind. Fools fold their hands and ruin themselves. Better one handful with tranquility than two handfuls with toil and chasing after the wind.

ECCLESIASTES 4:1-6 NIV

REFLECTIONS:

If you look around, you see this discomfort and unhappiness in the world. That's why it's so important to be the light of Jesus in this dark world!

REQUESTS:

Lord, may we set our hearts and minds on Jesus and share his love. Lord, this old world may knock us down, but you are always faithful in picking us back up and comforting us in our time of need. Bless these men today with the hope and peace they need to get through whatever they are facing today. May they see and feel your presence so they know they're not alone.

Lord, we love you and thank you for answering our prayers.
In Jesus' name. AMEN

FEBRUARY - DAILY DEVOTIONAL #3

Elijah was a human being, even as we are. He prayed earnestly that it would not rain, and it did not rain on the land for three and a half years. Again he prayed, and the heavens gave rain, and the earth produced its crops.

JAMES 5:16-18 NIV

REFLECTIONS:

Isn't it crazy how Elijah prayed earnestly, and it didn't rain for three and a half years? And then he prayed, and the earth produced a crop—a physical crop. Then Jesus came along and ministered and prayed for three and a half years, and his rain is still producing crops.

REQUESTS:

Lord, give us a vision and a heart to pray for and chase after, the spiritual harvest Jesus has sown and prepared for us to reap. Use us to continue sowing and watering the spiritual seeds that are being planted, as well as those that have already been planted. Protect these men and their families, keeping them warm and safe.

Lord, we love you and thank you for answering our prayers.
In Jesus' name. AMEN

FEBRUARY - DAILY DEVOTIONAL #4

The Pharisees challenged him, "Here you are, appearing as your own witness; your testimony is not valid." Jesus answered, "Even if I testify on my own behalf, my testimony is valid, for I know where I came from and where I am going. But you have no idea where I come from or where I am going. You judge by human standards; I pass judgment on no one.

JOHN 8:13-15 NIV

REFLECTIONS:

Is your testimony validated in Jesus? I know you know where you came from, but do you know where you're going?

REQUESTS:

Lord, when we share parts of our testimony, may they always conclude with a "but God" moment: "Yes, I did those things, but God delivered me despite myself." May our testimonies always finish by pointing to Christ, our Lord and Savior. Lord, may we see opportunities to share your glory with others. Bless these men with your peace and presence throughout their day.

Lord, we love you and thank you for answering our prayers.
In Jesus' name. AMEN

FEBRUARY - DAILY DEVOTIONAL #5

Trust in the LORD with all your heart and lean not on your own understanding; In all your ways submit to him, and he will make your paths straight.

PROVERBS 3:5-6 NIV

REFLECTIONS:

New cars come with some cool features. Some models come with a button that keeps the vehicle in its lane, but eventually, it'll prompt you to take control. Then some cars are self-driving—we all think that would be cool. You put your destination into the navigation system, and it'll drive you there. We're relying on a man-made vehicle to get us where we want to go.

However, do we struggle to commit to seeking Jesus to direct our paths for our day-to-day walk with him so that we may be his light in this dark world?

REQUESTS:

Lord, bless us with a deep desire and hunger for your direction and your Word. May we develop an attitude where, if you're not going with us, we aren't going. Lord, I ask you to bless each of these men and their families with peace and your protection over them.

Lord, we love you and thank you for answering our prayers.
In Jesus' name. AMEN

FEBRUARY - DAILY DEVOTIONAL #6

However, as it is written: "What no eye has seen, what no ear has heard, and what no human mind has conceived"—the things God has prepared for those who love him—these are the things God has revealed to us by his Spirit. The Spirit searches all things, even the deep things of God.

1 CORINTHIANS 2:9-10 NIV

REFLECTIONS:

I never saw God until I sought after him, and I never heard God until I listened for him. I never understood the things of God until I asked for wisdom.

Don't be like the older man who, when he died, only had 1 mile on his car because that was the distance from his house to the dealership. Unfortunately, the older man took the time to buy the car but never learned to drive. Many Christians take the time to get saved but never learn to walk with the Lord.

REQUESTS:

Lord, give us a thirst for your word and your wisdom that will never be satisfied, so we may never stop chasing after you. As we seek you and listen for you each day, may we see and hear from you so we walk with you daily. Let us always be prepared to give an answer to others about who we are and why we love you so much. Lord, I ask for your peace over these men. Please surround them with your presence.

Lord, we love you and thank you for answering our prayers.
In Jesus' name. AMEN

FEBRUARY - DAILY DEVOTIONAL #7

Moreover, the Father judges no one, but has entrusted all judgment to the Son, that all may honor the Son just as they honor the Father. Whoever does not honor the Son does not honor the Father, who sent him.

JOHN 5:22-23 NIV

REFLECTIONS:

As a country, we build memorials for fallen heroes to honor them. However, are we honoring them with our actions, or would they be ashamed of how our country looks now? Do we truly honor them, or are we just going through the motions? The same can be asked of our Christian walk:

- Does our life honor Jesus with our actions?
- Are we sharing Jesus with others?
- Or are we only *remembering* Jesus like we would a soldier who gave his life for our freedom?

REQUESTS:

Lord, may our walk with you be more about your light shining through us and touching others—not just about expressing words of remembrance that fall on deaf ears. Lord, bless us with a deep heart-moving desire to pray for the sick, seek the lost, and lift up our struggling brothers in Christ. May your peace rest upon us today, and your presence lead us.

Lord, we love you and thank you for answering our prayers.
In Jesus' name. AMEN

FEBRUARY - DAILY DEVOTIONAL #8

The teachers of the law and the Pharisees brought in a woman caught in adultery. They made her stand before the group and said to Jesus, "Teacher, this woman was caught in the act of adultery. In the Law Moses commanded us to stone such women. Now what do you say?" They were using this question as a trap, in order to have a basis for accusing him. But Jesus bent down and started to write on the ground with his finger. When they kept on questioning him, he straightened up and said to them, "Let any one of you who is without sin be the first to throw a stone at her." Again he stooped down and wrote on the ground.

JOHN 8:3-8 NIV

REFLECTIONS:

Where do you find yourself in this story? Are you standing by that friend everyone is talking about, praying and ministering to them, or are you the one gathering rocks? Or are you the person who thinks I don't want to be involved, so I'm not doing anything?

REQUESTS:

Lord, give us your heart, your compassion, and your love for others, through your Spirit within us. Let us not be found holding rocks or standing idle when we should be acting on your will. Lord, I ask you for eyes to see you and ears to hear you today.

Lord, we love you and thank you for answering our prayers.
In Jesus' name. AMEN

FEBRUARY - DAILY DEVOTIONAL #9

He who was seated on the throne said, "I am making everything new!" Then he said, "Write this down, for these words are trustworthy and true." He said to me: "It is done. I am the Alpha and the Omega, the Beginning and the End. To the thirsty I will give water without cost from the spring of the water of life. Those who are victorious will inherit all this, and I will be their God and they will be my children.

REVELATION 21:5-7 NIV

REFLECTIONS:

From the Old Testament to the New, our Father has been and is still doing something new. Are you allowing him to do something new in you? Or are you like the older man whose daughter gave him a new coat? He never wore it because he said the old one was more comfortable. We all received new coats when we accepted Jesus, but we've made our walk with Jesus comfortable, just the way we like it. So are we going to allow ourselves to get uncomfortable and allow God to make things new in our walk with him?

REQUESTS:

Lord, take us out of our comfort zone, so we may be willing vessels for you to use in your kingdom. May we be a light in places we never thought needed your light. Let us throw away our old coats as you continue to make things new. Please help us be willing and able to follow you in new directions to further your kingdom. You know what each of these men needs. Bless them beyond measure.

Lord, we love you and thank you for answering our prayers.
In Jesus' name. AMEN

FEBRUARY - DAILY DEVOTIONAL #10

"He himself bore our sins" in his body on the cross, so that we might die to sins and live for righteousness; "by his wounds you have been healed."

1 PETER 2:24 NIV

REFLECTIONS:

Most of us, including myself, have probably thought, "by his wounds you have been healed" meant a physical healing for the sick. While it does mean that, it goes even further. The wounds of sin can cause any kind of pain—physical, mental, or emotional.

Maybe it's a sin you have recently committed that is causing you hurt, or a sin someone else committed against you. Regardless, by Jesus' wounds, you are healed as you turn the sin and pain over to him.

REQUESTS:

Lord, help us take a deep look at what pains us and turn it all over to you so the healing may make us whole again. Bless these men with peace and your presence.

Lord, we love you and thank you for answering our prayers.
In Jesus' name. AMEN

FEBRUARY - DAILY DEVOTIONAL #11

With God we will gain the victory, and he will trample down our enemies.

PSALM 60:12 NIV

REFLECTIONS:

God has delivered all of us from something. Yes, he has forgiven us of sin, but, more specifically, he may have delivered you from addictions like alcohol, drugs, porn, or even legalism. Sometimes we stumble, but Jesus is there to pick us up, so we keep walking with him.

Here's what I hate: when you're listening to someone else's story, and show a little emotion for that person, that old devil asks the same old question—did God really deliver you? The devil tries to make you feel unworthy. I'm telling you now—that's a bold-faced lie.

REQUESTS:

Father, may the person feeling unworthy today be the most willing to share Jesus. May he be bold in telling his story and how you pulled him out of the pits of hell. Lord, may he be bold to say, "I'm not perfect and I slip up sometimes, but I'm headed in the right direction—towards heaven and our God who calls me his SON!"

Lord, we love you and thank you for answering our prayers.
In Jesus' name. AMEN

FEBRUARY - DAILY DEVOTIONAL #12

I am reminded of your sincere faith, which first lived in your grandmother Lois and in your mother Eunice and, I am persuaded, now lives in you also.

2 TIMOTHY 1:5 NIV

REFLECTIONS:

Most of the time, our testimony can be seen through our children or others we had a significant influence on. Yes, they may run out and do their own thing and make their own mistakes, but are we leaving them the hope of Jesus to run back to?

REQUESTS:

Lord, let us not be remembered for all the things we acquired or how crazy we were living for this world. But may our testimony of living for you, Jesus, be seen in our children and children's children from generation to generation.

Lord, we love you and thank you for answering our prayers.
In Jesus' name. AMEN

FEBRUARY - DAILY DEVOTIONAL #13

"Surely God does not reject one who is blameless or strengthen the hands of evildoers. He will yet fill your mouth with laughter and your lips with shouts of joy. Your enemies will be clothed in shame, and the tents of the wicked will be no more."

JOB 8:20-22 NIV

REFLECTIONS:

Without Jesus, God rejects all of us. Without our Savior, we are worthless and rejected. As we say in the Deep South, we are as "useless as tits on a boar hog." But through the blood of Jesus, we are found blameless and are accepted as his children, joint heirs to Jesus.

REQUESTS:

Lord, show these men today that they are accepted and show them how much they are worth to you. Lord, bless them with your peace and surround them with your presence, guiding them in the direction you would have them go.

Lord, we love you and thank you for answering our prayers.
In Jesus' name. AMEN

FEBRUARY - DAILY DEVOTIONAL #14

No, in all these things we are more than conquerors through him who loved us. For I am convinced that neither death nor life, neither angels nor demons, neither the present nor the future, nor any powers, neither height nor depth, nor anything else in all creation, will be able to separate us from the love of God that is in Christ Jesus our Lord.

ROMANS 8:37-39 NIV

REFLECTIONS:

I've heard and read this scripture too many times to count, and always understood it as a promise we can stand on as believers—and we can. But before we knew Jesus, he loved us and died for us. Praise God, nothing could keep us from coming to him, receiving his forgiveness, and being sealed in our salvation.

May this be our testimony: that as a lost person, we were still loved. We didn't clean ourselves up first, but we came to Jesus, and he cleaned us up and healed our broken hearts.

REQUESTS:

Lord, if anyone is feeling separated from you, may you open their eyes to see that you've never left their side. We love you because you first loved us. And we thank you for the prayers you have answered before we could ever think to ask.

Lord, we love you and thank you for answering our prayers.
In Jesus' name. AMEN

FEBRUARY - DAILY DEVOTIONAL #15

I am the door. If anyone enters by me, he will be saved and will go in and out and find pasture.

JOHN 10:9 ESV

REFLECTIONS:

Isn't it strange that as men we sit facing the door at a restaurant, but do just about everything we can to keep our backs to God's door? He is holding it open to bless us if we will walk through it.

REQUESTS:

Lord, bless these men today with eyes to see and ears to hear you calling us to a blessing. Give us a heart to be obedient to your calling. You know every need we have, and we ask you to provide a way where we see no way.

Lord, we love you and thank you for answering our prayers.
In Jesus' name. AMEN

FEBRUARY - DAILY DEVOTIONAL #16

Make every effort to live in peace with everyone and to be holy; without holiness no one will see the Lord. See to it that no one falls short of the grace of God and that no bitter root grows up to cause trouble and defile many.

HEBREWS 12:14-15 NIV

REFLECTIONS:

This verse says to live in peace with everyone, but many of us have peace with everyone but our families. Do you walk around at work being nice to everyone, joking and laughing until you get home? But your wife and kids (or whoever your family comprises) are wondering how you're going to act towards them when you come in the door?

A daily dose of coming home as a grumpy and hateful husband, father, son, or brother can cause a deep root of unforgiveness. The root starts with you. Therefore, before you attempt to help others cut off their root of bitterness, make sure you have cut off your own.

REQUESTS:

Lord, I ask you to bless these men with peace, guiding them to a freedom that comes with forgiving others and themselves. Watch over them and their families, protecting them from all harm.

Lord, we love you and thank you for answering our prayers.
In Jesus' name. AMEN

FEBRUARY - DAILY DEVOTIONAL #17

So, as the Holy Spirit says: "Today, if you hear his voice, do not harden your hearts as you did in the rebellion, during the time of testing in the wilderness, where your ancestors tested and tried me, though for forty years they saw what I did. That is why I was angry with that generation; I said, 'Their hearts are always going astray, and they have not known my ways.' So I declared on oath in my anger, 'They shall never enter my rest.'" See to it, . . . that none of you has a sinful, unbelieving heart that turns away from the living God. But encourage one another daily, . . . so that none of you may be hardened by sin's deceitfulness. We have come to share in Christ, if indeed we hold our original conviction firmly to the very end.

HEBREWS 3:7-14 NIV

REFLECTIONS:

There are so many Christians who play the "what if" game. We think, *I love the Lord, I trust him, and all my faith is in him, but what if this or that happens? What are we going to do?* Our hearts and minds get caught up in this thinking, just like the Israelites did in Moses' day. They played the "what if" game so much that God allowed that thinking to harden their hearts, and they strayed from God. It doesn't matter what the "if" is; we need to let God be God in the good times and bad, always seeking him and encouraging one another.

REQUESTS:

Lord, bless these men with peace today, so that no matter what happens, their hearts remain faithful to you and all you have planned for them.

Lord, we love you and thank you for answering our prayers.
In Jesus' name. AMEN

FEBRUARY - DAILY DEVOTIONAL #18

But whatever were gains to me I now consider loss for the sake of Christ. What is more, I consider everything a loss because of the surpassing worth of knowing Christ Jesus my Lord, for whose sake I have lost all things. I consider them garbage, that I may gain Christ and be found in him, not having a righteousness of my own that comes from the law, but that which is through faith in Christ—the righteousness that comes from God on the basis of faith. I want to know Christ—yes, to know the power of his resurrection and participation in his sufferings, becoming like him in his death, and so, somehow, attaining to the resurrection from the dead.

PHILIPPIANS 3:7-11 NIV

REFLECTIONS:

Paul is saying that whatever he lost or left behind was worth losing when he came to know Jesus as his Lord and Savior. Dying to self and living for Jesus is a way of dying and being resurrected into Jesus, just as he died and rose again and was resurrected to the Father. He did this so our sins could be paid in full. Do you feel the same way as Paul? Was what you left behind worth it?

REQUESTS:

Lord, you are so much more than what the world has to offer. I ask you for eyes to see and ears to hear your goodness and glory so we're not distracted by the world, but focused on attaining all that you have to offer us as your children. Lord, bless these men with all that they need to walk with you today.

Lord, we love you and thank you for answering our prayers.
In Jesus' name. AMEN

FEBRUARY - DAILY DEVOTIONAL #19

Do not be deceived: God cannot be mocked. A man reaps what he sows. Whoever sows to please their flesh, from the flesh will reap destruction; whoever sows to please the Spirit, from the Spirit will reap eternal life. Let us not become weary in doing good, for at the proper time we will reap a harvest if we do not give up. Therefore, as we have opportunity, let us do good to all people, especially to those who belong to the family of believers.

GALATIANS 6:7-10 NIV

REFLECTIONS:

In farmer terms, what is your planter full of this morning? Selfish desires that will only satisfy your fleshly desires, or selfless desires that put your wants to the side to bless others? Are you showing the love of Jesus, who is the perfect example of selflessness? Jesus stepped out of heaven to come live among us as a man and to be crucified as a sacrifice for our sins.

REQUESTS:

Lord, may we have opportunities to set our selfish desires aside and love others as you love us so selflessly. Bless these men and their families with your peace and presence.

Lord, we love you and thank you for answering our prayers. In Jesus' name. AMEN

FEBRUARY - DAILY DEVOTIONAL #20

With the tongue we praise our Lord and Father, and with it we curse human beings, who have been made in God's likeness. Out of the same mouth come praise and cursing. My brothers and sisters, this should not be. Can both fresh water and salt water flow from the same spring? My brothers and sisters, can a fig tree bear olives, or a grapevine bear figs? Neither can a salt spring produce fresh water.

JAMES 3:9-12 NIV

REFLECTIONS:

Take a moment and ask yourself this today: Are you going to be that man God saved and delivered out of death, hell, and the grave? Or are you going to act like, or be the man God needs to save from death, hell, and the grave?

REQUESTS:

Lord, bless each of these men as they lay down their worldly manhood and walk as the men you saved, so they too can share the gospel and tell of your goodness. Help those who are struggling because you are our help in time of need. Cover these men and their families with a blanket of peace and surround them with your presence.

Lord, we love you and thank you for answering our prayers.
In Jesus' name. AMEN

FEBRUARY - DAILY DEVOTIONAL #21

In your struggle against sin, you have not yet resisted to the point of shedding your blood. And have you completely forgotten this word of encouragement that addresses you as a father addresses his son? It says, "My son, do not make light of the Lord's discipline, and do not lose heart when he rebukes you, because the Lord disciplines the one he loves, and he chastens everyone he accepts as his son." Endure hardship as discipline; God is treating you as his children. For what children are not disciplined by their father? If you are not disciplined—and everyone undergoes discipline—then you are not legitimate, not true sons and daughters at all.

HEBREWS 12:4-8 NIV

REFLECTIONS:

I asked my momma one time why she whipped me so hard. Her answer stunned me, but after that, I didn't have to be whipped anymore. She told me viciously that the last whipping didn't last as long as was needed to keep me out of trouble. I didn't want to find out how hard the next one would feel.

God doesn't spank us, but just like my momma, his discipline is out of love and wanting the very best for us. So, just like a little kid, as children of God, we know when God is about to get our attention. This time, listen.

REQUESTS:

Lord, thank you that, as your children, you love and care about us enough to discipline us for our own good. Bless these men and their families with all that they need.

Lord, we love you and thank you for answering our prayers.
In Jesus' name. AMEN

FEBRUARY - DAILY DEVOTIONAL #22

As God's co-workers we urge you not to receive God's grace in vain. For he says, "In the time of my favor I heard you, and in the day of salvation I helped you." I tell you, now is the time of God's favor, now is the day of salvation.

2 CORINTHIANS 6:1-2 NIV

REFLECTIONS:

Men, do not take his grace and favor for granted, but with a humble heart, handle them as if they were your grandma's fine china.

REQUESTS:

Lord, may we show your same grace and favor to those around us, so we may be considered faithful and just in your sight. Fill each of these men's homes with your peace and presence, blessing them with all that they need.

Lord, we love you and thank you for answering our prayers. In Jesus' name. AMEN

FEBRUARY - DAILY DEVOTIONAL #23

Humble yourselves, therefore, under God's mighty hand, that he may lift you up in due time. Cast all your anxiety on him because he cares for you.

1 PETER 5:6-7 NIV

REFLECTIONS:

Set your hearts and minds on Jesus and his goodness as you work through sharing the gospel of Jesus Christ with others.

REQUESTS:

Lord, bless these men and their homes with your presence and peace, and keep their families safe from all harm.

Lord, we love you and thank you for answering our prayers.
In Jesus' name. AMEN

FEBRUARY - DAILY DEVOTIONAL #24

For, as I have often told you before and now tell you again even with tears, many live as enemies of the cross of Christ. Their destiny is destruction, their god is their stomach, and their glory is in their shame. Their mind is set on earthly things. But our citizenship is in heaven. And we eagerly await a Savior from there, the Lord Jesus Christ, who, by the power that enables him to bring everything under his control, will transform our lowly bodies so that they will be like his glorious body.

PHILIPPIANS 3:18-21 NIV

REFLECTIONS:

Men, let your life promote the cross and point people to Christ. Then he can change our hearts so we carry the forgiveness for others that the cross carries for us through Jesus Christ, our Lord and Savior.

REQUESTS:

Lord, bless each of these men and their families. Keep them warm and safe today. Bless them with peace and your presence throughout their home.

Lord, we love you and thank you for answering our prayers.
In Jesus' name. AMEN

FEBRUARY - DAILY DEVOTIONAL #25

Now when Daniel learned that the decree had been published, he went home to his upstairs room where the windows opened toward Jerusalem. Three times a day he got down on his knees and prayed, giving thanks to his God, just as he had done before. Then these men went as a group and found Daniel praying and asking God for help.

DANIEL 6:10-11 NIV

REFLECTIONS:

When the enemy comes at you, are you found to be a man of God like Daniel? One who is praying and seeking his guidance and help?

REQUESTS:

Lord, may we find you in the fire with us. Bless these men with peace and fill their homes with your presence. May we always remember it's not what we have, but who we have that really matters. Fill our hearts, Lord, with your goodness.

Lord, we love you and thank you for answering our prayers.
In Jesus' name. AMEN

FEBRUARY - DAILY DEVOTIONAL #26

"My prayer is not for them alone. I pray also for those who will believe in me through their message, that all of them may be one, Father, just as you are in me and I am in you. May they also be in us so that the world may believe that you have sent me. I have given them the glory that you gave me, that they may be one as we are one—I in them and you in me—so that they may be brought to complete unity. Then the world will know that you sent me and have loved them even as you have loved me.

"Father, I want those you have given me to be with me where I am, and to see my glory, the glory you have given me because you loved me before the creation of the world.

"Righteous Father, though the world does not know you, I know you, and they know that you have sent me. I have made you known to them, and will continue to make you known in order that the love you have for me may be in them and that I myself may be in them."

JOHN 17:20-26NIV

REFLECTIONS:

There is no better person to pray for us than Jesus himself. May each of you have a blessed day, knowing even before you were born, Jesus himself prayed for your success in spreading the gospel!

REQUESTS:

Lord, may this prayer come alive in us, giving us a more profound, consistent desire to tell people about Jesus. Bless these men with your peace and presence all around them.

Lord, we love you and thank you for answering our prayers.
In Jesus' name. AMEN

FEBRUARY - DAILY DEVOTIONAL #27

. . . even though God had said to him, "It is through Isaac that your offspring will be reckoned." Abraham reasoned that God could even raise the dead, and so in a manner of speaking he did receive Isaac back from death.

HEBREWS 11:18-19 NIV

REFLECTIONS:

Have you ever looked in the mirror and considered what it really means that Jesus raised you from the dead? When we were lost and following the world, we were tied up just like Isaac.

But before the world could kill us in our own sin, God intervened just like he did for Isaac. He provided a sacrifice—Jesus. When we accepted Jesus as our Lord and Savior, we were untied from the world and made free to walk with him.

REQUESTS:

Lord, we claim that freedom in Jesus. As the world tries to tie us back up, may we run to Jesus, and may the world see the paid-in-full stamp on our foreheads. As we walk through the valleys, may we hold tightly to our faith because we know even in the valleys we have victory. Bless these men as they face the day. May they have confidence that you are with them and you'll never leave them.

Lord, we love you and thank you for answering our prayers.
In Jesus' name. AMEN

FEBRUARY - DAILY DEVOTIONAL #28

Therefore Israel will be abandoned until the time when she who is in labor bears a son, and the rest of his brothers return to join the Israelites. He will stand and shepherd his flock in the strength of the LORD, in the majesty of the name of the LORD his God. And they will live securely, for then his greatness will reach to the ends of the earth.

MICAH 5:3-4 NIV

REFLECTIONS:

This is God's message to all other countries: No matter what, Jesus, the Great Shepherd, is watching over Israel, and he is protecting them. And through the blood of Jesus, we as his *adopted* children have been grafted into this promise of security and peace.

REQUESTS:

Lord, I don't know what these men and their families are facing, but I ask you to pour out your peace over them. Cover them with your blood, protecting them from all harm, and give them victory!

Lord, we love you and thank you for answering our prayers.
In Jesus' name. AMEN

MARCH - DAILY DEVOTIONAL #1

The remnant of Jacob will be in the midst of many peoples like dew from the LORD, like showers on the grass, which do not wait for anyone or depend on man. The remnant of Jacob will be among the nations, in the midst of many peoples, like a lion among the beasts of the forest, like a young lion among flocks of sheep, which mauls and mangles as it goes, and no one can rescue. Your hand will be lifted up in triumph over your enemies, and all your foes will be destroyed.

MICAH 5:7-9 NIV

REFLECTIONS:

I am not sure where we stand as the remnant of Jacob, but I do know the Lord is describing the world we're living in right now in this passage. Because the Lord has adopted us through the cross and the blood of Jesus, we can claim this promise of being lifted up in triumph as we draw closer and closer to the Lord, seeking his will.

REQUESTS:

Lord, as we start this day, we claim a triumphant heart—not a saddened heart beat down by this old world and all the uncertainty in it. We know we are going to have difficulties and may stumble, but you are faithful to pick us back up, guiding us in the way we should go. Lord, bless these men with your peace and victory over their struggles today.

Lord, we love you and thank you for answering our prayers.
In Jesus' name. AMEN

MARCH - DAILY DEVOTIONAL #2

"Why do you look at the speck of sawdust in your brother's eye and pay no attention to the plank in your own eye? How can you say to your brother, 'Brother, let me take the speck out of your eye,' when you yourself fail to see the plank in your own eye? You hypocrite, first take the plank out of your eye, and then you will see clearly to remove the speck from your brother's eye. . .. "

LUKE 6:41-42 NIV

REFLECTIONS:

So, according to my finite way of thinking, what this is saying is, "Why would you take an alcoholic to rehab when you drink more than he does?" In other words, instead of pointing a finger at someone, maybe we need to point it at the guy in the mirror.

REQUESTS:

Lord, you know what we need to fix within ourselves before we can help others. Please give us a willing heart to begin our own healing and deliverance so all that we do points to the cross and brings you glory. Lord, may we chase after you, seeking you in all that we do.

Lord, we love you and thank you for answering our prayers.
In Jesus' name. AMEN

MARCH - DAILY DEVOTIONAL #3

But when I speak to you, I will open your mouth and you shall say to them, 'This is what the Sovereign Lord says.' Whoever will listen let them listen, and whoever will refuse let them refuse; for they are a rebellious people.

EZEKIEL 3:27 NIV

REFLECTIONS:

An older man once told me the best quality of a man is the ability to listen. He said just hearing something is not enough, but the ability to listen will keep you out of a lot of trouble.

REQUESTS:

Lord, may we not just hear you speaking but give us a heart that is willing to listen and be obedient. I ask you to bless each of these men and their families with your presence and peace. Lord, only you truly know what they need, so I ask to bless them beyond measure!

Lord, we love you and thank you for answering our prayers.
In Jesus' name. AMEN

MARCH - DAILY DEVOTIONAL #4

Even in darkness light dawns for the upright, for those who are gracious and compassionate and righteous.

PSALM 112:4 NIV

REFLECTIONS:

Even in our darkest moments, the Lord's light shines on his children, but how do we react? Are we gracious and compassionate to others who are worse off than we are, or do we cover the light with selfishness and hatefulness?

REQUESTS:

Lord, today show your compassion and graciousness to others through us. May we be the light to someone who is in a darker place than we are. Let us never forget to tell you we love you.

Lord, we love you and thank you for answering our prayers.
In Jesus' name. AMEN

MARCH - DAILY DEVOTIONAL #5

During the days of Jesus' life on earth, he offered up prayers and petitions with fervent cries and tears to the one who could save him from death, and he was heard because of his reverent submission.

HEBREWS 5:7 NIV

REFLECTIONS:

Maybe it's because I'm getting older, but every once in a while I think about what my obituary might say. It's my hope that my prayer life has been so evident that my kids would write this: "He prayed often for God's will, like his life depended on it." I believe no amount of money or earthly possessions is greater than leaving your children an example of a diligent and faithful prayer life.

REQUESTS:

Lord, give us a heart and desire to seek you in prayer as often and as faithfully as Jesus did. Help us not be like the disciples sleeping, but to be praying when Jesus comes back. Lord, bless these men and their families today with your peace and presence, guiding them in the way they should go.

Lord, we love you and thank you for answering our prayers.
In Jesus' name. AMEN

MARCH - DAILY DEVOTIONAL #6

Therefore, since we have a great high priest who has ascended into heaven, Jesus the Son of God, let us hold firmly to the faith we profess. For we do not have a high priest who is unable to empathize with our weaknesses, but we have one who has been tempted in every way, just as we are—yet he did not sin. Let us then approach God's throne of grace with confidence, so that we may receive mercy and find grace to help us in our time of need.

HEBREWS 4:14-16 NIV

REFLECTIONS:

I've been to see a few counselors in my life, and the best ones were the ones who not only studied to get their degree but also had a life experience and walked through the fire of life problems. An alcoholic is probably easier to lead an AA meeting than someone who has never had a drink.

The same is true with Jesus. He found it necessary to at least go through every temptation we have ever been through without giving in to it. So, as his children, we would have confidence to come to him for strength and healing to overcome. In simple layman's terms, whatever your addiction is, the next time you feel the urge to give in, run to Jesus with confidence—he's your strength to overcome.

REQUESTS:

Lord, bless these men with your peace and confidence that in their weakness, Jesus is their strength to be victorious in all that they face. May your glory shine through us, giving light to a dark world.

Lord, we love you and thank you for answering our prayers.
In Jesus' name. AMEN

MARCH - DAILY DEVOTIONAL #7

See, I am doing a new thing! Now it springs up; do you not perceive it? I am making a way in the wilderness and streams in the wasteland. The wild animals honor me, the jackals and the owls, because I provide water in the wilderness and streams in the wasteland, to give drink to my people, my chosen, the people I formed for myself that they may proclaim my praise.

ISAIAH 43:19-21 NIV

REFLECTIONS:

You know it's hard, but we have to look beyond our circumstances and put our hope in the Lord. Whatever we face does not have to be a catastrophic event, but it can be as simple as anger, jealousy, or even good, old selfishness that can keep us from seeing what the Lord is creating new for us.

REQUESTS:

Lord, bless these men with eyes to see and hearts to follow you. Help them find the new things you're preparing for them so they may lay down the old. Bless them with ears to hear your voice and direct their steps. Lord, we love you. We thank you for what you are about to do for these men.

Lord, we love you and thank you for answering our prayers.
In Jesus' name. AMEN

MARCH - DAILY DEVOTIONAL #8

For Christ did not enter a sanctuary made with human hands that was only a copy of the true one; he entered heaven itself, now to appear for us in God's presence. Nor did he enter heaven to offer himself again and again, the way the high priest enters the Most Holy Place every year with blood that is not his own. Otherwise Christ would have had to suffer many times since the creation of the world. But he has appeared once for all at the culmination of the ages to do away with sin by the sacrifice of himself. Just as people are destined to die once, and after that to face judgment, so Christ was sacrificed once to take away the sins of many; and he will appear a second time, not to bear sin, but to bring salvation to those who are waiting for him.

HEBREWS 9:24-28 NIV

REFLECTIONS:

All that to ask this one question: How are you spending your time waiting for Jesus to come back?

REQUESTS:

Lord, in our time of waiting, may we be about your business and not our own. May wherever we go and whatever we do shine your light in this dark world. Lord, bless these men today beyond measure.

Lord, we love you and thank you for answering our prayers.
In Jesus' name. AMEN

MARCH - DAILY DEVOTIONAL #9

Therefore, since Christ suffered in his body, arm yourselves also with the same attitude, because whoever suffers in the body is done with sin. As a result, they do not live the rest of their earthly lives for evil human desires, but rather for the will of God. For you have spent enough time in the past doing what pagans choose to do—living in debauchery, lust, drunkenness, orgies, carousing and detestable idolatry. . . But they will have to give account to him who is ready to judge the living and the dead. For this is the reason the gospel was preached even to those who are now dead, so that they might be judged according to human standards in regard to the body, but live according to God in regard to the spirit.

1 PETER 4:1-6 NIV

REFLECTIONS:

Here's a simple question for today: Are you going to live for the world, seeking the Lord and his direction? If you're going to live for the world, that's not hard; there's a bar open somewhere. *Or* you could start your day with the Lord. That's much easier, and you don't have to go anywhere. Slide out of your bed, let your knees hit the floor, and begin to pray: Lord, I'm not leaving this house without you. I don't want to face any problems without you going ahead of me, beside me, behind me, and guiding me. Yes, we may fail, but he's always there to pick us back up. Don't let the world determine your next move; allow God to direct you.

REQUESTS:

Lord, bless these men today with peace that passes all understanding. Please give them your wisdom, even through the struggles.

Lord, we love you and thank you for answering our prayers.
In Jesus' name. AMEN

MARCH - DAILY DEVOTIONAL #10

And do not think you can say to yourselves, 'We have Abraham as our father.' I tell you that out of these stones God can raise up children for Abraham. The ax is already at the root of the trees, and every tree that does not produce good fruit will be cut down and thrown into the fire.

MATTHEW 3:9-10 NIV

REFLECTIONS:

An older man whom I used to work cows and sheep for, often said this: "You can talk the talk, but can you walk the walk?" In other words, you might be unable to tell people how to have a prayer life, or how to witness to someone and lead them to Christ, but is that truly a desire you have, or does it just sound like something good to do?

REQUESTS:

Lord, I ask you to help us each day to look a little more like you in our actions. We know God worked for six days and rested one day, but even on the day he rested, he was still God. So, may our walk with you be in the same manner, seven days a week.

Lord, we love you and thank you for answering our prayers.
In Jesus' name. AMEN

MARCH - DAILY DEVOTIONAL #11

If you really keep the royal law found in Scripture, "Love your neighbor as yourself," you are doing right. But if you show favoritism, you sin and are convicted by the law as lawbreakers. For whoever keeps the whole law and yet stumbles at just one point is guilty of breaking all of it. For he who said, "You shall not commit adultery," also said, "You shall not murder." If you do not commit adultery but do commit murder, you have become a lawbreaker. Speak and act as those who are going to be judged by the law that gives freedom, because judgment without mercy will be shown to anyone who has not been merciful. Mercy triumphs over judgment.

JAMES 2:8-13 NIV

REFLECTIONS:

In our current day and time, the court system hands out mercy. You can murder someone, and if you have the right lawyer, you get a slap on the wrist. But if you don't have or can't pay for a good lawyer, you're going to get the full punishment.

Well, with God, there is no time off for good behavior. Sin is sin, and it carries the full weight of God's punishment unless you have Jesus, who paid the price on the cross for you and me. Then, and only then, do you receive God's mercy.

REQUESTS:

Lord, I ask you to bless these men with your peace and presence. Draw them into a closer walk with you. Show them the depth of your mercy through their brothers in Christ.

Lord, we love you and thank you for answering our prayers.
In Jesus' name. AMEN

MARCH - DAILY DEVOTIONAL #12

There remains, then, a Sabbath-rest for the people of God; for anyone who enters God's rest also rests from their works, just as God did from his. Let us, therefore, make every effort to enter that rest, so that no one will perish by following their example of disobedience.

HEBREWS 4:9-11 NIV

REFLECTIONS:

Have you ever thought your mind was going to explode trying to hold up to a standard that is impossible to reach? And you get so frustrated, you want to pull your hair out. Have you ever felt like you can't catch a break, or you're burning your candle at both ends?

God's rest releases you from that and the burdens of this old world. His rest isn't just about your body; it's about your soul receiving his peace and your mind being cleared and filled with his thoughts.

REQUESTS:

Today, Lord, bless these men with your peace and presence as they go about their physical work. May you bless their minds and souls with your rest. Lord, you know each one of these men's needs. I ask you to bless them mightily today.

Lord, we love you and thank you for answering our prayers.
In Jesus' name. AMEN

MARCH - DAILY DEVOTIONAL #13

But while all this was going on, I was not in Jerusalem, for in the thirty-second year of Artaxerxes king of Babylon I had returned to the king. Some time later I asked his permission and came back to Jerusalem. Here I learned about the evil thing Eliashib had done in providing Tobiah a room in the courts of the house of God. I was greatly displeased and threw all Tobiah's household goods out of the room. I gave orders to purify the rooms, and then I put back into them the equipment of the house of God, with the grain offerings and the incense. I also learned that the portions assigned to the Levites had not been given to them, and that all the Levites and musicians responsible for the service had gone back to their own fields. So I rebuked the officials and asked them, "Why is the house of God neglected?" Then I called them together and stationed them at their posts.

NEHEMIAH 13:6-11 NIV

REFLECTIONS:

How does this apply to us? When Nehemiah left, no one took responsibility for upholding God's ways. They decided to do their own thing. While we don't have Moses or Nehemiah or any other guide like the Jews had, we have the Holy Spirit living in us to guide us and to help in all situations if we let him. But many times, just like the Jews, we still go about our own way, disregarding what the Holy Spirit has taught us.

REQUESTS:

Lord, today set our hearts back right. May we lay our will down and allow you to purify our hearts once again. Help us set the rooms in our hearts on you, and not the things of the flesh. Lord, bless these men and their families.

Lord, we love you and thank you for answering our prayers.
In Jesus' name. AMEN

MARCH - DAILY DEVOTIONAL #14

I also shook out the folds of my robe and said, "In this way may God shake out of their house and possessions anyone who does not keep this promise. So may such a person be shaken out and emptied!" At this the whole assembly said, "Amen," and praised the LORD. And the people did as they had promised.

NEHEMIAH 5:13 NIV

REFLECTIONS:

In this story, the Jews were taking from the poorer Jews. They were taking their land, their children, and putting them into slavery. So Nehemiah makes them give it all back with a promise to the Lord that it will include interest, and that they will take no more. Nehemiah gives an example of what their punishment would be; if they don't give it all back as promised, God would shake them until they're emptied.

REQUESTS:

So today, Lord, as your children, whatever we have taken from the world that is not of you or from you, shake us until we're empty and fill us back up with your glory. May we seek your desires for our lives and not our own. Sometimes we just need you to clean house in our hearts. Lord, bless these when men and their families with your peace and surround them with your presence. Guide them in their walk with you.

Lord, we love you and thank you for answering our prayers.
In Jesus' name. AMEN

MARCH - DAILY DEVOTIONAL #15

I urge, then, first of all, that petitions, prayers, intercession and thanksgiving be made for all people—for kings and all those in authority, that we may live peaceful and quiet lives in all godliness and holiness. This is good, and pleases God our Savior, who wants all people to be saved and to come to a knowledge of the truth. For there is one God and one mediator between God and mankind, the man Christ Jesus, who gave himself as a ransom for all people. This has now been witnessed to at the proper time. And for this purpose I was appointed a herald and an apostle—I am telling the truth, I am not lying—and a true and faithful teacher of the Gentiles. Therefore I want the men everywhere to pray, lifting up holy hands without anger or disputing.

1 TIMOTHY 2:1-8 NIV

REFLECTIONS:

Paul said a lot in this passage of scripture, but it's what he started and ended with that touches me. It should be the way we start and finish things. He started by telling us to pray and ended by saying we still need to pray. Since Jesus is our mediator, if we want to see him move mountains, we should pray and then pray some more.

REQUESTS:

Lord, you know every need this morning in our homes, in our families, and in our country. So, I ask you to meet our needs. We know we can't survive without you, so Lord, stir our hearts to seek your face daily in prayer so we know your will. Lord, bless these men with a fresh breath of hope today.

Lord, we love you and thank you for answering our prayers.
In Jesus' name. AMEN

MARCH - DAILY DEVOTIONAL #16

The tongue also is a fire, a world of evil among the parts of the body. It corrupts the whole body, sets the whole course of one's life on fire, and is itself set on fire by hell.

JAMES 3:6 NIV

REFLECTIONS:

So many people are using social media today to unload their thoughts. They say, "It was a harmless post," or "I was just venting." My favorite is, "I was just playing; they know I didn't mean anything by it." When we post, it's out there. It may not affect someone right now, but that same teasing post can be read 10-20 years from now. So it's as powerful as the tongue; it can either encourage or destroy someone.

REQUESTS:

Lord, may we use all sources of communication to glorify you by using what man created as a place to spread the gospel. Bless these men and their families today with peace and strength through their struggles, whatever they may be.

Lord, we love you and thank you for answering our prayers.
In Jesus' name. AMEN

MARCH - DAILY DEVOTIONAL #17

When I was a child, I talked like a child, I thought like a child, I reasoned like a child. When I became a man, I put the ways of childhood behind me.

1 CORINTHIANS 13:11 NIV

REFLECTIONS:

I believe I was around 14 when I heard an older man say, "I've seen grown men at 18 and I've seen kids at 50." Having a relationship with God is like growing up; you start as a young Christian and begin to grow as you walk with the Lord. Many of us are stuck in one spot between our earthly will and God's will, which stops the growing.

REQUESTS:

Lord, I ask you to get us unstuck so we can grow to our full potential in you, laying down childish ways, and continuing to grow in faith in you. Bless these men and their families with all that they need. Pour out your peace over them.

Lord, we love you and thank you for answering our prayers.
In Jesus' name. AMEN

MARCH - DAILY DEVOTIONAL #18

"Do not judge, or you too will be judged. For in the same way you judge others, you will be judged, and with the measure you use, it will be measured to you. "Why do you look at the speck of sawdust in your brother's eye and pay no attention to the plank in your own eye? How can you say to your brother, 'Let me take the speck out of your eye,' when all the time there is a plank in your own eye? You hypocrite, first take the plank out of your own eye, and then you will see clearly to remove the speck from your brother's eye.

MATTHEW 7:1-5 NIV

REFLECTIONS:

Ouch! These verses are pretty tough, but they're talking about true discipleship. If I look in the mirror and don't see the Christian I expect others to be, I have a choice. I can either ridicule them or I can be a true disciple.

   I can begin to pray and seek the Lord with all my heart, asking him to change me and cleanse me of my own self-righteousness. It won't make me perfect, but it will allow God to get the plank out of my eye so the Lord may use me to remove someone else's.

REQUESTS:

Lord, may we always seek you daily to keep ourselves in a useful position for your glory. An overweight and out-of-shape lineman is of no use to the team, so, Lord, help us keep in shape so we may be ready in season and out.

Lord, we love you and thank you for answering our prayers.
In Jesus' name. AMEN

MARCH - DAILY DEVOTIONAL #19

Let us then approach God's throne of grace with confidence, so that we may receive mercy and find grace to help us in our time of need.

HEBREWS 4:16 NIV

REFLECTIONS:

I have my phone alarm set for 4:16 p.m., reminding me to come to the Lord's throne in prayer. I encourage you to do the same, whatever time of day you think would be best for you. It may surprise you how well the rest of your day will go.

REQUESTS:

Lord, I ask you to bless these men with peace and fill their homes with your presence. Please help us make time to pause in our day to come to your throne seeking you.

Lord, we love you and thank you for answering our prayers.
In Jesus' name. AMEN

MARCH - DAILY DEVOTIONAL #20

Similarly, encourage the young men to be self-controlled. In everything set them an example by doing what is good. In your teaching show integrity, seriousness and soundness of speech that cannot be condemned, so that those who oppose you may be ashamed because they have nothing bad to say about us.

TITUS 2:6-8 NIV

REFLECTIONS:

Have you ever really thought about the saying, "practice what you preach?" That means, if you preach to live like Jesus, be a servant. If you take more pleasure in being served than serving, then you're probably not setting the right example.

REQUESTS:

Lord, may our actions begin to show proof of the goodness that we preach or tell others about. I ask you to bless these men with a desire to be an example of Christ in their daily walk. Open doors of opportunity to lead people to Jesus.

Lord, we love you and thank you for answering our prayers.
In Jesus' name. AMEN

MARCH - DAILY DEVOTIONAL #21

As for other matters, brothers and sisters, pray for us that the message of the Lord may spread rapidly and be honored, just as it was with you. And pray that we may be delivered from wicked and evil people, for not everyone has faith. But the Lord is faithful, and he will strengthen you and protect you from the evil one. We have confidence in the Lord that you are doing and will continue to do the things we command. May the Lord direct your hearts into God's love and Christ's perseverance.

2 THESSALONIANS 3:1-5 NIV

REFLECTIONS:

Paul wrote this to the Thessalonians, but it still applies to us today. We need to pray for revival for our land, that the Spirit of the Lord will spread across this nation and others. We need to pray for each other for the Lord to deliver us from even the evil people we are around each day in our workplaces and the towns we live in. Don't give up the good fight for the kingdom; God is on your side and with you. Don't fall into the trap of following your own ways.

REQUESTS:

Lord, I ask you to bless each of these men with peace. I know not all of them work or live in a place that loves Jesus, so I ask you to cover them with the blood of Jesus. Protect them from all harm. May they be a light in this dark and evil world. Lord, I pray for your peace and presence in their homes, blessing them beyond measure.

Lord, we love you and thank you for answering our prayers.
In Jesus' name. AMEN

MARCH - DAILY DEVOTIONAL #22

In reply Jesus said: "A man was going down from Jerusalem to Jericho, when he was attacked by robbers. They stripped him of his clothes, beat him and went away, leaving him half dead. A priest happened to be going down the same road, and when he saw the man, he passed by on the other side. So too, a Levite, when he came to the place and saw him, passed by on the other side. But a Samaritan, as he traveled, came where the man was; and when he saw him, he took pity on him. He went to him and bandaged his wounds, pouring on oil and wine. Then he put the man on his own donkey, brought him to an inn and took care of him."

LUKE 10:30-34 NIV

REFLECTIONS:

Many men have been beaten up and robbed by this old world. As Christian men, are we stopping and ministering to their need for Jesus, or are we crossing the road to avoid coming in contact with them?

REQUESTS:

Lord, give us a willing heart to be used by you to witness to men who are beaten up by this old world. Some may need Jesus, and some may just need help standing back up on their own two feet. So, Lord, give us eyes to see and ears to hear what they need so we do not miss an opportunity to see you be glorified!

Lord, we love you and thank you for answering our prayers.
In Jesus' name. AMEN

MARCH - DAILY DEVOTIONAL #23

. . . "Be dressed ready for service and keep your lamps burning, like servants waiting for their master to return from a wedding banquet, so that when he comes and knocks they can immediately open the door for him. It will be good for those servants whose master finds them watching when he comes. Truly I tell you, he will dress himself to serve, will have them recline at the table and will come and wait on them. It will be good for those servants whose master finds them ready, even if he comes in the middle of the night or toward daybreak. But understand this: If the owner of the house had known at what hour the thief was coming, he would not have let his house be broken into. You also must be ready, because the Son of Man will come at an hour when you do not expect him."

LUKE 12:35-40 NIV

REFLECTIONS:

Just as Jesus will come to serve us, we should always be ready to serve. As we wait for Jesus, we should have a watchful eye, and let us be found serving others just as he serves us!

REQUESTS:

Lord, bless these men today with eyes to see and ears to hear ways they can serve others, just as Jesus does, has, and will.

Lord, we love you and thank you for answering our prayers.
In Jesus' name. AMEN

MARCH - DAILY DEVOTIONAL #24

This is what the Lord says to me: "Go, post a lookout and have him report what he sees. When he sees chariots with teams of horses, riders on donkeys or riders on camels, let him be alert, fully alert." And the lookout shouted, "Day after day, my Lord, I stand on the watchtower; every night I stay at my post. Look, here comes a man in a chariot with a team of horses. And he gives back the answer: 'Babylon has fallen, has fallen! All the images of its gods lie shattered on the ground!'"

ISAIAH 21:6-9 NIV

REFLECTIONS:

Are we watching for the victories God is giving us, or are we going about our day doing our own thing, not seeing the battle we don't even know God is fighting for us? If it's not about us or our family, we may think it doesn't pertain to us. Well, idols are being worshiped from your house to Washington, D.C.; we may not see them, but God does.

REQUESTS:

Lord, may we always remember and never forget to give thanks and be watchful and mindful of the victories you give us.

Lord, we love you and thank you for answering our prayers.
In Jesus' name. AMEN

MARCH - DAILY DEVOTIONAL #25

You were running a good race. Who cut in on you to keep you from obeying the truth? That kind of persuasion does not come from the one who calls you. "A little yeast works through the whole batch of dough." I am confident in the Lord that you will take no other view. The one who is throwing you into confusion, whoever that may be, will have to pay the penalty.

GALATIANS 5:7-10 NIV

REFLECTIONS:

This goes along with the old saying, "You become who you hang around." Let me say that again. You become who you hang around. If you aspire to be a man after God's own heart, then surround yourself with like-minded men.

REQUESTS:

Lord, may we become more and more like you as we walk with you. May we be surrounded by like-minded men who are willing to say, "I need a brother who will hold me accountable; someone who will walk with me to my destination."

Lord, we love you and thank you for answering our prayers.
In Jesus' name. AMEN

MARCH - DAILY DEVOTIONAL #26

For I know my transgressions, and my sin is always before me. Against you, you only, have I sinned and done what is evil in your sight; so you are right in your verdict and justified when you judge. Surely I was sinful at birth, sinful from the time my mother conceived me. Yet you desired faithfulness even in the womb; you taught me wisdom in that secret place. Cleanse me with hyssop, and I will be clean; wash me, and I will be whiter than snow. Let me hear joy and gladness; let the bones you have crushed rejoice. Hide your face from my sins and blot out all my iniquity. Create in me a pure heart, O God, and renew a steadfast spirit within me. Do not cast me from your presence or take your Holy Spirit from me.

PSALM 51:3-11 NIV

REFLECTIONS:

I want you to read this as if David is arguing with God, saying how sinful he is over and over. Then he says, "Ok, Lord, I give up. Cleanse my heart, make it ever true, and please don't take your Spirit from me." We all have had those conversations before: "Why me, Lord?"

And the Lord continues to say, "Why not you?" So whatever God is calling you to do, say "Yes, Lord," and he will cleanse your heart.

REQUESTS:

Lord, bless these men and their families beyond measure. I ask you to continue to cleanse our hearts to be more like you.

Lord, we love you and thank you for answering our prayers.
In Jesus' name. AMEN

MARCH - DAILY DEVOTIONAL #27

But now many nations are gathered against you. They say, "Let her be defiled, let our eyes gloat over Zion!" But they do not know the thoughts of the LORD; they do not understand his plan, that he has gathered them like sheaves to the threshing floor. "Rise and thresh, Daughter Zion, for I will give you horns of iron; I will give you hooves of bronze, and you will break to pieces many nations." You will devote their ill-gotten gains to the LORD, their wealth to the Lord of all the earth.

MICAH 4:11-13 NIV

REFLECTIONS:

If you have ever wondered why it's so important for the U.S. to support Israel, here it is in this passage. In addition, this is why it's so important to seek a relationship with the Lord. Whether you're a country against Israel or just a hater of God's people, you're going to the threshing floor. I bet that ain't real fun being thrashed.

REQUESTS:

Lord, may our nation always remember and never forget to stand strong with Israel. Lord, as your children, may we always remember you have our backs. Lord, bless these men and their families with peace, and fill their homes with your presence.

Lord, we love you and thank you for answering our prayers.
In Jesus' name. AMEN

MARCH - DAILY DEVOTIONAL #28

Do not be deceived: God cannot be mocked. A man reaps what he sows. Whoever sows to please their flesh, from the flesh will reap destruction; whoever sows to please the Spirit, from the Spirit will reap eternal life. Let us not become weary in doing good, for at the proper time we will reap a harvest if we do not give up. Therefore, as we have opportunity, let us do good to all people, especially to those who belong to the family of believers.

GALATIANS 6:7-10 NIV

REFLECTIONS:

Do you ever wake up looking for an opportunity to do good or bless at least one person? Or do you wake up mad at the world and can't get past yourself, only looking for what you need and what you desire?

Well, think about Jesus. He didn't come into this world looking for what he needed because he really didn't *need* us. Still, he did come looking for what he *wants,* and that's a personal one-on-one relationship with each of us. So today, let someone see a little bit of Jesus in you by doing something good for them.

REQUESTS:

Lord, bless us with opportunities today to do good for others so they may see Jesus and his goodness.

Lord, we love you and thank you for answering our prayers.
In Jesus' name. AMEN

MARCH - DAILY DEVOTIONAL #29

... who build Zion with bloodshed, and Jerusalem with wickedness. Her leaders judge for a bribe, her priests teach for a price, and her prophets tell fortunes for money. Yet they look for the LORD's support and say, "Is not the LORD among us? No disaster will come upon us." Therefore because of you, Zion will be plowed like a field, Jerusalem will become a heap of rubble, the temple hill a mound overgrown with thickets.

MICAH 3:10-12 NIV

REFLECTIONS:

When you read this, it brings to mind the corruption in our country. Every president has claimed we are a blessed country, but they continue to be corrupt. But let's get a little closer to home. How often do we claim Jesus is with me or God is blessing my family, yet we dip our toe into corruption or sin?

Nothing bad may happen right away, so we say, "Surely God is with us." As we see here, be careful what you play with. God had to plow me under to get my attention.

REQUESTS:

Lord, bless our country and our leaders. Get their hearts right, but more importantly, get their hearts right, so not even their little toe wants to dip into sin. Bless these men with all that they need to be overcomers.

Lord, we love you and thank you for answering our prayers.
In Jesus' name. AMEN

MARCH - DAILY DEVOTIONAL #30

For we do not wrestle against flesh and blood, but against the rulers, against the authorities, against the cosmic powers over this present darkness, against the spiritual forces of evil in the heavenly places. Therefore take up the whole armor of God, that you may be able to withstand in the evil day, and having done all, to stand firm. Stand therefore, having fastened on the belt of truth, and having put on the breastplate of righteousness, and, as shoes for your feet, having put on the readiness given by the gospel of peace. In all circumstances take up the shield of faith, with which you can extinguish all the flaming darts of the evil one; and take the helmet of salvation, and the sword of the Spirit, which is the word of God, praying at all times in the Spirit, with all prayer and supplication. To that end, keep alert with all perseverance, making supplication for all the saints, . . .

EPHESIANS 6:12-18 ESV

REFLECTIONS:

Are you armored up? If you have a discipline of praying before you leave the house every day, you will be. However, if you don't start this routine, when you rush out without praying, you go out unprotected. Personally, my day is horrible until I stop, pray, and armor up.

REQUESTS:

Lord, bless these men with your protection. We know we battle against all things that we can and can't see. But when we armor up with your goodness, you always get the victory.

Lord, we love you and thank you for answering our prayers.
In Jesus' name. AMEN

MARCH - DAILY DEVOTIONAL #31

(What does "he ascended" mean except that he also descended to the lower, earthly regions? He who descended is the very one who ascended higher than all the heavens, in order to fill the whole universe.) So Christ himself gave the apostles, the prophets, the evangelists, the pastors and teachers, to equip his people for works of service, so that the body of Christ may be built up until we all reach unity in the faith and in the knowledge of the Son of God and become mature, attaining to the whole measure of the fullness of Christ. Then we will no longer be infants, tossed back and forth by the waves, and blown here and there by every wind of teaching . . . we will grow to become in every respect the mature body of him who is the head, that is, Christ. From him the whole body, joined and held together by every supporting ligament, grows and builds itself up in love, as each part does its work.

EPHESIANS 4:9-16 NIV

REFLECTIONS:

God, the Father, gave his only Son to a dying world as a sacrifice to save those who will call upon his name and receive him as their Lord and Savior. Jesus gave all of us who have been saved the calling to spread the gospel and to equip his people to serve in love as the body of Christ. So, being a Christian in the body of Christ is about all of us coming together, working together to give out of love.

REQUESTS:

Lord, guide us in our walk so we may learn and teach others. Guide us as we share with others the true love of Christ. We ask you to continually pour the love of Christ out through us so we may be found in Christ, not chasing what the world says the gospel is—to get all you can get. Lord, bless these men with all that they need to be the men of God you've called them to be.

Lord, we love you and thank you for answering our prayers.
In Jesus' name. AMEN

Some of the very things we beat ourselves up over, God wants to redeem and use for His purposes.

APRIL - DAILY DEVOTIONAL #1

Now that I, your Lord and Teacher, have washed your feet, you also should wash one another's feet. I have set you an example that you should do as I have done for you. Very truly I tell you, no servant is greater than his master, nor is a messenger greater than the one who sent him. Now that you know these things, you will be blessed if you do them.

JOHN 13:14-17 NIV

REFLECTIONS:

If the Lord moves on you to wash someone's feet as you pray for them, I suggest you do it without hesitation. It is one of the most precious blessings you could do for anyone and for yourself. It is one of the most beautiful acts of love you could ever do for someone, just as cooking a meal, mowing a lawn, or any other acts of service you can think of. They are special in their own way because they are done out of love for Jesus and the other person.

REQUESTS:

Lord, give us a heart of a servant. Being a servant is not always literally washing feet, but is serving others in a way that shows your love for them. Lord, I ask you to give us eyes to see and ears to hear where we may humbly serve others. Bless my brothers with your peace and presence. I ask for your protection over them and their families.

Lord, we love you and thank you for answering our prayers.
In Jesus' name. AMEN

APRIL - DAILY DEVOTIONAL #2

Jesus went out as usual to the Mount of Olives, and his disciples followed him. On reaching the place, he said to them, "Pray that you will not fall into temptation." He withdrew about a stone's throw beyond them, knelt down and prayed, "Father, if you are willing, take this cup from me; yet not my will, but yours be done." An angel from heaven appeared to him and strengthened him. And being in anguish, he prayed more earnestly, and his sweat was like drops of blood falling to the ground. When he rose from prayer and went back to the disciples, he found them asleep, exhausted from sorrow. "Why are you sleeping?" he asked them. "Get up and pray so that you will not fall into temptation."

LUKE 22:39-46 NIV

REFLECTIONS:

Every day when you wake up, pray for the Lord's guidance throughout the day, so that when temptation comes around, you will recognize it and rebuke it. Remember, temptations have many forms. Many temptations may seem like a blessing from God, but they are actually a curse from the enemy to try to trap you into sin. So pray every morning, asking for protection and guidance. Then pray at night, thanking the Lord for being with you all day.

REQUESTS:

Lord, may your Spirit strengthen us so we're not found sleeping or falling into the temptations of this world, but be found seeking you in all that we do. We thank you for Jesus, who, despite our guilt, paid the ultimate price of dying for our sins. He rose again in three days, so we may walk in his grace and mercy when we receive Jesus and the forgiveness of our sins. Lord, bless each of my brothers and their families with your peace and presence.

Lord, we love you and thank you for answering our prayers.
In Jesus' name. AMEN

APRIL - DAILY DEVOTIONAL #3

But he was pierced for our transgressions, he was crushed for our iniquities; the punishment that brought us peace was on him, and by his wounds we are healed.

ISAIAH 53:5 NIV

REFLECTIONS:

They say that by his stripes we are healed, and the blood of Jesus heals all hurts and washes away our sins. So the crown of thorns that was placed on his head—the wound and the blood—takes away your worries and anxiety. Jesus didn't have a place on his body that wasn't wounded or covered in blood. So whatever you think you have that can't be healed, Jesus did it at the cross.

Remember the lady who touched Jesus and was healed? How much more healed will you be when Jesus touches you? So no matter what a doctor tells you, you need to hang on to the peace you have from him.

REQUESTS:

Lord, may we find and walk in that peace that was given to us through Jesus being punished for our sins. We know we didn't earn it, and we surely don't deserve it. But you loved us enough that our forgiveness came from the mercy and grace you gave us through Jesus. Lord, bless my brothers with your presence, guiding them to a deeper walk with you . . ..

Lord, we love you and thank you for answering our prayers.
In Jesus' name. AMEN

APRIL - DAILY DEVOTIONAL #4

. . . and said to Jesus, "Teacher, this woman was caught in the act of adultery. In the Law Moses commanded us to stone such women. Now what do you say?" They were using this question as a trap, in order to have a basis for accusing him. But Jesus bent down and started to write on the ground with his finger. When they kept on questioning him, he straightened up and said to them, "Let any one of you who is without sin be the first to throw a stone at her." Again he stooped down and wrote on the ground. At this, those who heard began to go away one at a time, the older ones first, until only Jesus was left, with the woman still standing there. Jesus straightened up and asked her, "Woman, where are they? Has no one condemned you?" "No one, sir," she said. "Then neither do I condemn you," Jesus declared. "Go now and leave your life of sin."

JOHN 8:4-11 NIV

REFLECTIONS:

If you're like me, you may have had a thought pop into your head after reading this. What did Jesus write on the ground? In my own country boy way of thinking, I believe he wrote something from the Word. He answers every question the devil asks him with the Word. This is how we must respond to the world when we are questioned or condemned...with the Word.

REQUESTS:

Lord, bless these men with peace. When the devil or the world wants to throw rocks at them, may they run to you, because you took their condemnation to the cross!

Lord, we love you and thank you for answering our prayers.
In Jesus' name. AMEN

APRIL - DAILY DEVOTIONAL #5

There was a violent earthquake, for an angel of the Lord came down from heaven and, going to the tomb, rolled back the stone and sat on it. . . . The angel said to the women, "Do not be afraid, for I know that you are looking for Jesus, who was crucified. He is not here; he has risen, just as he said. Come and see the place where he lay. . . . "

MATTHEW 28:2, 5-6 NIV

REFLECTIONS:

I think many of us need a violent earthquake to shake us up a little and remind us we have a Savior in heaven who went to the cross to pay for our sins. We need to stop living as if we are children of this world, and start living in a way that shows we are children of the most high king Jesus. We need to act as someone who walked out of their grave because that's exactly what happened when we accepted Jesus as our Lord and Savior.

REQUESTS:

Lord, thank you that when the stone was rolled away, it wasn't for Jesus to get out. It wasn't just for the evidence that Jesus had risen. But, Lord, it is so when we get tired of living in the darkness of sin, we can be reminded that you will roll our stone away. We can look up and see the light of Jesus and walk out of our own grave and receive eternal life through Jesus. Lord, bless each of my brothers and their families today with your peace and presence.

Lord, we love you and thank you for answering our prayers.
In Jesus' name. AMEN

APRIL - DAILY DEVOTIONAL #6

Be patient, then, brothers and sisters, until the Lord's coming. See how the farmer waits for the land to yield its valuable crop, patiently waiting for the autumn and spring rains. You too, be patient and stand firm, because the Lord's coming is near. Don't grumble against one another, brothers and sisters, or you will be judged. The Judge is standing at the door! Brothers and sisters, as an example of patience in the face of suffering, take the prophets who spoke in the name of the Lord. As you know, we count as blessed those who have persevered. You have heard of Job's perseverance and have seen what the Lord finally brought about. The Lord is full of compassion and mercy.

JAMES 5:7-11 NIV

REFLECTIONS:

Have you ever gone into a situation and doubted God led you to this place because the conditions didn't feel right or didn't look right? And so you didn't put forth much of an effort to be patient and wait on God to move. God doesn't look for the right conditions or a particular feeling!

Consider Paul, who was a murderer when God spoke to him. Yet Paul was patient and followed after God to be healed. He might have run away, but God used him to spread the gospel throughout the known world at that time. Paul's letters helped to form what we know as the New Testament.

REQUESTS:

God, don't let us focus on how we feel or our situation. May our trust be in you; may we be obedient and patient in our time of waiting.

Lord, we love you and thank you for answering our prayers.
In Jesus' name. AMEN

APRIL - DAILY DEVOTIONAL #7

Jesus, once more deeply moved, came to the tomb. It was a cave with a stone laid across the entrance. "Take away the stone," he said. "But, Lord," said Martha, the sister of the dead man, "by this time there is a bad odor, for he has been there four days." Then Jesus said, "Did I not tell you that if you believe, you will see the glory of God?" So they took away the stone. Then Jesus looked up and said, "Father, I thank you that you have heard me. I knew that you always hear me, but I said this for the benefit of the people standing here, that they may believe that you sent me." When he had said this, Jesus called in a loud voice, "Lazarus, come out!" The dead man came out, his hands and feet wrapped with strips of linen, and a cloth around his face. Jesus said to them, "Take off the grave clothes and let him go."

JOHN 11:38-44 NIV

REFLECTIONS:

Which side of the stone are you on? You are either: 1) stuck in a cave of the world, separating yourself from God, family, and friends, or 2) you're pleading with Jesus to call someone out of their cave they're hiding in.

REQUESTS:

So, Lord, I ask you to give the one stuck in their cave whatever that looks like, ears to hear your calling, eyes to see the darkness they're in, and a heart to be obedient to come out of the darkness into your light to be healed. Lord, for the one who is pleading with you in prayer, I ask you to give them peace, as you are glorified by answering their prayers. Lord, bless these men and their families. May all that we do bring glory to you.

Lord, we love you and thank you for answering our prayers.
In Jesus' name. AMEN

APRIL - DAILY DEVOTIONAL #8

For an overseer, as God's steward, must be above reproach. He must not be arrogant or quick-tempered or a drunkard or violent or greedy for gain, but hospitable, a lover of good, self-controlled, upright, holy, and disciplined. He must hold firm to the trustworthy word as taught, so that he may be able to give instruction in sound doctrine and also to rebuke those who contradict it.

TITUS 1:7-9 ESV

REFLECTIONS:

Everything around us is God's. In the passage above, Paul was referring to a position in the church. But, as men, we should all approach our everyday life with this same mindset. Through Jesus, we have been made overseers of his kingdom.

REQUESTS:

Lord, we ask for wisdom in all that you have blessed us with to oversee our families, our jobs, and especially our walk with you. Lord, bless us with eyes to see and ears to hear your direction and will for our lives.

Lord, we love you and thank you for answering our prayers.
In Jesus' name. AMEN

APRIL - DAILY DEVOTIONAL #9

The LORD said to Moses, "Why do you cry to me? Tell the people of Israel to go forward. Lift up your staff, and stretch out your hand over the sea and divide it, that the people of Israel may go through the sea on dry ground. And I will harden the hearts of the Egyptians so that they shall go in after them, and I will get glory over Pharaoh and all his host, his chariots, and his horsemen. And the Egyptians shall know that I am the LORD, when I have gotten glory over Pharaoh, his chariots, and his horsemen."

EXODUS 14:15-18 ESV

REFLECTIONS:

Moses learned that the raising of the hands was in obedience and worship of God. This action should still be used today. If we truly trust him, we can walk through the problem with God leading us. Unbeknownst to Moses, he embodied Psalm 23 even before it existed.

REQUESTS:

Lord, as we worship this morning, we lift our hands, seeking your guidance through our current struggles.

Lord, we love you and thank you for answering our prayers.
In Jesus' name. AMEN

APRIL - DAILY DEVOTIONAL #10

The very fact that you have lawsuits among you means you have been completely defeated already. Why not rather be wronged? Why not rather be cheated? Instead, you yourselves cheat and do wrong, and you do this to your brothers and sisters. Or do you not know that wrongdoers will not inherit the kingdom of God? Do not be deceived: Neither the sexually immoral nor idolaters nor adulterers nor men who have sex with men or thieves nor the greedy nor drunkards nor slanderers nor swindlers will inherit the kingdom of God. And that is what some of you were. But you were washed, you were sanctified, you were justified in the name of the Lord Jesus Christ and by the Spirit of our God.

1 CORINTHIANS 6:7-11 NIV

REFLECTIONS:

In this passage, the key word is "were." We were people who didn't honor God and would not inherit his kingdom. But now we're not those things! And this is not because of something *we* did. Christ's willingness to go to the cross and bear our shame saved us from death, the grave, and an eternity in hell.

REQUESTS:

Lord, we accept your forgiveness. We honor you for taking our place on the cross. May our lives reflect the love you have for all. Lord, bless these men with all that they need (and then some)!

Lord, we love you and thank you for answering our prayers.
In Jesus' name. AMEN

APRIL - DAILY DEVOTIONAL #11

He replied, "Because you have so little faith. Truly I tell you, if you have faith as small as a mustard seed, you can say to this mountain, 'Move from here to there,' and it will move. Nothing will be impossible for you."

MATTHEW 17:20 NIV

REFLECTIONS:

Wouldn't it be awesome to have the boldness that David, the shepherd boy, had when he spoke to Goliath? His little faith in a big God brought David victory over his giant!

Often, I quote this scripture because I fear the mountain. But the Lord didn't give us a spirit of fear. We must give God what little faith we have and ask him to help us move mountains.

REQUESTS:

Lord, help us stand firm in you and boldly face our mountains with your confidence. Bless us with your presence and peace.

Lord, we love you and thank you for answering our prayers. In Jesus' name. AMEN

APRIL - DAILY DEVOTIONAL #12

Now the crowd that was with him when he called Lazarus from the tomb and raised him from the dead continued to spread the word. Many people, because they had heard that he had performed this sign, went out to meet him. So the Pharisees said to one another, "See, this is getting us nowhere. Look how the whole world has gone after him!"

JOHN 12:17-19 NIV

REFLECTIONS:

Here, Jesus calls forth his dear friend, Lazarus, from the tomb. And the raising of Lazarus from the dead caused the entire world to be amazed.

The day we received Jesus as Lord and Savior, he called us out of our personal tombs and gave us eternal life through the forgiveness of sins. Are people amazed at the change they see in us, following our being raised from our spiritual death? May our story resonate globally, and may we see a revival that cannot be contained.

REQUESTS:

Lord, bless these men with your presence and goodness. Today, may Your glory shine on them. Bless them with all that they need to serve you this day.

Lord, we love you and thank you for answering our prayers.
In Jesus' name. AMEN

APRIL - DAILY DEVOTIONAL #13

During the days of Jesus' life on earth, he offered up prayers and petitions with fervent cries and tears to the one who could save him from death, and he was heard because of his reverent submission.

HEBREWS 5:7 NIV

REFLECTIONS:

Men, prayer isn't something we do just because everyone else is doing it. Or because we think it is necessary to appease God.

No matter if we're praying over a family meal or praying in our closet by ourselves seeking his will, may we always have a reverent and submissive heart like Jesus.

REQUESTS:

Lord, may we learn to pray as often as you did so that we stay fully connected to your will. Lord, today bless us all with eyes to see and ears to hear your glory; may it penetrate us to the core of our being.

Lord, we love you and thank you for answering our prayers.
In Jesus' name. AMEN

APRIL - DAILY DEVOTIONAL #14

So he started out, and on his way he met an Ethiopian eunuch, an important official in charge of all the treasury of the Kandake (which means "queen of the Ethiopians"). This man had gone to Jerusalem to worship, and on his way home was sitting in his chariot reading the Book of Isaiah the prophet. The Spirit told Philip, "Go to that chariot and stay near it." Then Philip ran up to the chariot and heard the man reading Isaiah the prophet. "Do you understand what you are reading?" Philip asked. "How can I," he said, "unless someone explains it to me?" So he invited Philip to come up and sit with him.

ACTS 8:27-31 NIV

REFLECTIONS:

There are four things we gain from this passage. This is a reminder that we need:

1. Ears to hear God's direction,
2. Eyes to see the need,
3. Understanding of the Word, and last,
4. The boldness to stand in the gap like Philip and tell the good news of Jesus.

REQUESTS:

Lord, we ask for these qualities of a man of God, so in our daily walk, we can be a witness of Jesus. Lord, bless each of us with your peace and presence all around us.

Lord, we love you and thank you for answering our prayers.
In Jesus' name. AMEN

APRIL - DAILY DEVOTIONAL #15

So do not worry, saying, 'What shall we eat?' or 'What shall we drink?' or 'What shall we wear?' For the pagans run after all these things, and your heavenly Father knows that you need them. But seek first his kingdom and his righteousness, and all these things will be given to you as well. Therefore do not worry about tomorrow, for tomorrow will worry about itself. Each day has enough trouble of its own.

MATTHEW 6:31-34 NIV

REFLECTIONS:

Let's not be like Peter, who worried more about getting back in the boat instead of standing in the presence of Jesus. We should strive to be like Daniel, who pursued God even while in the lion's den.

REQUESTS:

Lord, you know our every need, those we have and those we will have. And so, we place them all at your feet. We don't want our needs to be a distraction to us. Free our hearts and minds so that we may seek you first in all things.

Lord, we love you and thank you for answering our prayers.
In Jesus' name. AMEN

APRIL - DAILY DEVOTIONAL #16

A certain man from Cyrene, Simon, the father of Alexander and Rufus, was passing by on his way in from the country, and they forced him to carry the cross.

MARK 15:21 NIV

REFLECTIONS:

The Lord never forces us to respond. However, he's given us a heart to help those who are struggling and are carrying a cross. He provides what we require to live victoriously and to have strength daily.

REQUESTS:

This old world should never win. Lord, give us eyes to see and ears to hear the opportunities to share the gospel and love others as Jesus loves us. Bless these men with your presence and peace today.

Lord, we love you and thank you for answering our prayers.
In Jesus' name. AMEN

APRIL - DAILY DEVOTIONAL #17

Therefore, since we are surrounded by such a great cloud of witnesses, let us throw off everything that hinders and the sin that so easily entangles. And let us run with perseverance the race marked out for us, fixing our eyes on Jesus, the pioneer and perfecter of faith. For the joy set before him he endured the cross, scorning its shame, and sat down at the right hand of the throne of God. Consider him who endured such opposition from sinners, so that you will not grow weary and lose heart.

HEBREWS 12:1-3 NIV

REFLECTIONS:

Excess weight can burden us as we run our race. Our lives are weighed down by fear, worry, and anxiety. But Jesus died to remove these burdens. As today's scripture teaches, we must throw off everything that holds us back or entangles us. Do you constantly eliminate things that prevent you from following Christ?

REQUESTS:

Lord, may we find the joy Jesus found as he endured the cross and its shame for our guilt, so we know that we're never alone in the troubles and hardships of this world. May we fix our eyes and hearts on Jesus—the one who goes before us, walks with us, and follows after us.

Lord, we love you and thank you for answering our prayers.
In Jesus' name. AMEN

APRIL - DAILY DEVOTIONAL #18

After forty years had passed, an angel appeared to Moses in the flames of a burning bush in the desert near Mount Sinai. When he saw this, he was amazed at the sight. As he went over to get a closer look, he heard the Lord say: "I am the God of your fathers, the God of Abraham, Isaac and Jacob."Moses trembled with fear and did not dare to look.

ACTS 7:30-32 NIV

REFLECTIONS:

As individual men and as the body of Christ, we should never take God's presence for granted. We should have a reverent heart and act like we're at the burning bush on sacred ground.

REQUESTS:

Lord, many things changed, but you remain constant. We should show you the same awareness and respect that Moses did. For we, too, are standing on holy ground. Lord, bless us today in our homes and places of worship, with a heart-changing moment like Moses at the burning bush!

Lord, we love you and thank you for answering our prayers.
In Jesus' name. AMEN

APRIL - DAILY DEVOTIONAL #19

A furious squall came up, and the waves broke over the boat, so that it was nearly swamped. Jesus was in the stern, sleeping on a cushion. The disciples woke him and said to him, "Teacher, don't you care if we drown?" He got up, rebuked the wind and said to the waves, "Quiet! Be still!" Then the wind died down and it was completely calm.

MARK 4:37-39 NIV

REFLECTIONS:

Now that's something unique to put on our resume: "Slept through a major storm and didn't panic or wake up!" But it's also unlikely that most of us have done that. We tend to wake up and cry out to God in fear.

Jesus is faithful. He took care of his disciples in the midst of a storm, and he will take care of us, as well. Are you speaking to your storms in the name of Jesus? Are you telling them to "Be still?"

REQUESTS:

Lord, thank you for your constant peace through trials; turning to you instead of hiding from fear grants us that peace. Provide us with a tranquility that can calm the wind in the midst of a storm. Prepare our hearts for the next storm. Allow us to have victory over our trials.

Lord, we love you and thank you for answering our prayers.
In Jesus' name. AMEN

APRIL - DAILY DEVOTIONAL #20

For though we live in the world, we do not wage war as the world does. The weapons we fight with are not the weapons of the world. On the contrary, they have divine power to demolish strongholds. We demolish arguments and every pretension that sets itself up against the knowledge of God, and we take captive every thought to make it obedient to Christ.

2 CORINTHIANS 10:3-5 NIV

REFLECTIONS:

In our world, we use physical weapons to fight an enemy: guns, knives, tanks, and bombs, etc. But in the spiritual world, our weapon is the power of the Holy Spirit within us. God speaks to us through the Holy Spirit to lead us in battle, whether it is to speak through us, to defend the gospel, uplift the broken-hearted, or preach to the lost.

REQUESTS:

Lord, without the power of your Holy Spirit within us, we are useless in battle. Transform us by the renewing of minds today so that our thoughts are your thoughts and our ways are your ways. Bless each of us with the divine power we need to stand against the world.

Lord, we love you and thank you for answering our prayers.
In Jesus' name. AMEN

APRIL - DAILY DEVOTIONAL #21

A cry is heard on the barren heights, the weeping and pleading of the people of Israel, because they have perverted their ways and have forgotten the Lord their God. "Return, faithless people; I will cure you of backsliding."

"Yes, we will come to you, for you are the Lord our God. Surely the idolatrous commotion on the hills and mountains is a deception; surely in the Lord our God is the salvation of Israel. From our youth, shameful gods have consumed the fruits of our ancestors' labor—their flocks and herds, their sons and daughters . . .. "

JEREMIAH 3:21-24 NIV

REFLECTIONS:

The character of a man is determined by what he does when no one is looking. Because the Lord is always watching.

REQUESTS:

Lord, help us not to be storefront Christian men who forget you or turn from you when no one is looking. It consumes our children and their children's children. May our faith and salvation be unwavering, God, whether someone is watching or not. You are our God; may we serve no other. We repent of our backsliding and hypocrisy. Lord, bless us all with a heart that chases after you.

Lord, we love you and thank you for answering our prayers.
In Jesus' name. AMEN

APRIL - DAILY DEVOTIONAL #22

Blessed is the one who trusts in the LORD, who does not look to the proud, to those who turn aside to false gods.

PSALM 40:4 NIV

REFLECTIONS:

It's easy to trust the Lord with all things when they are running smoothly and like a well-oiled machine. But when a wrench gets thrown into that, we need help. We should always turn to him and surround ourselves with Godly men who will stand and pray with us in those rough times.

REQUESTS:

Lord, the world has its ways of dealing with troubles, but most of them are only temporary fixes that lead to more troubles. So, Lord, assure us that you have our back and will be with us through thick and thin.

Lord, we love you and thank you for answering our prayers.
In Jesus' name. AMEN

APRIL - DAILY DEVOTIONAL #23

Likewise, the tongue is a small part of the body, but it makes great boasts. Consider what a great forest is set on fire by a small spark. The tongue also is a fire, a world of evil among the parts of the body. It corrupts the whole body, sets the whole course of one's life on fire, and is itself set on fire by hell.

JAMES 3:5-6 NIV

REFLECTIONS:

The Lord spoke to beggars and thieves in positive ways, and never did he say they could do better without bringing healing to them physically and spiritually. It's easier to say they need to find a job than to offer help.

REQUESTS:

Lord, I ask you to forgive me where I have failed to speak Jesus into the lives of the less fortunate. Lord, I ask you for eyes to see and ears to hear you, so we will know the genuine needs of those around us. May we speak and show Jesus to them. When we go to our places of worship, fill us with your presence, pour out your Spirit, and may we leave there forever changed.

Lord, we love you and thank you for answering our prayers.
In Jesus' name. AMEN

APRIL - DAILY DEVOTIONAL #24

It is for freedom that Christ has set us free. Stand firm, then, and do not let yourselves be burdened again by a yoke of slavery. Mark my words! I, Paul, tell you that if you let yourselves be circumcised, Christ will be of no value to you at all. Again I declare to every man who lets himself be circumcised that he is obligated to obey the whole law. You who are trying to be justified by the law have been alienated from Christ; you have fallen away from grace. For through the Spirit we eagerly await by faith the righteousness for which we hope. For in Christ Jesus neither circumcision nor uncircumcision has any value. The only thing that counts is faith expressing itself through love.

GALATIANS 5:1-6 NIV

REFLECTIONS:

There is freedom from the world's ways of living in Jesus. Let us share that freedom that leads to eternal life with Christ. The freedom he gives is so much more than what the world offers, which leads to death.

REQUESTS:

Lord, thank you that you are always there to pick us up when we get ahead of you and your direction for us. Bless each one of these men with peace and your presence all around them. Lord, where they are struggling, give them strength and wisdom to overcome the struggle.

Lord, we love you and thank you for answering our prayers.
In Jesus' name. AMEN

APRIL - DAILY DEVOTIONAL #25

He said to them, "Go into all the world and preach the gospel to all creation. Whoever believes and is baptized will be saved, but whoever does not believe will be condemned. And these signs will accompany those who believe: In my name they will drive out demons; they will speak in new tongues; they will pick up snakes with their hands; and when they drink deadly poison, it will not hurt them at all; they will place their hands on sick people, and they will get well."

MARK 16:15-18 NIV

REFLECTIONS:

When believers come together and begin to pray as the Body of Christ, these signs do follow. We begin to see deliverance from bondage. When we walked in the world's ways, we had a worldly language that did not bring glory to the Lord, but now we have a new language of praising him and giving him all the glory.

The body truly stands on the promise that "no weapon formed against us shall prosper," whether earthly or spiritual. And as the body of Christ is praying together in unity, the sick are being healed.

REQUESTS:

Lord, give us the eyes to see and ears to hear more of what's happening through the body of Christ and less of what's happening in the world. Lord, may your glory shine through all believers when we come together as one body.

Lord, we love you and thank you for answering our prayers.
In Jesus' name. AMEN

APRIL - DAILY DEVOTIONAL #26

"When you enter the land of Canaan, which I am giving you as your possession, and I put a spreading mold in a house in that land, the owner of the house must go and tell the priest, 'I have seen something that looks like a defiling mold in my house.' The priest is to order the house to be emptied before he goes in to examine the mold, so that nothing in the house will be pronounced unclean. After this the priest is to go in and inspect the house. . . . "

LEVITICUS 14:34-36 NIV

REFLECTIONS:

We need continual reporting of any sin in our lives, so it doesn't defile others around us, as with mold. One little spot needs to be taken care of before it spreads throughout the house. The same is true with sin, so it does not spread throughout our hearts and minds.

REQUESTS:

Lord, may we have a willing heart to allow Jesus to come inspect every room of our hearts, leaving nothing hidden.

Lord, we love you and thank you for answering our prayers.
In Jesus' name. AMEN

APRIL - DAILY DEVOTIONAL #27

And now, Israel, what does the LORD your God ask of you but to fear the LORD your God, to walk in obedience to him, to love him, to serve the LORD your God with all your heart and with all your soul, . . .

DEUTERONOMY 10:12 NIV

REFLECTIONS:

In this passage, the LORD is asking us to do three things to show that we "fear" him:

1. Walk in obedience to him,
2. To love him, and
3. To serve him with all of our heart and all of our soul.

God is still asking us to do this very thing today! Are you ready to respond in faithfulness to him?

REQUESTS:

Lord, may we be obedient and attentive in taking care of business by following these requests. As we grow in you, may we have eyes to see and ears to hear more ways to serve and love others. Let them see in us that we serve and love you, Lord, with all our hearts. Bless these men with your peace and presence as they grow and learn to serve others.

Lord, we love you and thank you for answering our prayers.
In Jesus' name. AMEN

APRIL - DAILY DEVOTIONAL #28

If you remain in me and my words remain in you, ask whatever you wish, and it will be done for you. This is to my Father's glory, that you bear much fruit, showing yourselves to be my disciples. "As the Father has loved me, so have I loved you. Now remain in my love. If you keep my commands, you will remain in my love, just as I have kept my Father's commands and remain in his love. I have told you this so that my joy may be in you and that your joy may be complete. My command is this: Love each other as I have loved you. . . .

JOHN 15:7-12 NIV

REFLECTIONS:

Jesus laid down his life for us to be saved from death, hell, and the grave. So let us lay ourselves down to serve, and to love others so they may see Jesus through our love and actions. May we find *your* pure joy in serving.

REQUESTS:

Lord, I ask you to give us eyes to see and ears to hear. Show us how to lay down our selfish desires for our own lives so we may serve others and show your unconditional love.

Lord, we love you and thank you for answering our prayers.
In Jesus' name. AMEN

APRIL - DAILY DEVOTIONAL #29

Now faith is confidence in what we hope for and assurance about what we do not see. This is what the ancients were commended for. By faith we understand that the universe was formed at God's command, so that what is seen was not made out of what was visible.

HEBREWS 11:1-3 NIV

REFLECTIONS:

Many people live in a fantasy world (or now a virtual world) where they make things up as they go. When it gets boring or trouble comes, they hit reset. In reality, we need a hard reset because the only real life we have is in the Lord.

REQUESTS:

As men of God, forgive us, Lord, where we have failed in showing our faith and the hope we have in you. May we be men known for being real in you, Lord. Not men whose world around them is falling apart because their fantasy world won't let them see it. Lord, may our hope and faith always be in you.

Lord, we love you and thank you for answering our prayers.
In Jesus' name. AMEN

APRIL - DAILY DEVOTIONAL #30

The earth is the LORD's, and everything in it, the world, and all who live in it; for he founded it on the seas and established it on the waters. Who may ascend the mountain of the LORD? Who may stand in his holy place? The one who has clean hands and a pure heart, who does not trust in an idol or swear by a false god. They will receive blessing from the LORD and vindication from God their Savior. Such is the generation of those who seek him, who seek your face, God of Jacob.

PSALM 24:1-6 NIV

REFLECTIONS:

What are you seeking today?

REQUESTS:

Lord, may we be men who seek you daily to walk with us, guiding us to do your good work in your kingdom. May we be men who lead the next generation in seeking you and your glory. Lord, bless these men with your peace and your presence throughout their day, so someone may see Jesus in the joy they carry.

Lord, we love you and thank you for answering our prayers.
In Jesus' name. AMEN

MAY - DAILY DEVOTIONAL #1

Trust in the LORD with all your heart and lean not on your own understanding; in all your ways submit to him, and he will make your paths straight.

PROVERBS 3:5-6 NIV

REFLECTIONS:

Google Maps gives us choices on how to get somewhere on a road trip. But on this trip of life, Jesus gives us a clear path when we're walking in and always seeking his direction.

REQUESTS:

Today, Lord, we commit all our steps to you. Lead us, Good Shepherd. Bless these men and their families with everything that they need.

Lord, we love you and thank you for answering our prayers.
In Jesus' name. AMEN

MAY - DAILY DEVOTIONAL #2

Rejoice always, pray continually, give thanks in all circumstances; for this is God's will for you in Christ Jesus.

1 THESSALONIANS 5:16-18 NIV

REFLECTIONS:

How much would you have if you woke up this morning, and you only had in your possession what you had thanked God for yesterday?

REQUESTS:

Lord, thank you that through your mercy and grace, we don't really have to worry about that. But when you asked me that last night, it hit me like a ton of bricks. Lord, we don't want to take anything you've blessed each one of us with for granted. Give us a thankful heart and bless these men and their families with all that they need.

Lord, we love you and thank you for answering our prayers. In Jesus' name. AMEN

MAY - DAILY DEVOTIONAL #3

... but I gave them this command: Obey me, and I will be your God and you will be my people. Walk in obedience to all I command you, that it may go well with you. But they did not listen or pay attention; instead, they followed the stubborn inclinations of their evil hearts. They went backward and not forward.

JEREMIAH 7:23-24 NIV

REFLECTIONS:

If you look this scripture up, God is talking about the Jewish people when they were walking around in circles with Moses. But in more ways than one, he's also describing us as a church and as individuals. How many times have we been disobedient and wanted to do it our way and not God's? And we lost ground instead of moving forward. Praise the Lord for his grace and mercy.

REQUESTS:

Lord, we ask you to forgive us when we are stubborn towards you. I ask, Lord, as we grow in you and seek your direction, we begin to take each step with you, instead of thinking our way might be better. Bless these men and their families with your peace and presence throughout their homes and families.

Lord, we love you and thank you for answering our prayers.
In Jesus' name. AMEN

MAY - DAILY DEVOTIONAL #4

When Jesus saw her weeping, and the Jews who had come along with her also weeping, he was deeply moved in spirit and troubled. "Where have you laid him?" he asked. "Come and see, Lord," they replied. Jesus wept.

JOHN 11:33-35 NIV

. . . who comforts us in all our troubles, so that we can comfort those in any trouble with the comfort we ourselves receive from God. For just as we share abundantly in the sufferings of Christ, so also our comfort abounds through Christ.

2 CORINTHIANS 1:4-5 NIV

REFLECTIONS:

The verse "Jesus wept" is the shortest verse in the Bible, yet it's probably one of the most powerful. It shows when we grieve, he grieves with us. And even while grieving with us, he is there to be the Great Comforter and the answer to our prayers.

REQUESTS:

Today, Lord, if any of these men and their families are hurting or grieving, I ask you to comfort them and fill the emptiness and helplessness they may be feeling. Lord, we thank you for always being there for us.

Lord, we love you and thank you for answering our prayers.
In Jesus' name. AMEN

MAY - DAILY DEVOTIONAL #5

Finally, brothers and sisters, whatever is true, whatever is noble, whatever is right, whatever is pure, whatever is lovely, whatever is admirable—if anything is excellent or praiseworthy—think about such things.

PHILIPPIANS 4:8 NIV

REFLECTIONS:

All of Jesus' thoughts and desires were on others and his will for them, but our thoughts and desires are selfish and often more about ourselves than others.

REQUESTS:

Lord, I ask you to forgive us for being single-minded with thoughts only of ourselves. Help us have the mind of Christ and think more highly of others. May we seek more of your desires for others than we do for ourselves. Lord, bless these young men with all that they need.

Lord, we love you and thank you for answering our prayers.
In Jesus' name. AMEN

MAY - DAILY DEVOTIONAL #6

For we know that since Christ was raised from the dead, he cannot die again; death no longer has mastery over him. The death he died, he died to sin once for all; but the life he lives, he lives to God. In the same way, count yourselves dead to sin but alive to God in Christ Jesus. Therefore do not let sin reign in your mortal body so that you obey its evil desires.

ROMANS 6:9-12 NIV

REFLECTIONS:

When we come to Jesus and we turn from our sinful life, there's not a sin he can't deliver us from if we accept Jesus as our Lord and Savior and receive his forgiveness. Who or what are you seeking?

REQUESTS:

Lord, may we be men who seek you daily to walk with us, guiding us to do your good work in your Kingdom. May we be men who lead the next generation in seeking you and your glory. I don't know what any of these men are struggling with, but help them lay it at your feet so they may walk in your freedom. Bless them with your peace and presence throughout their day, so someone may see Jesus in the joy they carry.

Lord, we love you and thank you for answering our prayers.
In Jesus' name. AMEN

MAY - DAILY DEVOTIONAL #7

Therefore I glory in Christ Jesus in my service to God. I will not venture to speak of anything except what Christ has accomplished through me in leading the Gentiles to obey God by what I have said and done—by the power of signs and wonders, through the power of the Spirit of God. So from Jerusalem all the way around to Illyricum, I have fully proclaimed the gospel of Christ. It has always been my ambition to preach the gospel where Christ was not known, so that I would not be building on someone else's foundation. Rather, as it is written: "Those who were not told about him will see, and those who have not heard will understand."

ROMANS 15:17-21 NIV

REFLECTIONS:

Just as Paul witnessed to others about Jesus, we are to do the same; it should be our desire, like a fire in us, to look for the hearts that have never heard the gospel of Jesus Christ.

REQUESTS:

Lord, I ask you to lead us to the one who has never heard the gospel. Please lead us to the hearts that need seeds planted so they may begin searching for you. May your glory shine on these men so much that others ask what's different about you. Lord, bless these men and their families with your peace and presence throughout their homes.

Lord, we love you and thank you for answering our prayers.
In Jesus' name. AMEN

MAY - DAILY DEVOTIONAL #8

All you need to say is simply 'Yes' or 'No'; anything beyond this comes from the evil one.

MATTHEW 5:37 NIV

REFLECTIONS:

Does it depend on who is asking as to how you answer a question about your faith or beliefs? In other words, is your answer the same whether you're at a Christian concert or sitting at the bar having a beer at Twin Peaks? Or maybe it depends on whether you're in your hometown vs. a town of complete strangers.

So are you a Christian, a child of God, who believes every word of the Bible all the time? Or do you have to think about how to answer the question? It's a simple question—it's either yes or no. But it sends many of us into a tornado of thoughts. Only you know how to respond yes or no.

REQUESTS:

Lord, bless us all with confidence in who we are in you. Whether it's our pastor asking or the bartender at our favorite watering hole, let our yes be yes and our no be no. Lord, may your peace rest on my brothers today. I ask you to fill their homes with your presence.

Lord, we love you and thank you for answering our prayers.
In Jesus' name. AMEN

MAY - DAILY DEVOTIONAL #9

What benefit did you reap at that time from the things you are now ashamed of? Those things result in death!

ROMANS 6:21 NIV

REFLECTIONS:

We need to ask ourselves the next question, even now after we've accepted Jesus as Lord and Savior: why are we still trying to reap benefits from things we are still doing that we are ashamed of? Every morning, we need to lay those things we struggle with at the feet of Jesus. During the day, when we begin to contemplate picking them back up, we lay them back down. Our hardest battle is against our own flesh, and we can't win without Jesus.

REQUESTS:

Lord, bless my brothers with the strength to lay down their struggles each and every day at your feet so they can all be made complete in you. Bless them with your presence and peace today.

Lord, we love you and thank you for answering our prayers.
In Jesus' name. AMEN

MAY - DAILY DEVOTIONAL #10

About midnight Paul and Silas were praying and singing hymns to God, and the other prisoners were listening to them. Suddenly there was such a violent earthquake that the foundations of the prison were shaken. At once all the prison doors flew open, and everyone's chains came loose. The jailer woke up, and when he saw the prison doors open, he drew his sword and was about to kill himself because he thought the prisoners had escaped. But Paul shouted, "Don't harm yourself! We are all here!" The jailer called for lights, rushed in and fell trembling before Paul and Silas. He then brought them out and asked, "Sirs, what must I do to be saved?"

ACTS 16:25-30 NIV

REFLECTIONS:

Do you feel locked up today? That could mean anything for each of us—sin, anxiety, worry, or an addiction, and the list could go on. Paul and Silas took their eyes off what had them locked up and began to pray and worship, and they were set free. And ultimately, the jailer and his whole family were set free. Just as the jailer was watching Paul and Silas, people are watching you as you are set free. They, too, may come to know their freedom in Jesus. Begin to worship the Lord in prayer and song, and may your doors fly open.

REQUESTS:

Lord, many of us may not even know that we're locked up by something as little as our thoughts or as big as an addiction. During our prayer and worship, set us free, and may our freedom bring others to their freedom in Jesus. Protect my brothers and their families from any and all harm. Lord, bless them with your peace and presence.

Lord, we love you and thank you for answering our prayers.
In Jesus' name. AMEN

MAY - DAILY DEVOTIONAL #11

Brothers and sisters, as an example of patience in the face of suffering, take the prophets who spoke in the name of the Lord. As you know, we count as blessed those who have persevered. You have heard of Job's perseverance and have seen what the Lord finally brought about. The Lord is full of compassion and mercy.

JAMES 5:10-11 NIV

REFLECTIONS:

Whatever you're going through, hang on and keep seeking the Lord. He has not forgotten you or walked away from you. He's in front of you, opening a path for you. He is beside you, walking with you, so you're not alone, and he is behind you, protecting you.

REQUESTS:

Lord, I ask you to bless my brothers today, no matter what they're facing. Today, may your hand be upon them, encouraging them, guiding them to the blessings that are right around the corner. Lord, I ask you to surround them with your peace and fill their homes with your presence.

Lord, we love you and thank you for answering our prayers.
In Jesus' name. AMEN

MAY - DAILY DEVOTIONAL #12

My dear brothers and sisters, take note of this: Everyone should be quick to listen, slow to speak and slow to become angry, because human anger does not produce the righteousness that God desires.

JAMES 1:19-20 NIV

"In your anger do not sin": Do not let the sun go down while you are still angry, and do not give the devil a foothold.

EPHESIANS 4:26-27 NIV

REFLECTIONS:

Have you ever thought about the day Jesus was crucified? He never once showed himself to be mad or deeply angered. In our minds, he had every right to "be a man" at those who were hurting him. But Jesus never showed hate or anger toward his Father for putting him in the position he was in.

In fact, I would have been thinking, "If I get off the cross alive, I'm gonna get each and every one of these dudes in a dark alley," but Jesus forgave them. And not only them, but us too. Think about if he had let that root of anger set in. Today is the perfect day to turn loose of the anger that's been rooted so deep and so long that we've grown to live with it.

REQUESTS:

Lord, today I ask you to pull back the covers we've put over our anger so we may get a hold of it and give it all to you so your goodness can fill that spot in our hearts and we can be forever set free. Lord, bless my brothers with the strength and peace to lay it down at your feet and never to pick it up again.

Lord, we love you and thank you for answering our prayers.
In Jesus' name. AMEN

MAY - DAILY DEVOTIONAL #13

The commandments, "You shall not commit adultery," "You shall not murder," "You shall not steal," "You shall not covet," and whatever other command there may be, are summed up in this one command: "Love your neighbor as yourself."

ROMANS 13:9 NIV

REFLECTIONS:

A shiny new penny is worth the same as a dull one. The shiny new penny will eventually get dull, too, because it has no way or power to shine the dullness back up. Likewise, as neighbors, we are worth the same as everyone around us.

But we are either spending all our time shining ourselves up to look better than others, or we are using the love we receive from Jesus to help our neighbors. We hope they feel and see the shine of the light of Jesus in us, by us loving on them as we have been loved on through Jesus.

REQUESTS:

Lord, there are two kinds of unconditional love. The first one is the unconditional love that says, "No matter what or who it hurts, I'm gonna love myself more than anyone else," because conceit tells us we're better than and worth more than anyone else. The second is the unconditional love you gave us at the cross, Lord. May you help us to show that unconditional love to all who are around us, so we may never forget where our blessings came from.

Lord, we love you and thank you for answering our prayers.
In Jesus' name. AMEN

MAY - DAILY DEVOTIONAL #14

The Jews there were amazed and asked, "How did this man get such learning without having been taught?" Jesus answered, "My teaching is not my own. It comes from the one who sent me. Anyone who chooses to do the will of God will find out whether my teaching comes from God or whether I speak on my own. Whoever speaks on their own does so to gain personal glory, but he who seeks the glory of the one who sent him is a man of truth; there is nothing false about him.

JOHN 7:15-18 NIV

REFLECTIONS:

This is a self-examination scripture. Do you seek glory for yourself for the things you do, or are you doing God's work to glorify him who sent you?

REQUESTS:

Lord, I ask you to fill us with the Spirit of truth. May all the things we do ultimately give glory to your kingdom. Lord, I ask you to continue to direct our paths to do your good work so we may show the truth that's in us. Lord, bless my brothers with peace and surround them with your presence.

Lord, we love you and thank you for answering our prayers.
In Jesus' name. AMEN

MAY - DAILY DEVOTIONAL #15

Once safely on shore, we found out that the island was called Malta. The islanders showed us unusual kindness. They built a fire and welcomed us all because it was raining and cold. Paul gathered a pile of brushwood and, as he put it on the fire, a viper, driven out by the heat, fastened itself on his hand. When the islanders saw the snake hanging from his hand, they said to each other, "This man must be a murderer; for though he escaped from the sea, the goddess Justice has not allowed him to live." But Paul shook the snake off into the fire and suffered no ill effects.

ACTS 28:1-5 NIV

REFLECTIONS:

When the Spirit of the Lord begins to move, those who can't stand the heat begin to try to destroy you or make you look back at other situations. We can either yield to their attacks or be like Paul and shake them loose. We must continue to focus on what God has called us to do, and that's share the gospel of Jesus with those who will listen.

REQUESTS:

Lord, bless each of my brothers with peace as the enemy tries to mess up their testimony. Cover them with the blood of Jesus to protect them from any harm. Let those around them be astonished that what the enemy has done didn't destroy them, but made them stronger in their faith in you. Lord, fill my brothers' homes with your presence; bring all their households to Jesus.

Lord, we love you and thank you for answering our prayers.
In Jesus' name. AMEN

MAY - DAILY DEVOTIONAL #16

It is written: "I believed; therefore I have spoken." Since we have that same spirit of faith, we also believe and therefore speak, because we know that the one who raised the Lord Jesus from the dead will also raise us with Jesus and present us with you to himself.

2 CORINTHIANS 4:13-14 NIV

REFLECTIONS:

Have you ever sat down in the evening and thought about your day, and asked yourself how many times did I speak Jesus or life into someone's life? It's not a competition or a requirement, but it should be second nature to see the good and speak about it.

REQUESTS:

Lord, may we not get so caught up in our day that we don't take time to see just how good you are to us and speak about it. May your goodness in us overflow to others around us. May we be the hands and feet of Jesus, and share your peace and comfort with those who are hurting. Lord, bless my brothers with eyes to see and ears to hear your goodness today.

Lord, we love you and thank you for answering our prayers.
In Jesus' name. AMEN

MAY - DAILY DEVOTIONAL #17

Dear friends, do not be surprised at the fiery ordeal that has come on you . . . But rejoice in as much as you participate in the sufferings of Christ, so that you may be overjoyed when his glory is revealed. If you are insulted because of the name of Christ, you are blessed, for the Spirit of glory and of God rests on you. If you suffer, it should not be as a murderer . . . However, if you suffer as a Christian, do not be ashamed, but praise God that you bear that name. For it is time for judgment to begin with God's household; and if it begins with us, what will the outcome be for those who do not obey the gospel of God? And, "If it is hard for the righteous to be saved, what will become of the ungodly and the sinner?" So then, those who suffer according to God's will should commit themselves to their faithful Creator and continue to do good.

1 PETER 4:12-19 NIV

REFLECTIONS:

Sometimes we go through such pain that we may question if God exists, but truthfully, we know he does. When we came to know Jesus as our Lord and Savior, we were not promised that roads would be smooth and all our days would be perfect. But we were promised that he would never leave us nor forsake us. If we spend our time in prayer, when the pain and rough times come, we are in a position to seek and hear from the one who can get us through the mess as more than conquerors. Develop a habit of talking to the Lord every day.

REQUESTS:

Lord, just as Christ suffered on the cross for our salvation and to honor your will, may we also honor your will and count it all joy as we seek you. You know what battles my brothers are fighting. Strengthen them and surround them with prayer warriors who will seek you with them and give them peace.

Lord, we love you and thank you for answering our prayers.
In Jesus' name. AMEN

MAY - DAILY DEVOTIONAL #18

A good man brings good things out of the good stored up in his heart, and an evil man brings evil things out of the evil stored up in his heart. For the mouth speaks what the heart is full of.

LUKE 6:45 NIV

REFLECTIONS:

It's this simple: the Jesus in your heart should never be like that little screwdriver in your toolbox, that you can never find until you empty it, because it's always at the very bottom. Then we either put the junk back in and throw the screwdriver back in with it, or we drop the screwdriver back in when we're done and put the junk back on top.

Does your heart need cleaning so Jesus doesn't fall to the bottom, or are you going to leave the junk out? Really listen to what you're speaking today, and that'll give you the answer if you don't already know it.

REQUESTS:

Lord, may we all clean our hearts, so even without words, it's obvious to those around us that we walk with you. Lord, bless my brothers' eyes to see and ears to hear you.

Lord, we love you and thank you for answering our prayers.
In Jesus' name. AMEN

MAY - DAILY DEVOTIONAL #19

Though I am free and belong to no one, I have made myself a slave to everyone, to win as many as possible. To the Jews I became like a Jew, to win the Jews. To those under the law I became like one under the law (though I myself am not under the law), so as to win those under the law. To those not having the law I became like one not having the law (though I am not free from God's law but am under Christ's law), so as to win those not having the law. To the weak I became weak, to win the weak. I have become all things to all people so that by all possible means I might save some. I do all this for the sake of the gospel, that I may share in its blessings.

1 CORINTHIANS 9:19-23 NIV

REFLECTIONS:

What limits you from being all in on sharing the gospel with any and all you possibly can? I hope and pray that when I get to heaven, no one comes up to me and thanks me for nothing. If it hadn't been for someone else, I wouldn't have found Jesus. Are your daily actions leaving a wake of hurts that you can't see, or do they leave behind hope and peace? There are three things we do every day: we either build, destroy, or do nothing. As Christians, we want it all to be for the kingdom of God.

REQUESTS:

Lord, may we all be more like Paul, who would do anything to share the gospel with even just one person. Lord, forgive us where we fall short. Continue to put opportunities in front of us to share Jesus with others, despite ourselves. Bless my brothers today with your love, grace, and mercy. You know their every need and prayer, so bless them with your glorious riches.

Lord, we love you and thank you for answering our prayers.
In Jesus' name. AMEN

MAY - DAILY DEVOTIONAL #20

Consequently, faith comes from hearing the message, and the message is heard through the word about Christ.

ROMANS 10:17 NIV

And we know that in all things God works for the good of those who love him, who have been called according to his purpose.

ROMANS 8:28 NIV

REFLECTIONS:

You say, "I've read or heard both scriptures, and nothing ever goes my way." Well, if you had a plate full of food and you threw it away, eventually you're going to starve to death. But if I hand you a plate of food and you receive it as a meal and eat it, you get full, and you know you won't starve to death.

Now handle God's Word the same way if you receive it and digest it. Don't just read it or hear it and let it go through one ear and out the other. Receive it and let it grow within you.

REQUESTS:

Lord, bless these men and their families today with your peace and goodness, and surround them with your presence. May your words—whether we read them or hear them—be received and move us around to a position to receive your blessings. Lord, I ask you, whatever my brothers are going through, may you work all out for their good according to your will.

Lord, we love you and thank you for answering our prayers.
In Jesus' name. AMEN

MAY - DAILY DEVOTIONAL #21

What I am saying is that as long as an heir is underage, he is no different from a slave, although he owns the whole estate. The heir is subject to guardians and trustees until the time set by his father. So also, when we were underage, we were in slavery under the elemental spiritual forces of the world. But when the set time had fully come, God sent his Son, born of a woman, born under the law, to redeem those under the law, that we might receive adoption to sonship. Because you are his sons, God sent the Spirit of his Son into our hearts, the Spirit who calls out, *"Abba*, Father." So you are no longer a slave, but God's child; and since you are his child, God has made you also an heir.

GALATIANS 4:1-7 NIV

REFLECTIONS:

We've all heard that saying, "You can't pick who you're kin to," but God did. Jesus helped him through the adoption process, securing our inheritance in heaven. When we accept Jesus as our Lord and Savior, we are sealed in our adoption, becoming children of God and joint heirs with Christ. And in him we are no longer slaves to this world.

REQUESTS:

Lord, help us to learn how to walk humbly in our inheritance and share the love of Jesus. May our lives reflect who Jesus is and not what this world says we have to look like. Bless my brothers today with your peace and presence, guiding them in their walk with you.

Lord, we love you and thank you for answering our prayers.
In Jesus' name. AMEN

MAY - DAILY DEVOTIONAL #22

Praise be to the God and Father of our Lord Jesus Christ, who has blessed us in the heavenly realms with every spiritual blessing in Christ. For he chose us in him before the creation of the world to be holy and blameless in his sight. In love he predestined us for adoption to sonship through Jesus Christ, in accordance with his pleasure and will—to the praise of his glorious grace, which he has freely given us in the One he loves. In him we have redemption through his blood, the forgiveness of sins, in accordance with the riches of God's grace that he lavished on us. With all wisdom and understanding, he made known to us the mystery of his will according to his good pleasure, which he purposed in Christ, . . .

EPHESIANS 1:3-9 NIV

REFLECTIONS:

When the devil brings up our past, he's not saying anything God didn't know about before the beginning of time. That should make you smile. Look at it this way: which child do you have, or might *not* have had, if you knew ahead of time what trouble they would get into when they grew up? Or, to be more blunt, would your parents have brought you into the world, knowing your deeds? Yes. Yes. And yes! God could have said, "I'm not creating the heavens and earth because those guys are just too much trouble," but through Jesus and the cross, he showed he loves us despite our faults.

REQUESTS:

Lord, may your unconditional love shine through us. May we share your love and goodness with others. When the enemy comes to accuse us, may we not be knocked down but rejoice in the victory through Jesus, our Lord and Savior. Bless my brothers today with peace and your presence.

Lord, we love you and thank you for answering our prayers.
In Jesus' name. AMEN

MAY - DAILY DEVOTIONAL #23

Do nothing out of selfish ambition or vain conceit. Rather, in humility value others above yourselves, not looking to your own interests but each of you to the interests of the others.

PHILIPPIANS 2:3-4 NIV

REFLECTIONS:

When we read this Scripture, we always get convicted for the things we possess, materialistically, anyway. But what about Jesus and the forgiveness and joy he's given us through the cross and his resurrection? Do you ever feel bad or convict yourself for keeping it all inside?

We should leap for joy when we are asked to speak of Jesus. I may not have the means to give something huge like a house or a car, but I can lead others to the One who can bless them beyond their wildest dreams. So, practice humility today and tell someone about Jesus if the opportunity arises.

REQUESTS:

Lord, humble us in all our ways so that sharing Jesus is our number one goal in our walk with you. May our eyes always be on the cross and Jesus, so we use what you have blessed us for your glory, first. Bless my brothers today. You know their every need, so I ask you to bless them beyond their understanding.

Lord, we love you and thank you for answering our prayers.
In Jesus' name. AMEN

MAY - DAILY DEVOTIONAL #24

Be still before the LORD and wait patiently for him; do not fret when people succeed in their ways, when they carry out their wicked schemes.

PSALM 37:7 NIV

REFLECTIONS:

I know people who can't wait for a pan of cookies to get done, so they eat the raw cookie dough. I have to admit, it's pretty good, but the home-baked cookies are worth waiting for. Some folks even go so far as to buy already packaged cookies. Those are good, but I never felt the love in a packaged cookie that I did when my mom or grandmother made them. The same is with prayer. Don't get in such a hurry that you only get a taste of the dough, or you try to manufacture an answer. Wait for the Lord to come with a hot plate of cookies. His answers and direction are always best—for generations to come! So, continue to wait.

REQUESTS:

Lord, help us in our waiting to stay focused and steadfast in prayer, for we know you have plans for us. May we not get impatient as we watch the world continue to move around us, but find joy in the waiting. We know when you move, there is power that changes lives. Lord, bless each one of my brothers with peace as they wait for whatever answer they are seeking from you.

Lord, we love you and thank you for answering our prayers.
In Jesus' name. AMEN

MAY - DAILY DEVOTIONAL #25

And I will ask the Father, and he will give you another advocate to help you and be with you forever—the Spirit of truth. The world cannot accept him, because it neither sees him nor knows him. But you know him, for he lives with you and will be in you. I will not leave you as orphans; I will come to you.

JOHN 14:16-18 NIV

REFLECTIONS:

It's powerful to think Jesus is telling us all about the Holy Spirit coming to be with us and in us, and then he says matter-of-factly, "That's not all you're getting. I will not leave you as orphans, but I will come to you when you're lonely, scared, hurting, feeling empty, or having any or all the emotions and feelings that an orphan has. Remember, Jesus came to fill those voids of helplessness and to heal your hurts.

REQUESTS:

Lord, thank you for Jesus; help us remember and never forget that throughout history, sons were given to die for our freedom, not excluding Jesus, who died for our ultimate freedom. Lord, bless each and every family that has lost sons and daughters fighting for the freedoms we take for granted. Lord, thank you for Jesus, who died for our ultimate freedom from Hell! Let us never ever take that freedom for granted. Bless my brothers today with your peace and presence. Fill their homes with your goodness.

Lord, we love you and thank you for answering our prayers.
In Jesus' name. AMEN

MAY - DAILY DEVOTIONAL #26

... for all have sinned and fall short of the glory of God, and all are justified freely by his grace through the redemption that came by Christ Jesus.

ROMANS 3:23-24 NIV

REFLECTIONS:

How many times have we looked at someone's appearance, thought they are nothing but a druggy and a thug, and we take wide circles around them to keep away like they have the plague? You know what I'm talking about; we even do it to our neighbors. We whisper, "Did you hear about this or that? What kind of trashy person does that?"

In reality, we're all in the same boat; the only difference is someone took the time to tell you and me about Jesus and his saving grace. So you have been given hope to share. Can you do it, or are you just too perfect and clean to help your brother or sister get free?

REQUESTS:

Lord, whatever is prideful in our hearts, take it from us. Please change our hearts and remove the barriers that prevent us from assisting those we need to help. Oh God, may we begin to show the love Jesus has for us all and not the hate the world promotes. Lord, bless my brothers today with opportunities to share your unconditional love.

Lord, we love you and thank you for answering our prayers.
In Jesus' name. AMEN

MAY - DAILY DEVOTIONAL #27

A man was there by the name of Zacchaeus; he was a chief tax collector and was wealthy. He wanted to see who Jesus was, but because he was short he could not see over the crowd. So he ran ahead and climbed a sycamore-fig tree to see him, since Jesus was coming that way. When Jesus reached the spot, he looked up and said to him, "Zacchaeus, come down immediately. I must stay at your house today."

LUKE 19:2-5 NIV

REFLECTIONS:

Zacchaeus was not only short, but he was a hated tax collector. So even though he was short, he also took a chance on someone not liking him enough to knock him out of that tree. What are you willing to do to see Jesus?

We don't have to wait for him to walk by. We can spend time in God's Word, in prayer, and we can also ask him to not just come into our homes, but to come into our hearts, if you've never done that before. So whatever you think your tree is that you need to climb to see Jesus, do it today and every day.

REQUESTS:

Lord, give us a heart to chase after you. May you give us eyes to see what you'd have us do to further your kingdom. May we have ears to hear you speaking to us. Lord, we invite you into our day. Let us not get ahead of you, but may we be led by your Word. Lord, bless my brothers with your peace and presence in their homes and in their families.

Lord, we love you and thank you for answering our prayers.
In Jesus' name. AMEN

MAY - DAILY DEVOTIONAL #28

He withdrew about a stone's throw beyond them, knelt down and prayed, "Father, if you are willing, take this cup from me; yet not my will, but yours be done." An angel from heaven appeared to him and strengthened him. And being in anguish, he prayed more earnestly, and his sweat was like drops of blood falling to the ground.

LUKE 22:41-44 NIV

REFLECTIONS:

How are you praying today? Are you praying for yourselves so you may not be tempted, and are you praying for those who are struggling? Jesus was a stone's throw away from them, and they were falling asleep. They had no clue the weight that Jesus had on him.

The same is true in our lives today. We have family, friends, and even strangers facing pressures that we think we understand. So don't just pray once for them, pray continuously.

REQUESTS:

Lord, I lift my brothers to you. Many of them may be facing things I couldn't even fathom, so I ask you to strengthen them, and I ask for your intervention or healing. Whatever it is, Lord, we know you can move the mountain. Lord, bless my brothers and their families with your peace and presence today.

Lord, we love you and thank you for answering our prayers.
In Jesus' name. AMEN

MAY - DAILY DEVOTIONAL #29

LORD, I have heard of your fame; I stand in awe of your deeds, LORD. Repeat them in our day, in our time make them known; in wrath remember mercy.

HABAKKUK 3:2 NIV

REFLECTIONS:

Most lost people have heard of God, and most think the stories are cool, but they don't really know that he is real. So how different are we as Christians if we don't show and tell others that he is a real God and that it's true Jesus went to the cross for our forgiveness so we may be rescued from the pits of hell?

God is doing what he's always done, pointing us to Jesus. Are you allowing him to use you to tell of his glory so that we can be a part of it through Jesus? Don't just talk about God as a has-been, but a God who was, who is, and who is to come.

REQUESTS:

Lord, I ask you to continue to use us to tell others of your rescue story that comes through Jesus and the cross. May our lives preach Jesus is real and alive, sitting at the Father's right hand, until it's time for you to come back. Lord, use us! I ask you to bless my brothers today with your peace and presence.

Lord, we love you and thank you for answering our prayers.
In Jesus' name. AMEN

MAY - DAILY DEVOTIONAL #30

Even if I should choose to boast, I would not be a fool, because I would be speaking the truth. But I refrain, so no one will think more of me than is warranted by what I do or say, or because of these surpassingly great revelations. Therefore, in order to keep me from becoming conceited, I was given a thorn in my flesh, a messenger of Satan, to torment me. Three times I pleaded with the Lord to take it away from me. But he said to me, "My grace is sufficient for you, for my power is made perfect in weakness." Therefore I will boast all the more gladly about my weaknesses, so that Christ's power may rest on me. That is why, for Christ's sake, I delight in weaknesses, in insults, in hardships, in persecutions, in difficulties. For when I am weak, then I am strong.

2 CORINTHIANS 12:6-10 NIV

REFLECTIONS:

All of us have a thorn. I don't know if Paul's was a physical or spiritual thorn, but I do know what mine is. Instead of asking God to heal me or deliver me from it, I've learned to be grateful for it, because it's God's way of keeping me humble, not breaking my arm patting myself on the back, for who I have become and what I've done. I know it's all because of Jesus, who died so that we may be made perfect.

REQUESTS:

Lord, I ask you to bless my brothers. Help my brothers not to be crippled by their thorn, but to embrace the humbling it brings. I ask you to bless them in ways they've never thought of, as you use their weakness to minister to others. Lord, I ask you to fill their homes with your peace and presence today.

Lord, we love you and thank you for answering our prayers.
In Jesus' name. AMEN

MAY - DAILY DEVOTIONAL #31

I am writing these things to you about those who are trying to lead you astray. As for you, the anointing you received from him remains in you, and you do not need anyone to teach you. But as his anointing teaches you about all things and as that anointing is real, not counterfeit—just as it has taught you, remain in him. And now, dear children, continue in him, so that when he appears we may be confident and unashamed before him at his coming.

1 JOHN 2:26-28 NIV

REFLECTIONS:

Not every preacher or teacher is telling the truth. That's why we have to measure everything by God's word and his Spirit within us. We also need to be in a place where we are ready and willing to accept the truth, because whether you're a child of God or not, sometimes the truth of God's Word hurts. The truth should always move us towards God and not against him.

REQUESTS:

Lord, I ask for our hearts to chase after the truth and not what sounds good or what we want to hear. We ask for wisdom through your Spirit so we may measure all that we face by what we're told in your Word. Bless my brothers today with your overwhelming goodness and peace.

Lord, we love you and thank you for answering our prayers.
In Jesus' name. AMEN

What God has for you, is for you. Trust His timing. Trust His plan.

JUNE - DAILY DEVOTIONAL #1

Whoever believes in the Son of God accepts this testimony. Whoever does not believe God has made him out to be a liar, because they have not believed the testimony God has given about his Son. And this is the testimony: God has given us eternal life, and this life is in his Son. Whoever has the Son has life; whoever does not have the Son of God does not have life.

1 JOHN 5:10-13 NIV

REFLECTIONS:

The Word says that those who believe in the Son of God have a "testimony." That is a solemn declaration of what has occurred or what someone has done in your life. What is your testimony? Do you have something powerful that the Lord has done in your life that you can declare?

REQUESTS:

Lord, may you use us to testify of your great mercy and grace so the good news of Jesus is spread through our families, our communities, and our country. Bless each of these men and their families with an outpouring of your love and grace over them.

Lord, we love you and thank you for answering our prayers.
In Jesus' name. AMEN

JUNE - DAILY DEVOTIONAL #2

Guard your steps when you go to the house of God. Go near to listen rather than to offer the sacrifice of fools, who do not know that they do wrong. Do not be quick with your mouth, do not be hasty in your heart to utter anything before God. God is in heaven and you are on earth, so let your words be few.

ECCLESIASTES 5:1-2 NIV

REFLECTIONS:

The most significant character trait we can receive from the Lord is the ability to listen, not just with our ears, but more importantly, with our hearts. More often than not, when we only listen with our ears, it goes in one ear and out the other. However, when we listen with our hearts, it sinks in and causes change.

REQUESTS:

Lord, today may our ears and mouths be closed, but open our hearts to receive and hear your life-changing words. Bless these men and their families with your peace and your presence in their homes today.

Lord, we love you and thank you for answering our prayers.
In Jesus' name. AMEN

JUNE - DAILY DEVOTIONAL #3

Now if the ministry that brought death, which was engraved in letters on stone, came with glory, . . . will not the ministry of the Spirit be even more glorious? If the ministry that brought condemnation was glorious, how much more glorious is the ministry that brings righteousness! . . . And if what was transitory came with glory, how much greater is the glory of that which lasts! Therefore, since we have such a hope, we are very bold. We are not like Moses, who would put a veil over his face . . . Even to this day when Moses is read, a veil covers their hearts. But whenever anyone turns to the Lord, the veil is taken away. Now the Lord is the Spirit, and where the Spirit of the Lord is, there is freedom. And we all, who with unveiled faces contemplate the Lord's glory, are being transformed into his image with ever-increasing glory, which comes from the Lord, who is the Spirit.

2 CORINTHIANS 3:7-18 NIV

REFLECTIONS:

Moses shone with God's glory because he stood in the very presence of the Lord. Even though we have the Holy Spirit living in us, we must still *seek* the presence of the Lord and allow him to live through us so his glory will shine on us and through us. How do we do that? First, develop a time to seek the Lord in prayer and in his Word. As we do this, we shine with his glory. Eventually, it opens doors to tell people more about Jesus and how he has changed us.

REQUESTS:

Lord, may your transforming glory shine through us into a dying world. May they see you in us and ask us where our hope comes from. Bless these men with strength through your Spirit to continue to be transformed from who they once were to who they are in you. Bless them with your peace and presence today.

Lord, we love you and thank you for answering our prayers.
In Jesus' name. AMEN

JUNE - DAILY DEVOTIONAL #4

Are we beginning to commend ourselves again? Or do we need, like some people, letters of recommendation to you or from you? You yourselves are our letter, written on our hearts, known and read by everyone. You show that you are a letter from Christ, the result of our ministry, written not with ink but with the Spirit of the living God, not on tablets of stone but on tablets of human hearts. Such confidence we have through Christ before God. Not that we are competent in ourselves to claim anything for ourselves, but our competence comes from God. He has made us competent as ministers of a new covenant—not of the letter but of the Spirit; for the letter kills, but the Spirit gives life.

2 CORINTHIANS 3:1-6 NIV

REFLECTIONS:

Have you ever seen or worked with someone who nearly breaks their own arm every day trying to pat themselves on the back for the work they do? They are glory seekers. There is no glory in being a Christian or a follower of Christ if we are truly following him. All glory goes to him. Now, the blessing comes when those around us come to know Christ through our obedience.

REQUESTS:

Lord, may our walk with you be like a letter that has come to life. May we not have any confidence in the paper or the ink, but may all our confidence come from your Spirit that lives in us, guiding us. Lord, may each of my brothers fellowship with other believers and be strengthened in their spirit. Bless them with your peace and fill their home with your presence. Lord, shine your glory through them.

Lord, we love you and thank you for answering our prayers.
In Jesus' name. AMEN

JUNE - DAILY DEVOTIONAL #5

In fact, everyone who wants to live a godly life in Christ Jesus will be persecuted, while evildoers and impostors will go from bad to worse, deceiving and being deceived. But as for you, continue in what you have learned and have become convinced of, because you know those from whom you learned it, and how from infancy you have known the Holy Scriptures, which are able to make you wise for salvation through faith in Christ Jesus.

2 TIMOTHY 3:12-15 NIV

REFLECTIONS:

What is your stress relief from this rough world we live in? Mine used to be to go to the bar and get hammered. In fact, it was a daily routine. But when that wore off, the problems were usually bigger, and I got into a vicious cycle that was sucking the life out of me.

So now, when problems come and the walls are caving in, I don't walk; I run to the Father. That is where you can find peace in the middle of the storms of life. No matter what the world is telling you to do, run to Jesus to find your answers.

REQUESTS:

Lord, I ask you to be with each of my brothers as struggles come. Let it not sway them from or weaken their faith, but only make them stronger by digging into you through the Word. Lord, I ask you to make them more than conquerors in Jesus. Lord, pour into them and their families your peace and surround them in your presence.

Lord, we love you and thank you for answering our prayers.
In Jesus' name. AMEN

JUNE - DAILY DEVOTIONAL #6

Now this I know: The LORD gives victory to his anointed. He answers him from his heavenly sanctuary with the victorious power of his right hand.

PSALM 20:6 NIV

REFLECTIONS:

It's hard to even feel or think about being an anointed child of God in the middle of the storm, but that's exactly what our battle cry should be. I am a blood-bought, Spirit-filled, anointed child of God through the blood of Jesus.

If you start claiming that over your family, your home, and your job, the storms may not stop, but you'll see the hand of God walking you to Victory Lane. So remember, seek him in the storm.

REQUESTS:

Lord, thank you for the victories and peace that come with sitting in your presence. Lord, bless my brothers with your presence and hope of glory.

Lord, we love you and thank you for answering our prayers.
In Jesus' name. AMEN

JUNE - DAILY DEVOTIONAL #7

When the people heard this, they were cut to the heart and said to Peter and the other apostles, "Brothers, what shall we do?" Peter replied, "Repent and be baptized, every one of you, in the name of Jesus Christ for the forgiveness of your sins. And you will receive the gift of the Holy Spirit. The promise is for you and your children and for all who are far off—for all whom the Lord our God will call." With many other words he warned them; and he pleaded with them, "Save yourselves from this corrupt generation." Those who accepted his message were baptized, and about three thousand were added to their number that day.

ACTS 2:37-41 NIV

REFLECTIONS:

If you want to speak to someone about Jesus and there is a language barrier, remember Jesus came to serve, not to be served. So, ask the Lord to show you how you could serve them in such a way that they would see and hear Jesus.

REQUESTS:

Lord, just like on the day of Pentecost, may our words of Jesus be heard in other languages, giving understanding to those around us with whom we have a language barrier. May they hear the true gospel of Jesus and be set free from sin, from generation to generation. Lord, speak the gospel clearly through us as we share with others the love, the grace, and mercy of Jesus. Bless these men and their families with your peace and presence.

Lord, we love you and thank you for answering our prayers.
In Jesus' name. AMEN

JUNE - DAILY DEVOTIONAL #8

Consider it pure joy, my brothers and sisters, whenever you face trials of many kinds, because you know that the testing of your faith produces perseverance. Let perseverance finish its work so that you may be mature and complete, not lacking anything.

JAMES 1:2-4 NIV

REFLECTIONS:

Trials can do one of two things. They either steal all your joy and knock you off the path the Lord is leading you down, or they can be a confirmation that your obedience to the Lord has gotten the enemy all stirred up. And he is now trying to knock you off your game. So no matter what life throws at you, be persistent in chasing after the Lord, no matter how rough it gets.

REQUESTS:

Lord, thank you that when we are persevering towards you with a purpose of serving others and doing your good work, we can count all trials and stumbling blocks pure joy. Even then, you are with us, and when you're with us, we shall and will not be defeated. Because you go before us, you walk with us, and you come behind us, protecting and guiding us. Lord, bless each of my brothers and their families. I pray for a victory today that only you can give in their lives.

Lord, we love you and thank you for answering our prayers.
In Jesus' name. AMEN

JUNE - DAILY DEVOTIONAL #9

Love must be sincere. Hate what is evil; cling to what is good. Be devoted to one another in love. Honor one another above yourselves. Never be lacking in zeal, but keep your spiritual fervor, serving the Lord. Be joyful in hope, patient in affliction, faithful in prayer. Share with the Lord's people who are in need. Practice hospitality. Bless those who persecute you; bless and do not curse. Rejoice with those who rejoice; mourn with those who mourn. Live in harmony with one another. Do not be proud, but be willing to associate with people of low position. Do not be conceited.

ROMANS 12:9-16 NIV

REFLECTIONS:

Have you ever been in line at McDonald's and the car in front of you pays for your ticket, and you pay for the car's meal that's behind you? I have, and I always feel better about paying for the car behind me than my meal being paid for. It feels better to give than to receive when you know whose child you are, because Jesus taught us to serve by giving, not taking. So love others and give with a cheerful heart.

REQUESTS:

Lord, may we never forget we don't have to be the most popular guy on the block or the loudest in the room. Let us not call attention to ourselves, but may we be hidden in your presence as you serve others through us. Lord, may we be quick to be obedient to help those you show us need help. Let our thoughts make us thankful for our blessings and see how we can share them with others. But let our thoughts not be of how much better we are than someone else. Lord, protect these men and their families today.

Lord, we love you and thank you for answering our prayers.
In Jesus' name. AMEN

JUNE - DAILY DEVOTIONAL #10

For everything that was written in the past was written to teach us, so that through the endurance taught in the Scriptures and the encouragement they provide we might have hope. May the God who gives endurance and encouragement give you the same attitude of mind toward each other that Christ Jesus had, so that with one mind and one voice you may glorify the God and Father of our Lord Jesus Christ.

ROMANS 15:4-6 NIV

REFLECTIONS:

We may attend other churches, but we are all called to be one body—the body of Jesus. It's an amazing sight when the hands and feet of Jesus come together to serve with one purpose: to share the love of Jesus. So as you leave your homes, look for ways to serve and share the love of Christ.

REQUESTS:

Lord, bless my brothers and their families as we prepare our hearts and minds to step out and serve others this coming week. We know you are ready, and you've prepared the place for us to do your good work. Lord, bless my brothers and their families with peace and protection from all attacks and distractions.

Lord, we love you and thank you for answering our prayers.
In Jesus' name. AMEN

JUNE - DAILY DEVOTIONAL #11

Therefore if you have any encouragement from being united with Christ, if any comfort from his love, if any common sharing in the Spirit, if any tenderness and compassion, then make my joy complete by being like-minded, having the same love, being one in spirit and of one mind. Do nothing out of selfish ambition or vain conceit. Rather, in humility value others above yourselves, not looking to your own interests but each of you to the interests of the others. In your relationships with one another, have the same mindset as Christ Jesus: Who, being in very nature God, did not consider equality with God something to be used to his own advantage; rather, he made himself nothing by taking the very nature of a servant, being made in human likeness. And being found in appearance as a man, he humbled himself by becoming obedient to death—even death on a cross!

PHILIPPIANS 2:1-8 NIV

REFLECTIONS:

Looking beyond ourselves is very hard for many of us. How many times a day do you get so focused on yourself that you can't see past your nose? Jesus could have called down the army in heaven to get off the cross. But, he was thinking more of your forgiveness and your getting into heaven than getting down off the cross. So today, try to walk humbly and consider the needs of another as greater than your own.

REQUESTS:

Lord, create in us a servant's heart through your Spirit that's within us. Give us eyes to see a man's heart, looking past his worldly stature. Give us ears to hear, not what his mouth is saying, but what his heart is longing for. As we see and hear men's hearts, please share your wisdom and words so we can best serve them and bring them to Jesus.

Lord, we love you and thank you for answering our prayers.
In Jesus' name. AMEN

JUNE - DAILY DEVOTIONAL #12

Praise be to the God and Father of our Lord Jesus Christ, the Father of compassion and the God of all comfort, who comforts us in all our troubles, so that we can comfort those in any trouble with the comfort we ourselves receive from God. For just as we share abundantly in the sufferings of Christ, so also our comfort abounds through Christ.

2 CORINTHIANS 1:3-5 NIV

REFLECTIONS:

As men, we always want to fix it. Whatever the problem is, we will beat our heads against the wall trying to fix it when someone we care about is hurting. The best tool you have sometimes is to wrap your arms around those who are hurting, and listen, don't speak. (And if you're like me, I don't use this tool very much or very well.)

Don't say, "It's going to be ok," because right now in that moment, it's not. I have found the best comfort from God is when he lets us scream out and cry, and he listens. That's why God gave us two ears and one mouth so we would do more listening than talking.

REQUESTS:

Lord, today, may we turn to you for our comfort. You know each of our hearts, and we know you can help us overcome our hurts, our emptiness, our fears, and our lack of understanding. I ask for your peace over each of my brothers today, and that your presence fill their homes. Lord, may your glory shine on each of my brothers and their families today.

Lord, we love you and thank you for answering our prayers.
In Jesus' name. AMEN

JUNE - DAILY DEVOTIONAL #13

Praise be to the God and Father of our Lord Jesus Christ, the Father of compassion and the God of all comfort, who comforts us in all our troubles, so that we can comfort those in any trouble with the comfort we ourselves receive from God. For just as we share abundantly in the sufferings of Christ, so also our comfort abounds through Christ.

2 CORINTHIANS 1:3-5 NIV

REFLECTIONS:

Have you ever said, "I would not wish this kind of pain on anyone," but for whatever reason, someone you know doesn't have to go through the pain alone now that you've been through it? How can I comfort someone who has lost a parent or a child when I've never been through it? I cannot imagine the pain.

So, whatever has happened to you, to bring healing, allow the Lord to use you to comfort those you know who are hurting the same way you hurt. Remember, Jesus came down to be fully man, not only to go to the cross but also to experience just about everything we have, so he could know our pain firsthand and could comfort us with understanding. Therefore, seek your calling and how he wants to use you.

REQUESTS:

Lord, today, may we turn to you for our comfort. You know each of our hearts, and I know you can help us overcome our hurts, our emptiness, our fears, and our lack of understanding. So I ask for peace over each of my brothers today, and your presence to fill their homes. Lord, may your glory shine on each of my brothers and their families today.

Lord, we love you and thank you for answering our prayers.
In Jesus' name. AMEN

JUNE - DAILY DEVOTIONAL #14

But as surely as God is faithful, our message to you is not "Yes" and "No." For the Son of God, Jesus Christ, who was preached among you by us-by me and Silas and Timothy-was not "Yes" and "No," but in him it has always been "Yes." For no matter how many promises God has made, they are "Yes" in Christ. And so through him the "Amen" is spoken by us to the glory of God. Now it is God who makes both us and you stand firm in Christ. He anointed us, set his seal of ownership on us, and put his Spirit in our hearts as a deposit, guaranteeing what is to come.

2 CORINTHIANS 1:18-22 NIV

REFLECTIONS:

God is never in a hurry to fulfill a promise. If you don't believe me, ask Abraham, who had to wait 25 years for his son. So wherever you are in God's promise to you, remember God never lies, and he is never ever late. In the waiting, there are blessings; God gives you eyes to see them. You can praise him in the hallway until the right door opens.

REQUESTS:

Lord, You and you alone are our yes. Even when we doubt a promise, your yes is yes. So Lord, today, may those who feel like you have left them remember your promise, "I will never leave you nor forsake you." Lord, bless my brothers and their families with peace, and may your presence fill their homes with your glory.

Lord, we love you and thank you for answering our prayers.
In Jesus' name. AMEN

JUNE - DAILY DEVOTIONAL #15

" . . . Have I not commanded you? Be strong and courageous. Do not be afraid; do not be discouraged, for the LORD your God will be with you wherever you go."

JOSHUA 1:9 NIV

REFLECTIONS:

Daniel prayed in the lion's den, and three Hebrew boys danced in the fiery furnace with Jesus without fear of being eaten or burned. So, if our God is for you, who can be against you? When fear, worry, or anxiety begin to creep up on you, remind yourself you are a blood-bought child of God. "Whom or what shall I fear?"

Each day, ask God to give you the strength to overcome all you will be facing, so fear itself will be afraid of you. Not because of who you are but because of *whose* you are.

REQUESTS:

Lord, your word still stands today. As Christians, we need to be seeking your direction, not with fear, but with great courage, because you promise to never leave nor forsake us. Lord, I ask you to bless my brothers with eyes to see and ears to hear your direction for their daily walk with you. May they step with such confidence that no matter what they face, you've already made a way.

Lord, we love you and thank you for answering our prayers.
In Jesus' name. AMEN

JUNE - DAILY DEVOTIONAL #16

And let us consider how we may spur one another on toward love and good deeds, not giving up meeting together, as some are in the habit of doing, but encouraging one another—and all the more as you see the Day approaching.

HEBREWS 10:24-25 NIV

REFLECTIONS:

Do you ever pick up your phone and call someone you know and say, "Man, how are you doing? Is there anything I can do for you?" Or maybe tell them you just wanted them to know you were thinking about them and wanted to make sure they're doing well. I usually send them a text asking how they're doing. If they're really heavy on my heart and mind, I will send a prayer in a text.

Even as men, we don't like to admit it, but we do like knowing someone cares or that someone noticed things aren't quite right. So today, step out of your comfort zone and ask God who he wants you to check on.

REQUESTS:

Lord, today I lift my brothers in Christ to you. I ask you to pour into them your peace and strength. I do not know what they're going through, but, Lord, I know you are not just the light at the end of the tunnel, but you are also the light through the tunnel. May their eyes be focused on you and not the darkness trying to consume them. Lord, may their victories bring healing not just to them but to those all around them.

Lord, we love you and thank you for answering our prayers.
In Jesus' name. AMEN

JUNE - DAILY DEVOTIONAL #17

And God raised us up with Christ and seated us with him in the heavenly realms in Christ Jesus, in order that in the coming ages he might show the incomparable riches of his grace, expressed in his kindness to us in Christ Jesus. For it is by grace you have been saved, through faith—and this is not from yourselves, it is the gift of God—not by works, so that no one can boast. For we are God's handiwork, created in Christ Jesus to do good works, which God prepared in advance for us to do.

EPHESIANS 2:6-10 NIV

REFLECTIONS:

You may never get asked to teach a Sunday school class, or you may never get asked to take up an offering or be a greeter at the door of the church. Do not let any of those things bother you. Instead, ask God what he wants you to do.

He may want you to be a light for him in your workplace. If you deal with the public a lot, maybe he needs you to be a light in the dark world you deal with every day. No matter what it is, he has prepared you for the job, and the Holy Spirit inside you will not lead you wrong if you will listen to what he is telling you.

REQUESTS:

Lord, every day we have breath in our lungs, you have a purpose for us. May we have eyes to see that purpose, whether it's to share Jesus with someone, to pray with someone, or to bless someone in a way they didn't see coming. Lord, whatever it is, may it bring glory to your name. Lord, bless my brothers with peace, and may your presence fill their homes.

Lord, we love you and thank you for answering our prayers.
In Jesus' name. AMEN

JUNE - DAILY DEVOTIONAL #18

He replied, "Isaiah was right when he prophesied about you hypocrites; as it is written: "'These people honor me with their lips, but their hearts are far from me. . . . You have let go of the commands of God and are holding on to human traditions." . . . For Moses said, 'Honor your father and mother,' and, 'Anyone who curses their father or mother is to be put to death.' But you say that if anyone declares that what might have been used to help their father or mother is Corban (that is, devoted to God)—then you no longer let them do anything for their father or mother. Thus you nullify the word of God by your tradition that you have handed down. And you do many things like that."

MARK 7:6-13 NIV

REFLECTIONS:

Remember to seek the Lord your God with all your heart and lean not on your own understanding. If we change what God has told us because we think it's too hard, or our way is better, we will no longer have God's peace. When we follow God's truth, it brings peace in the midst of the storm, and we find hope in his presence around us. But when we manipulate the truth for our benefit, God's blessing of peace is held back until we repent and receive his forgiveness. Thankfully, God's grace is sufficient because he considered our rebellious nature when he called us to do his good work.

REQUESTS:

Lord, we need you today. Show up in our lives; may our human hearts and minds not set limitations on what you can and cannot do with us. We ask you to forgive us where we've limited you in our personal lives, our families, and our churches. Use us beyond our limitations so we can see your goodness!

Lord, we love you and thank you for answering our prayers.
In Jesus' name. AMEN

JUNE - DAILY DEVOTIONAL #19

" . . . For I know the plans I have for you," declares the LORD, "plans to prosper you and not to harm you, plans to give you hope and a future. Then you will call on me and come and pray to me, and I will listen to you. You will seek me and find me when you seek me with all your heart. . . . "

JEREMIAH 29:11-13 NIV

REFLECTIONS:

Everyday prayer should be as important as putting on your pants before you head out the door. Start your prayer by inviting God into your day. Pray for your family, for wisdom, peace, and guidance. Moses told God one time, "If you're not going with us, we're not going." That should be your mindset every day.

And when you're through praying, sit for a minute and listen for God to speak to you. If you want to follow the Lord's guidance down this path of life, as we call it, we have to be present with him.

REQUESTS:

Lord, may we not head out on a plan and hope you are in it, or assume you're in it. But may we seek you with all our hearts so we may know your plans and know that you and you alone are directing our plans. Lord, bless these men today as they go about their day, and may you protect their families from all harm.

Lord, we love you and thank you for answering our prayers.
In Jesus' name. AMEN

JUNE - DAILY DEVOTIONAL #20

. . . for it is God who works in you to will and to act in order to fulfill his good purpose.

PHILIPPIANS 2:13 NIV

REFLECTIONS:

If you want to fulfill God's calling on your life, the next time he begins to speak to you, don't run or ignore him. Raise your hands and say, "Here I am, Lord. Use me."

Have you ever gone to a place only to think, *Why am I here*? Next time, don't leave right away. Ask the Lord, "What is my purpose here?" You may need to pray for the building and everyone in it, or there may be a specific person he wants you to talk to about Jesus.

So next time it happens, look for the Lord in that moment, and he will be there.

REQUESTS:

Lord, may we fulfill your purpose by having a personal relationship with you. May the fruit of that relationship be our witness to the salvation in Jesus and the love you have shared with us. May we then share it with others. Lord, thank you that we always have a purpose wherever we go—to shine the light of Jesus. Lord, bless my brothers with a purpose today.

Lord, we love you and thank you for answering our prayers.
In Jesus' name. AMEN

JUNE - DAILY DEVOTIONAL #21

"Blessed are you when people insult you, persecute you and falsely say all kinds of evil against you because of me. . . . "

MATTHEW 5:11 NIV

REFLECTIONS:

Remember, Jesus never promised we wouldn't be persecuted, but what he did say was, "I'll be there in the lion's den with you," (or in the hectic workplace). The point is, if your life is going through a rough patch and people are pointing fingers at you, Jesus is with you. As he brings you through it, blessings will be poured out over you.

Jesus is not just here for the good times in your life; he's here to be your strength and protector through the rough times. So hold your head up high because you are a child of God and joint heirs with Christ. Chase after him even in the storms of life.

REQUESTS:

Lord, may our eyes and ears be on you and not what the world says about us, trying to frustrate our calling to serve you. As we walk with you, may your goodness go before us. Walk with us and come behind us. Lord, these men with your peace and presence today.

Lord, we love you and thank you for answering our prayers.
In Jesus' name. AMEN

JUNE - DAILY DEVOTIONAL #22

Keep me safe, LORD, from the hands of the wicked; protect me from the violent, who devise ways to trip my feet. The arrogant have hidden a snare for me; they have spread out the cords of their net and have set traps for me along my path. I say to the LORD, "You are my God." Hear, LORD, my cry for mercy. Sovereign LORD, my strong deliverer, you shield my head in the day of battle. Do not grant the wicked their desires, LORD; do not let their plans succeed.

PSALM 140:4-8 NIV

REFLECTIONS:

Every time you feel the weight of the world on your shoulders and everyone is looking at you like everything going wrong is your fault, run to God, our Father. One thing that we all need to remember and never forget, when we are seeking after the Lord with our whole heart, is that the enemy is going to attack and try to cause us to stumble. But when we are obedient to God, he deals with the consequences, which means whatever happens, he is protecting you. Don't walk in fear of stumbling, but walk in faith that he is with you.

REQUESTS:

Lord, may we draw near to you. May we follow so close to you that your light blocks out any other light that may be trying to lead us down a crooked path. Lord, may our feet be planted on your plan for our day, and when we stumble, may we reach out for your hand and not the world's for help to get up. Guide us to moments in the day where we can say, "Surely God was with us." Bless these men with your presence and peace, keeping them focused on the things above.

Lord, we love you and thank you for answering our prayers.
In Jesus' name. AMEN

JUNE - DAILY DEVOTIONAL #23

This is what the LORD says to me with his strong hand upon me, warning me not to follow the way of this people: "Do not call conspiracy everything this people calls a conspiracy; do not fear what they fear, and do not dread it. . . . "

ISAIAH 8:11-12 NIV

REFLECTIONS:

If you turn on the TV and watch the news, you can see all kinds of questionable things. When it begins to pull you away from what you stand for, turn it off—the TV and social media. Meditate on God's Word. He has told us everything that is going to happen, and we are seeing more of it come true every day.

So, it's ok to watch and see what's going on, but if it bothers you, ask God to show you the truth of it all. You are identified as a child of the living God, so in your walk, compare everything against his Word.

REQUESTS:

Lord, may we seek your ways and your direction so we are not caught up in the things of this world. May your presence around us reveal the darkness, so we may walk in your light and not follow what the world does. Lord, let your peace be like a blanket over these men and their families. May your steps and direction be clear for them to follow.

Lord, we love you and thank you for answering our prayers.
In Jesus' name. AMEN

JUNE - DAILY DEVOTIONAL #24

I listen carefully to what God the LORD is saying, for he speaks peace to his faithful people. But let them not return to their foolish ways.

PSALM 85:8 NLT

REFLECTIONS:

Every day before I leave my home for work, I pray for God's peace over my home. I ask him to let anyone who comes to my door, whether it's the mail lady, UPS, FedEx, or one of those annoying door-knocking salespeople, feel his peace as they walk up my steps.

I also ask him to show them where that peace comes from. "The peace I have, I leave with you," is what Jesus said, so if you have Jesus, you have his peace. Ask him to show you how to live in it and share it.

REQUESTS:

Lord, may we have ears to hear and a heart to receive the peace you're speaking to us today. Lord, no matter what is going on, good or bad, we all need your peace today. May your peace hold us steadfast in you.

Lord, we love you and thank you for answering our prayers.
In Jesus' name. AMEN

JUNE - DAILY DEVOTIONAL #25

Now may the Lord of peace himself give you peace at all times and in every way. The Lord be with all of you.

2 THESSALONIANS 3:16 NIV

REFLECTIONS:

God's Word mentions the word "peace" 429 times. I am pretty sure God wants us to experience his peace daily. Peace comes when you know that you know that you're walking with the Lord. It also comes knowing that through thick and thin, he will never leave you nor forsake you.

When you spend time in prayer, that peace becomes more evident, not just to those around you but also to yourself. Do not be afraid of peace; embrace it. And if your world stays in that peace, I promise God has not left you.

REQUESTS:

Lord, no matter what my brothers are going through today or what they face down the road, may your peace always come to the top and comfort them. For without peace, there is no rest or comfort. So, Lord, bless them beyond measure with your peace that transcends all understanding.

Lord, we love you and thank you for answering our prayers.
In Jesus' name. AMEN

JUNE - DAILY DEVOTIONAL #26

You adulterous people, don't you know that friendship with the world means enmity against God? Therefore, anyone who chooses to be a friend of the world becomes an enemy of God. Or do you think Scripture says without reason that he jealously longs for the spirit he has caused to dwell in us? But he gives us more grace. That is why Scripture says: "God opposes the proud but shows favor to the humble." Submit yourselves, then, to God. Resist the devil, and he will flee from you. Come near to God and he will come near to you. Wash your hands, you sinners, and purify your hearts, you double-minded. Grieve, mourn and wail. Change your laughter to mourning and your joy to gloom. Humble yourselves before the Lord, and he will lift you up.

JAMES 4:4-10 NIV

REFLECTIONS:

I saw a prayer that made sense to me, and you pray it as soon as you wake: Lord, get in my head before I do and mess things up! If I'm not careful, I start thinking and planning my day before I ask the Lord to lead me through my day. I know that may sound ignorant, but trust me. Your day will be so much better if you ask him to lead you through it. I went from dreading my day to looking forward to it, because with God leading, I got to serve others with a happy heart instead of a dreadful heart. So, choose now who's leading your day, you or God.

REQUESTS:

Lord, change our hearts. Whatever is in us that's not of you, may it be removed by humbling ourselves before you. Let our worldly behavior become Godly behavior so those who are around us will see Jesus more clearly.

Lord, we love you and thank you for answering our prayers.
In Jesus' name. AMEN

JUNE - DAILY DEVOTIONAL #27

I have no greater joy than to hear that my children are walking in the truth.

3 JOHN 1:4 NIV

REFLECTIONS:

It doesn't matter if you're a dad, a stepdad, or just a really cool uncle. Be an example of Christ to them, show them all the peace and mercy he has shown you. As men, we don't have to be tough and macho for our kids to listen to us, but we need to be real and honest with them. I pray every day that as my children see the real me, they will see Jesus and come to know him as their Lord and Savior.

REQUESTS:

Lord, may we be an example to our children, as we walk in your truth and in a personal relationship with you. May the truth of Jesus flow through our families like a flowing river, never stopping and only getting fuller from generation to generation. Lord, I ask you to bless my brothers with your peace and presence.

Lord, we love you and thank you for answering our prayers.
In Jesus' name. AMEN

JUNE - DAILY DEVOTIONAL #28

For if, by the trespass of the one man, death reigned through that one man, how much more will those who receive God's abundant provision of grace and of the gift of righteousness reign in life through the one man, Jesus Christ!

ROMANS 5:17 NIV

REFLECTIONS:

It's funny that you can send in your DNA to see where your bloodline comes from or who you are kin to. How cool would it be if it showed where your bloodline switched from being from the bloodline of Adam to the bloodline of Jesus? It's scary to think of it that way because there would be some gaps on either side if you've accepted Christ as your Lord and Savior. All those who have done the same would show up.

But if you haven't accepted Christ, you'd only see those who didn't. So to ensure there are no gaps, begin to pray and witness to your kids so they, too, will come to know Christ, and teach their kids so that from generation to generation they will be saved. Be the start of the bloodline that is never broken through Jesus.

REQUESTS:

Lord, thank you that it is not by our own actions that we are saved, but through the obedience of Jesus Christ our Savior, that we have been made whole again. We didn't deserve it, but your grace and mercy saved us despite ourselves. So Lord, bless my brothers with your presence and peace today. Help us always remember and never forget, even though we can't see you and we may not always feel you, you are still working on our behalf.

Lord, we love you and thank you for answering our prayers.
In Jesus' name. AMEN

JUNE - DAILY DEVOTIONAL #29

But now apart from the law the righteousness of God has been made known, . . . This righteousness is given through faith in Jesus Christ to all who believe. There is no difference between Jew and Gentile, for all have sinned and fall short of the glory of God, and all are justified freely by his grace through the redemption that came by Christ Jesus. God presented Christ as a sacrifice of atonement, through the shedding of his blood—to be received by faith. He did this to demonstrate his righteousness, because in his forbearance he had left the sins committed beforehand unpunished—he did it to demonstrate his righteousness . . . to be just and the one who justifies those who have faith in Jesus.

ROMANS 3:21-26 NIV

REFLECTIONS:

Think how hard it was for God to ask his son to be a sacrifice for our sins. Then think about how hard it was to hear Jesus say, "Yes, Father, I will go and take their punishment." The reason he did that is not because of anything we could have done to earn it, but because God himself desired a personal relationship with us. To do that, he had to have a pure and holy sacrifice, which was Jesus. So the next time you look at your own son or look at your mom, think about how painful it would be to give your son up as a sacrifice. Don't take your salvation lightly; Tell others about Jesus!

REQUESTS:

Lord, thank you for Jesus, who was willing to go to the cross and be crucified for all our sins to be forgiven through your grace and mercy, so we may have a personal relationship with you. Through our faith in Christ, we are adopted into your family. Thank you, Lord, that we didn't have to earn it, but simply receive it. Bless my brothers with your joy of salvation.

Lord, we love you and thank you for answering our prayers.
In Jesus' name. AMEN

JUNE - DAILY DEVOTIONAL #30

I denied myself nothing my eyes desired; I refused my heart no pleasure. My heart took delight in all my labor, and this was the reward for all my toil. Yet when I surveyed all that my hands had done and what I had toiled to achieve, everything was meaningless, a chasing after the wind; nothing was gained under the sun.

ECCLESIASTES 2:10-11 NIV

REFLECTIONS:

Our lives should be the evidence a lost person sees to know Jesus is real and that he loves them. The time we have left here should be about taking as many to heaven as we can, because nothing we've gained in earthly possessions can go with us. We need to look for opportunities to share Jesus with friends, family, and strangers who don't know him.

REQUESTS:

Lord, may we fix our eyes upon you, and may our hearts be steadfast in our love for you. May our work be kingdom work. As we go about our days, may we be prepared to share the love of Jesus with others whom you lead across our paths. Bless my brothers with your peace and presence, and may your joy fill their hearts.

Lord, we love you and thank you for answering our prayers.
In Jesus' name. AMEN

JULY - DAILY DEVOTIONAL #1

Let the peace of Christ rule in your hearts, since as members of one body you were called to peace. And be thankful.

COLOSSIANS 3:15 NIV

REFLECTIONS:

When the storms of life hit, where do you run? I used to run to the first place I could drown my troubles away with alcohol. But you know what? I figured out that whatever or whomever you run to, other than Jesus, causes you to spin your tires and dig a deeper hole of trouble. When you run to Jesus and seek him throughout the storm, it is so peaceful that you begin to think the storm is over.

I know a man who once told his neighbor that if God's peace was present, a tornado could pass right by his house and he would never know it. His neighbor told him, "I believe you because a block past your house, a tornado passed by two days ago." For a month, you could see where it had cut a trail in the open field. So start every day asking God that no matter what happens, may his peace never leave you.

REQUESTS:

Lord, may your peace be like a blanket laid over all of us today. May we be thankful that the guy in the mirror is not as bad off as he feels. The guy in the mirror is a blood-bought and paid-for child of God, created in the image of our Father. So Lord, if we can't find one thing to be thankful for, may we be thankful for the one who prayed without ceasing for the man in the mirror to get where he is today. Lord, bless my brothers and their families today with your presence.

Lord, we love you and thank you for answering our prayers.
In Jesus' name. AMEN

JULY - DAILY DEVOTIONAL #2

With whom will you compare me or count me equal? To whom will you liken me that we may be compared? Some pour out gold from their bags and weigh out silver on the scales; they hire a goldsmith to make it into a god, and they bow down and worship it. They lift it to their shoulders and carry it; they set it up in its place, and there it stands. From that spot it cannot move. Even though someone cries out to it, it cannot answer; it cannot save them from their troubles. . . . "

ISAIAH 46:5-7 NIV

REFLECTIONS:

I don't know of anything that compares to our God. There's no other like him. There is nothing or anyone other than our God who would give up their son to save the world. So today, let's do a heart check. What do you value more than Jesus? Whatever it is, there is your God.

REQUESTS:

Lord, whatever consumes the attention of our hearts more than you, show us so we may put it in its rightful place. May we be consumed by your presence and peace today in all that we do, so we may do it all for you. Bless these men with eyes to see and ears to hear you; bless them with all that they need.

Lord, we love you and thank you for answering our prayers.
In Jesus' name. AMEN

JULY - DAILY DEVOTIONAL #3

While they were eating, Jesus took bread, and when he had given thanks, he broke it and gave it to his disciples, saying, "Take and eat; this is my body." Then he took a cup, and when he had given thanks, he gave it to them, saying, "Drink from it, all of you. This is my blood of the covenant, which is poured out for many for the forgiveness of sins. . . . "

MATTHEW 26:26-28 NIV

REFLECTIONS:

It doesn't matter if you take the Lord's supper every Sunday, once a month, or quarterly. Always remember and never forget, one day we are going to be sitting at the table with him as he breaks bread with all of us who are his children.

Don't just go through the ritualistic motions of the Lord's supper. Keep your heart and mind clear of all unrighteousness. Because of the shedding of his blood and his body being broken for forgiveness, we are made righteous through Jesus. The next time you partake in the Lord's supper, picture yourself and your family sitting at the table he has prepared for you.

REQUESTS:

Lord, whether we gather with family or we are alone, may we remember that even Jesus could give thanks in the most troublesome times. So, I ask you to give each one of us the strength to look beyond our hurting hearts and give thanks for the blessings you have given us through Jesus.

Lord, we love you and thank you for answering our prayers.
In Jesus' name. AMEN

JULY - DAILY DEVOTIONAL #4

You, my brothers and sisters, were called to be free. But do not use your freedom to indulge the flesh; rather, serve one another humbly in love. For the entire law is fulfilled in keeping this one command: "Love your neighbor as yourself."

GALATIANS 5:13-14 NIV

REFLECTIONS:

We should always remember and never forget what it cost for our freedom, spiritually and earthly. Many have fought and died in battles for earthly freedom, many moms and dads have given their sons and daughters so we may live in freedom—just as God gave his son as a sacrifice for payment for our sin debt, so we may be free and free indeed when we come to know him as our Lord and Savior. So today, may you show your gratefulness for your freedom by forgiving those you are holding in the bondage of unforgiveness.

REQUESTS:

Lord, thank you for our freedom. Jesus humbled himself as a man and went to the cross for our sins, so that we didn't have to. We also thank you for the soldiers who, just like Jesus, humbled themselves and fought for our freedom as a country. Lord, please forgive us where we have looked away from what it cost for our freedom, just doing whatever we want with no regard to the distance we're putting between ourselves and your will. Return our hearts to you, both individually and as a group, so our spiritual freedom is meaningful. Lord, bless these men today with a yearning for you!

Lord, we love you and thank you for answering our prayers.
In Jesus' name. AMEN

JULY - DAILY DEVOTIONAL #5

" . . . You are under a curse—your whole nation—because you are robbing me. Bring the whole tithe into the storehouse, that there may be food in my house. Test me in this," says the LORD Almighty, "and see if I will not throw open the floodgates of heaven and pour out so much blessing that there will not be room enough to store it. I will prevent pests from devouring your crops, and the vines in your fields will not drop their fruit before it is ripe," says the LORD Almighty. "Then all the nations will call you blessed, for yours will be a delightful land," says the LORD Almighty."

MALACHI 3:9-12 NIV

REFLECTIONS:

There are just some promises we don't claim because of selfishness, and in the end, it costs us more not to give than to give. We should think of it this way: give and it will be given back, don't give and it will be taken from you. I'm as guilty as anyone of saying, "I'll do it next week. It'll be easier then. I don't have any time this week." We have to think of it this way: blessed are both the giver and the one who receives it. We are the first receiver and the second giver because he gave it to us first. So, bless the giver and give God what's his. You will never be able to out-give the Lord, I promise.

REQUESTS:

Lord, I lift up our homes, towns, counties, states, and our country. Let a mighty wind of your Spirit blow across our nation and turn our hearts back to you. Lord, let revival start with my heart, my home, my town, my county, and my state. Lord, guide us back to you. May each of my brothers be blessed as they seek your will today.

Lord, we love you and thank you for answering our prayers.
In Jesus' name. AMEN

JULY - DAILY DEVOTIONAL #6

We know that the whole creation has been groaning as in the pains of childbirth right up to the present time. Not only so, but we ourselves, who have the first fruits of the Spirit, groan inwardly as we wait eagerly for our adoption to sonship, the redemption of our bodies. For in this hope we were saved. But hope that is seen is no hope at all. Who hopes for what they already have? But if we hope for what we do not yet have, we wait for it patiently. In the same way, the Spirit helps us in our weakness. We do not know what we ought to pray for, but the Spirit himself intercedes for us through wordless groans. And he who searches our hearts knows the mind of the Spirit, because the Spirit intercedes for God's people in accordance with the will of God. And we know that in all things God works for the good of those who love him, who have been called according to his purpose.

ROMANS 8:22-28 NIV

REFLECTIONS:

As you are reading this devotion, the Spirit is in front of God himself interceding for you. Whatever you are going through, he is working it out for your good as you seek him. If you're a father now or when you become one, you will do everything you can to bring out positive results for your children. Most of the time, we fail, but our Father in heaven never fails. The outcome may not be the way we expected, but it's not about us; it's about his glory. So never forget we have one standing before the Lord 24/7 on our behalf.

REQUESTS:

Lord, search our hearts, make them ever true with you. Lord, bless my brothers with peace in their hearts, knowing you are their great hope, and their hope is in you. You are guiding us to a better place with you.

Lord, we love you and thank you for answering our prayers.
In Jesus' name. AMEN

JULY - DAILY DEVOTIONAL #7

Therefore, confess your sins to one another and pray for one another, that you may be healed. The prayer of a righteous person has great power as it is working. Elijah was a man with a nature like ours, and he prayed fervently that it might not rain, and for three years and six months it did not rain on the earth. Then he prayed again, and heaven gave rain, and the earth bore its fruit.

JAMES 5:16-18 ESV

REFLECTIONS:

Having a group of men, or one good friend that you can speak openly with about things you battle and things you can't turn loose, is important in our walk with the Lord. It helps us keep our eyes on Jesus.

When our eyes are on Jesus, we pray without doubt and in full confidence that the Lord hears us and he will answer. You are as precious to the Lord as Elijah. Don't wait until you're out of options to go to the Lord in prayer. Make that your first choice, not your last.

REQUESTS:

Lord, thank you that we could never become righteous on our own, but through the shedding of the blood of Jesus and the forgiveness of our sins, we are made righteous in you. Lord, may we never doubt that you hear our prayers and move on our behalf. Lord, bless my brothers and their families. May your goodness be poured out over them, and may you keep them safe from all harm. Bless them beyond measure.

Lord, we love you and thank you for answering our prayers.
In Jesus' name. AMEN

JULY - DAILY DEVOTIONAL #8

"See, it is I who created the blacksmith who fans the coals into flame and forges a weapon fit for its work. And it is I who have created the destroyer to wreak havoc; no weapon forged against you will prevail, and you will refute every tongue that accuses you. This is the heritage of the servants of the LORD, and this is their vindication from me," declares the LORD.

ISAIAH 54:16-17 NIV

REFLECTIONS:

The next time you want to give someone the "what for," stop and pray. They are listening, so watch what happens to their hateful attitude. Sometimes our reactions stand in the way of our protector.

God will not hurt them physically, but what he will do is get a hold of their heart and change them completely. So before you jump out there and do something you'll regret, trust God to fight your battle.

REQUESTS:

Lord, this morning, arm us with your armor so we are protected from the one who came to kill, steal, and destroy. Whatever we are already battling and face today, let us fight on our knees only seeking you in the fire so we may sit at your table. YOU, Lord, have already won the battle. So, Lord, let us continue to keep our eyes and hearts on you and do your good work, sharing the love and mercy of Jesus.

Lord, we love you and thank you for answering our prayers.
In Jesus' name. AMEN

JULY - DAILY DEVOTIONAL #9

Answer me, LORD, out of the goodness of your love; in your great mercy turn to me.

PSALM 69:16 NIV

REFLECTIONS:

We as people are so funny; we don't like to wait until it's something we really want. We will stand in long lines to get tickets to hear someone sing a song we can hear on the radio. We will also stand in long lines to ride a 30-second water slide, only to get up and stand in line again.

But when it comes to the Lord, we make him wait and wait until we've dug ourselves in a hole so deep that the only way to look is up. And then the instant we say "Amen," we think we should instantly be out of the hole. Maybe we should try some humility and allow the Lord to work it out for us in his timing, which is always on time.

REQUESTS:

Lord, as it has been spoken, when people cried for your mercy, you brought healing. So, I ask, Lord, may your ears be attentive to our cries and may your hand bring healing and deliverance to our broken and hurting hearts. Lord, may your peace rest upon my brothers today, and may your presence wrap around us, holding us up so we may be a light in a dark world.

Lord, we love you and thank you for answering our prayers.
In Jesus' name. AMEN

JULY - DAILY DEVOTIONAL #10

. . . if my people, who are called by my name, will humble themselves and pray and seek my face and turn from their wicked ways, then I will hear from heaven, and I will forgive their sin and will heal their land.

2 CHRONICLES 7:14 NIV

REFLECTIONS:

Being humble takes discipline to remind yourself that life is not all about you and what you selfishly desire. When we humble ourselves, we choose God's way, which is always better than our own. Being humble is being attentive to the needs of others first before our own, just as Jesus was attentive to our needs before his own when he went to the cross for our sins. So begin to humble yourself and do something good for the person you think you are better than.

REQUESTS:

Lord, being humble is realizing the truth: knowing and believing that we can't do anything prosperous without you leading and guiding us in the way we should go. Lord, may each of my brothers be truthful and honest with you today, laying down everything that's holding them back from submerging themselves in you. Lord, bless my brothers beyond measure today with peace and your presence.

Lord, we love you and thank you for answering our prayers.
In Jesus' name. AMEN

JULY - DAILY DEVOTIONAL #11

But now be strong, Zerubbabel,' declares the LORD. 'Be strong, Joshua son of Jozadak, the high priest. Be strong, all you people of the land,' declares the LORD, 'and work. For I am with you,' declares the LORD Almighty. 'This is what I covenanted with you when you came out of Egypt. And my Spirit remains among you. Do not fear.'
"This is what the LORD Almighty says: 'In a little while I will once more shake the heavens and the earth, the sea and the dry land. I will shake all nations, and what is desired by all nations will come, and I will fill this house with glory,' says the LORD Almighty. 'The silver is mine and the gold is mine,' declares the LORD Almighty. 'The glory of this present house will be greater than the glory of the former house,' says the LORD Almighty. 'And in this place I will grant peace,' declares the LORD Almighty."

HAGGAI 2:4-9 NIV

REFLECTIONS:

Be strong, all you people. The Lord is not saying get a gym membership and work out every day like clockwork. He says, "Be strong in me, read my Word, seek my presence and peace," because he is with us. So many of us are wrapped up in what we want out of this old world, we put God on hold, and that, my friend, weakens us spiritually. So to stay strong in the tough times, the hard times, and in the good times, we must seek first the kingdom of God and his righteousness.

REQUESTS:

Lord, give us a selfless heart so we may seek those who need the peace we have; that peace that tells us when the earth and heaven do shake, we are standing on the solid rock that never moves. Lord, I ask you to bless my brothers beyond measure with your peace and presence, guiding them in the way they should go with you.

Lord, we love you and thank you for answering our prayers.
In Jesus' name. AMEN

JULY - DAILY DEVOTIONAL #12

Keep your lives free from the love of money and be content with what you have, because God has said, "Never will I leave you; never will I forsake you." So we say with confidence, "The Lord is my helper; I will not be afraid. What can mere mortals do to me?" Remember your leaders, who spoke the word of God to you. Consider the outcome of their way of life and imitate their faith. Jesus Christ is the same yesterday and today and forever.

HEBREWS 13:5-8 NIV

REFLECTIONS:

I have known several successful men, respectable men of God. On the outside, they appeared to barely be making ends meet. From the cars they drove to the house where they lived, it appeared they were broke as broke could be, but they were faithful to the Lord. Although many of them had bank accounts bigger than Texas, they gave silently to many organizations. Nobody ever knew it until the day of their funeral, and those organizations recognized them.

That is contentment with what you have. These men taught me it is more important to serve the Lord and use their blessings for the Lord's kingdom than to be selfish and use them for their own good.

REQUESTS:

Lord, thank you that you are always with us. In the roughest of times and in the best of times, your strength and power never waver. May we be an example of total dependence on you to the next generation. Lord, bless my brothers with your peace, and may you make your presence known to them so they know they're truly not alone as they go through today.

Lord, we love you and thank you for answering our prayers.
In Jesus' name. AMEN

JULY - DAILY DEVOTIONAL #13

Even though we speak like this, dear friends, we are convinced of better things in your case—the things that have to do with salvation. God is not unjust; he will not forget your work and the love you have shown him as you have helped his people and continue to help them. We want each of you to show this same diligence to the very end, so that what you hope for may be fully realized. We do not want you to become lazy, but to imitate those who through faith and patience inherit what has been promised.

HEBREWS 6:9-12 NIY

REFLECTIONS:

You've already seen what this world has to offer. Do you really think it's that much better than the place Jesus said he was going to prepare for you in heaven? Are you hoping to enjoy as many worldly things as possible and get into heaven by the skin of your teeth? Many people live that way; I lived that way for a long time.

I want to challenge you for two weeks. Work as hard for the Lord as you do chasing the worldly things you like and want, and see how God changes your perspective. He never said we had to do without, but our priorities need to be in line with his plan.

REQUESTS:

Lord, as the hands and feet of Jesus give us eyes to see the needs of others, and as we help in tending to those needs, may we have ears to hear beyond words—the deeper cry for help. May we serve others with the heart of Jesus. Help us be totally selfless in the way we help others. You know every need this morning, so I ask you to help those needs through the hearts of your people.

Lord, we love you and thank you for answering our prayers.
In Jesus' name. AMEN

JULY - DAILY DEVOTIONAL #14

He said, "Look! I see four men walking around in the fire, unbound and unharmed, and the fourth looks like a son of the gods." Nebuchadnezzar then approached the opening of the blazing furnace and shouted, "Shadrach, Meshach and Abednego, servants of the Most High God, come out! Come here!" So Shadrach, Meshach and Abednego came out of the fire, . . . They saw that the fire had not harmed their bodies, nor was a hair of their heads singed; their robes were not scorched, and there was no smell of fire on them. Then Nebuchadnezzar said, "Praise be to the God of Shadrach, Meshach and Abednego, who has sent his angel and rescued his servants! They trusted in him and defied the king's command and were willing to give up their lives rather than serve or worship any god except their own God."

DANIEL 3:25-28 NIV

REFLECTIONS:

The best testimony of our Father in heaven is for people to see you walk out of the fires of life, not weaker but stronger. It leaves them speechless, because they cannot deny the fact that only God the Father could have done that. Keep praying, keep seeking, and allow God to use you in ways you haven't seen yet. Remember, if you're moving in obedience to him, he's the best fire insurance you could ever have, and it's free.

REQUESTS:

Lord, help us as the body of Christ get on our knees and seek you with one set of ears and eyes—clearly as a nation of Christ followers so that other countries will know our God. Lord, may revival start in our homes, our neighborhoods, our churches, and in our towns until it spreads and consumes us.

Lord, we love you and thank you for answering our prayers.
In Jesus' name. AMEN

JULY - DAILY DEVOTIONAL #15

You, my brothers and sisters, were called to be free. But do not use your freedom to indulge the flesh; rather, serve one another humbly in love. For the entire law is fulfilled in keeping this one command: "Love your neighbor as yourself."

GALATIANS 5:13-14 NIV

REFLECTIONS:

Jesus came to set us free from death, hell, and the grave. But what he didn't come to set us free from is the consequence of our sinful actions. What that means is that if you have an affair and your wife files for divorce, that's a consequence of your actions. The Lord may have given your wife a forgiving heart, and she may not want a divorce, but you have destroyed her trust. Your actions have consequences, and it takes time to rebuild trust.

So when the world offers you something that's against God's will for you, consider the consequences of your actions before making that decision. I bet you'll find it's not worth it, whatever it is.

REQUESTS:

Lord, may you give us wisdom in the decisions we make every day. May we see the cost of our actions if they are against what you have commanded us to do. Open doors for us to serve others. Let us not pick and choose who we serve, but serve all who you send our way. Bless each of my brothers and their families with your peace and surround them with your presence.

Lord, we love you and thank you for answering our prayers.
In Jesus' name. AMEN

JULY - DAILY DEVOTIONAL #16

Devote yourselves to prayer, being watchful and thankful. And pray for us, too, that God may open a door for our message, so that we may proclaim the mystery of Christ, for which I am in chains. Pray that I may proclaim it clearly, as I should. Be wise in the way you act toward outsiders; make the most of every opportunity. Let your conversation be always full of grace, seasoned with salt, so that you may know how to answer everyone.

COLOSSIANS 4:2-6 NIV

REFLECTIONS:

I will guarantee you that if you get up ten minutes earlier than you do right now and pray a simple prayer five days in a row, your days will have more peace in them. Ten minutes will turn into 15 to 20 minutes. Your prayer could be something like this: "Good morning, Lord. Thank you for today. Please watch over my family and keep them safe. Also, use me today however you desire to do your good work."

REQUESTS:

Lord, I ask you to bless my brothers today. Give them opportunities to tell the mystery of Christ. Please give us self-control over our actions and our words so we can show grace and mercy to those around us. Lord, I ask you to cover these men and their families with a blanket of grace and peace.

Lord, we love you and thank you for answering our prayers.
In Jesus' name. AMEN

JULY - DAILY DEVOTIONAL #17

But now that you know God—or rather are known by God—how is it that you are turning back to those weak and miserable forces? Do you wish to be enslaved by them all over again? You are observing special days and months and seasons and years!

GALATIANS 4:9-10 NIV

REFLECTIONS:

Just like the prodigal son, many of us have left our comfortable place with God and his blessings of protection and dove headfirst back into our old ways, and it's sucking the life out of us. So, pull your head out of the slop bucket and hit your knees in prayer, asking the Lord to forgive you and return to who you were called by him to be. Remember it's his grace and mercy that saved, and it's his grace and mercy that will restore. What are you waiting for? You have nothing to lose and everything to gain.

REQUESTS:

Lord, I lift my brothers this morning and ask you to give them strength to turn away from their old ways and focus on the new life we have in you today. Yesterday is gone, and tomorrow is not promised, so may we walk with you today, instead of searching for what the world has to offer. Lord, bless my brothers and their families with your peace and presence today.

Lord, we love you and thank you for answering our prayers.
In Jesus' name. AMEN

JULY - DAILY DEVOTIONAL #18

For our struggle is not against flesh and blood, but against the rulers, against the authorities, against the powers of this dark world and against the spiritual forces of evil in the heavenly realms. Therefore put on the full armor of God, so that when the day of evil comes, you may be able to stand your ground, and after you have done everything, to stand. Stand firm then, with the belt of truth buckled around your waist, with the breastplate of righteousness in place, and with your feet fitted with the readiness that comes from the gospel of peace. In addition to all this, take up the shield of faith, with which you can extinguish all the flaming arrows of the evil one. Take the helmet of salvation and the sword of the Spirit, which is the word of God. And pray in the Spirit on all occasions with all kinds of prayers and requests. With this in mind, be alert and always keep on praying for all the Lord's people.

EPHESIANS 6:12-18 NIV

REFLECTIONS:

Our Father has equipped us with the sword of his Word. As we spend more time in the Word, he dresses us in his armor, but the greatest weapon we have is prayer. When we are in direct communication with our Father (and our Father loves it when we talk to him), as we pray, he wraps his arms around us so no arrows of the enemy can do any harm. Spend time with him and don't forget to listen because he speaks too.

REQUESTS:

God, help my brothers and their families today by giving them your armor so they can find victory through prayer. You know what each of my brothers and their families' needs are spiritually and physically, so I ask you to bless them today, shining your glory over them.

Lord, we love you and thank you for answering our prayers.
In Jesus' name. AMEN

JULY - DAILY DEVOTIONAL #19

As a prisoner for the Lord, then, I urge you to live a life worthy of the calling you have received. Be completely humble and gentle; be patient, bearing with one another in love. Make every effort to keep the unity of the Spirit through the bond of peace. There is one body and one Spirit, just as you were called to one hope when you were called; one Lord, one faith, one baptism; one God and Father of all, who is over all and through all and in all. But to each one of us grace has been given as Christ apportioned it.

EPHESIANS 4:1-7 NIV

REFLECTIONS:

Have you ever heard the saying, God broke the mold when he made—? They're usually talking about a really good guy. But it's true for all of us. There's no other person who is exactly like you.

So don't be anything less than the best version of you in Jesus. If you do that, people will see Jesus flowing through you like a river, pouring out his peace and love. The question is, are you happy with who you are as a person? And if you're not, are you willing to change?

REQUESTS:

Lord, may you open our hearts and minds to receive your peace that passes all understanding. If we don't have peace, the rest of it is out the window. So, Lord, I ask you to cover these men and their families like a blanket because when we have peace, we also have comfort like a heavy blanket provides. Lord, bless each of my brothers and their families with all that they need today.

Lord, we love you and thank you for answering our prayers.
In Jesus' name. AMEN

JULY - DAILY DEVOTIONAL #20

So Christ himself gave the apostles, the prophets, the evangelists, the pastors and teachers, to equip his people for works of service, so that the body of Christ may be built up until we all reach unity in the faith and in the knowledge of the Son of God and become mature, attaining to the whole measure of the fullness of Christ. Then we will no longer be infants, tossed back and forth by the waves, and blown here and there by every wind of teaching and by the cunning and craftiness of people in their deceitful scheming. Instead, speaking the truth in love, we will grow to become in every respect the mature body of him who is the head, that is, Christ. From him the whole body, joined and held together by every supporting ligament, grows and builds itself up in love, as each part does its work.

EPHESIANS 4:11-16 NIV

REFLECTIONS:

When God looks down at the church as a whole, what does he see? We are supposed to be the body of Jesus, but do we actually look like Jesus, or do we look like a 1000-count puzzle with all the pieces in the wrong places? When each of us quits thinking we should do more than we are called to do, then all the pieces would fit in the tight spots, and we would have a complete body of Jesus. So, seek what the Lord is calling you to do, and then seek him even more so you may be the best at your calling.

REQUESTS:

Lord, may we be the hands and feet of Jesus, pouring ourselves out to those who are hurting and to those who are lost and need Jesus. Pour us out, Lord, like a drink offering. As you do, draw us closer together as one body.

Lord, we love you and thank you for answering our prayers.
In Jesus' name. AMEN

JULY - DAILY DEVOTIONAL #21

For it is by grace you have been saved, through faith—and this is not from yourselves, it is the gift of God—not by works, so that no one can boast. For we are God's handiwork, created in Christ Jesus to do good works, which God prepared in advance for us to do.

EPHESIANS 2:8-10 NIV

REFLECTIONS:

God's Word says that if all the things Jesus did were recorded, the books would fill up the entire world. In saying that, I bet most of us might have a couple of pages worth of stuff recorded that we've allowed God to do through us. We can't change what has already been done in our story, but we can change our future story by seeking the Lord and what is still prepared for us to do. Start your day with prayer, seeking direction for the day.

REQUESTS:

Lord, open our hearts so we may begin to see and understand the depth of the truth that there is absolutely nothing we did to deserve the salvation and forgiveness we receive through Jesus and the cross. But it has everything to do with your endless love and the desire to have a personal relationship with each of us so we may continue to share your great love with others. Lord, bless my brothers with your peace and healing in their hearts so they may be prepared to do your good work.

Lord, we love you and thank you for answering our prayers.
In Jesus' name. AMEN

JULY - DAILY DEVOTIONAL #22

I keep asking that the God of our Lord Jesus Christ, the glorious Father, may give you the Spirit of wisdom and revelation, so that you may know him better. I pray that the eyes of your heart may be enlightened in order that you may know the hope to which he has called you, the riches of his glorious inheritance in his holy people, and his incomparably great power for us who believe. That power is the same as the mighty strength he exerted when he raised Christ from the dead and seated him at his right hand in the heavenly realms, far above all rule and authority, power and dominion, and every name that is invoked, not only in the present age but also in the one to come.

EPHESIANS 1:17-21 NIV

REFLECTIONS:

There is nothing or anyone greater or more powerful than the Lord himself, and he wants a personal relationship with you. Even if you had been the only person here on earth, Jesus would have come and given himself up as a sacrifice for the pardon of your sin. Because God loves you so much, he thinks you are worth using all his resources to give you the opportunity to take the time to get to know him more and more each day. So what are you waiting for?

REQUESTS:

Lord, as we chase after you, may we have eyes to see your glorious riches in their fullness, and may we have ears to hear you speaking to us more clearly. May our hearts be filled with your peace.

Lord, we love you and thank you for answering our prayers.
In Jesus' name. AMEN

JULY - DAILY DEVOTIONAL #23

But when Christ came as high priest . . . he went through the greater and more perfect tabernacle that is not made with human hands, . . . He did not enter by means of the blood of goats and calves; but he entered the Most Holy Place once for all by his own blood, thus obtaining eternal redemption. The blood of goats and bulls . . . sprinkled on those who are ceremonially unclean sanctify them so that they are outwardly clean. How much more, then, will the blood of Christ, who through the eternal Spirit offered himself unblemished to God, cleanse our consciences from acts that lead to death, so that we may serve the living God! For this reason Christ is the mediator of a new covenant, that those who are called may receive the promised eternal inheritance—now that he has died as a ransom to set them free from the sins committed under the first covenant.

HEBREWS 9:11-15 NIV

REFLECTIONS:

Can you imagine having to go before the priests and allowing them to sprinkle the blood of animals all over you so you would be ceremonially clean? The cleansing wouldn't last as long as the smell of the blood that was sprinkled on your clothes. Imagine Jesus going to pay the price once and for all. And as we accept him as our Lord and Savior, we are filled with his Spirit, which cleanses us from the inside out, freeing us from sin debt once and for all. So today, where are you in your journey with Jesus? Only you and he truly know.

REQUESTS:

Lord, thank you that Jesus is still sitting at your right hand in the Holy of Holies interceding for us. You desired a relationship with us so much that you went to the cross and died for our sins. We choose to seek you and your guidance so we can be free, as your blood provides.

Lord, we love you and thank you for answering our prayers.
In Jesus' name. AMEN

JULY - DAILY DEVOTIONAL #24

" . . . If you love me, keep my commands. And I will ask the Father, and he will give you another advocate to help you and be with you forever—the Spirit of truth. The world cannot accept him, because it neither sees him nor knows him. But you know him, for he lives with you and will be in you. I will not leave you as orphans; I will come to you. Before long, the world will not see me anymore, but you will see me. Because I live, you also will live. On that day you will realize that I am in my Father, and you are in me, and I am in you. Whoever has my commands and keeps them is the one who loves me. The one who loves me will be loved by my Father, and I too will love them and show myself to them. . . . "

JOHN 14:15-21 NIV

REFLECTIONS:

This sums up salvation. When you accept Jesus as Lord and Savior, you never live a day that he's not in you or around. He is always present, wanting to lead you in the direction you should go. Ask Jesus to reveal himself to you and speak to you. Then get into his Word and I promise, if you will seek him earnestly, you will see him all around you, feel him in you, and most importantly, hear him speaking to you.

REQUESTS:

Lord, thank you that you are with us and in us. Bless each one of these men by revealing yourself more and more to them. Lord, I don't know what my brothers are going through or dealing with today or this week, but you do. Pour out your comfort, peace, discernment, and wisdom as they need it. Bless their families and fill their homes with your presence, protecting them from all harm. Lord, whether we are in a valley or on the mountaintop, may your goodness and glory always shine through us.

Lord, we love you and thank you for answering our prayers.
In Jesus' name. AMEN

JULY - DAILY DEVOTIONAL #25

Listen! The LORD is calling to the city . . . "Heed the rod and the One who appointed it. Am I still to forget your ill-gotten treasures, you wicked house, and the short ephah, which is accursed? Shall I acquit someone with dishonest scales, with a bag of false weights? Your rich people are violent; your inhabitants are liars and their tongues speak deceitfully. Therefore, I have begun to destroy you, to ruin you because of your sins. You will eat but not be satisfied; your stomach will still be empty. You will store up but save nothing, because what you save I will give to the sword. You will plant but not harvest; you will press olives but not use the oil, you will crush grapes but not drink the wine. You have observed the statutes of Omri and all the practices of Ahab's house; you have followed their traditions. Therefore I will give you over to ruin and your people to derision; you will bear the scorn of the nations."

MICAH 6:9-16 NIV

REFLECTIONS:

If you think you're good and have no reason to pray, then look around and pray for our country and those who are in office, from the mayor of your town to the President of the United States. Then pray for your family and Godly wisdom, because the world, as we know it today, may not be the same tomorrow. So seek the Lord daily so you don't miss a blessing. God may have a plan to move you to a better place.

REQUESTS:

These verses from the Old Testament are very similar to what's happening in America now. Move our country into revival as fierce as the day of Pentecost. May thousands turn from their wicked ways and seek your desires for this world. We pray for people in positions of authority. Lord, I lift up my brothers and their families; may revival of your land begin within each of us.

Lord, we love you and thank you for answering our prayers.
In Jesus' name. AMEN

JULY - DAILY DEVOTIONAL #26

Day after day every priest stands and performs his religious duties; again and again he offers the same sacrifices, which can never take away sins. But when this priest had offered for all time one sacrifice for sins, he sat down at the right hand of God, and since that time he waits for his enemies to be made his footstool. For by one sacrifice he has made perfect forever those who are being made holy. The Holy Spirit also testifies to us about this. First, he says: "This is the covenant I will make with them after that time, says the Lord. I will put my laws in their hearts, and I will write them on their minds." Then he adds: "Their sins and lawless acts I will remember no more." And where these have been forgiven, sacrifice for sin is no longer necessary.

HEBREWS 10:11-18 NIV

REFLECTIONS:

I hope you're not waiting on something better in life, or that you think you have time to consider your options. Why wait to find out who Jesus is and what he's done for you? If you have never accepted him as your Lord and Savior, there is no better time than right now. To you who already know Jesus but still have your hand in the cookie jar of the world, turn your hearts back to Jesus and chase after him. See how better the cookies he blesses you with compare to the world's.

REQUESTS:

Lord, I ask you to help us in our weakness of committing lawless acts towards the cross. It's like we're writing checks we can't cash. Help our finite minds comprehend the depth of Jesus being crucified for our sins and the depth of his resurrection, providing us new life in him. Bless those who are hurting today. Meet them right where they are and comfort them, pouring your peace into them.

Lord, we love you and thank you for answering our prayers.
In Jesus' name. AMEN

JULY - DAILY DEVOTIONAL #27

Now there lived in that city a man poor but wise, and he saved the city by his wisdom. But nobody remembered that poor man. So I said, "Wisdom is better than strength." But the poor man's wisdom is despised, and his words are no longer heeded. The quiet words of the wise are more to be heeded than the shouts of a ruler of fools. Wisdom is better than weapons of war, but one sinner destroys much good.

ECCLESIASTES 9:15-18 NIV

REFLECTIONS:

The Lord tells us to ask for wisdom, and he will bless us. Some men sit quietly in rooms, and they seem to be smart until they speak, and then you realize they don't have a lick of sense. So seek the Lord's wisdom in all things, so when you begin to speak, God's wisdom pours out of you.

But always remember and never forget that the amount of words you speak doesn't make you wise. From whom you draw your wisdom determines your strength of knowledge, so seek Jesus and draw your wisdom and strength from him in prayer.

REQUESTS:

Lord, the world may despise us and it may not ever remember who we are, but may it remember that we showed them who you are. Lord, pour out your wisdom over us, so we may not be lovers of our own voice, but be obedient to allow you to speak through us in your timing. Bless my brothers with your peace and presence all around them as they go about their day!

Lord, we love you and thank you for answering our prayers.
In Jesus' name. AMEN

JULY - DAILY DEVOTIONAL #28

For who knows what is good for a person in life, during the few and meaningless days they pass through like a shadow? Who can tell them what will happen under the sun after they are gone?

ECCLESIASTES 6:12 NIV

REFLECTIONS:

It always makes me sad to think about all the good ol' boys who have died, never knowing Jesus. What is a good ol' boy? The guy who'll give you the shirt off his back, even though it's the only one he has. He is the guy who helps without being asked or elevates someone else's dreams over his own, but never complains. He hides his own pain so he's not a bother to anyone else.

Do you know that guy? If that good ol' boy's name isn't written in the Lamb's book of life, all the good deeds he did and all the shirts he gave off his back are meaningless. That's why I cry when I think about them. So don't just be a good ol' boy, be one who knows Jesus.

REQUESTS:

Lord, thank you that we know the answer is you. Thank you for reminding us that as we live for you, our days here on earth are not meaningless. Only you know what will happen, whether we're here or not. Lord, may we not get so caught up in the what-ifs, the could-haves, and the should-haves, but let us be focused on what is here and now. Lord, help us to take the steps you have laid out for us so we can do your good work.

Lord, we love you and thank you for answering our prayers.
In Jesus' name. AMEN

JULY - DAILY DEVOTIONAL #29

I thank my God every time I remember you. . . . because of your partnership in the gospel from the first day until now, being confident of this, that he who began a good work in you will carry it on to completion until the day of Christ Jesus.

PHILIPPIANS 1:3, 5-6 NIV

REFLECTIONS:

Whether we know each other or not, we are partners in sharing the gospel and brothers in Christ Jesus. So I thank God for you, my brother. If you want to know if God is still working on you, pinch yourself. If it hurts, then you're still alive and he's still working out the kinks.

So, keep striving toward Jesus because no matter what, he will never leave you or forsake you. So whatever has got you at a standstill or in neutral, ask God to give you a push start and keep going.

REQUESTS:

Lord, you know our every need and you know what we're dealing with, whether it is sickness, a loss, or an unwanted addiction. Lord, it doesn't matter what it is; you are our hope, our healer, our deliverer, but most of all, you are our peace. Lord, I ask you to pour out your peace over each of my brothers as you help them in their time of need today. Surround them with your presence and fill their hearts with joy only you can give.

Lord, we love you and thank you for answering our prayers.
In Jesus' name. AMEN

JULY - DAILY DEVOTIONAL #30

Now listen, you who say, "Today or tomorrow we will go to this or that city, spend a year there, carry on business and make money." Why, you do not even know what will happen tomorrow. What is your life? You are a mist that appears for a little while and then vanishes. Instead, you ought to say, "If it is the Lord's will, we will live and do this or that." As it is, you boast in your arrogant schemes. All such boasting is evil. If anyone, then, knows the good they ought to do and doesn't do it, it is sin for them.

JAMES 4:13-17 NIV

REFLECTIONS:

That doesn't mean if you think you ought to give someone a whipping, you should go ahead and do it. What it *does* mean is if you're standing behind someone at the grocery store or in a restaurant and God lays on your heart to pay their bill, and you don't, it is sin. That's what that means. You knew you ought to be obedient, but weren't. I'm as guilty as anyone, but I'm working on it, or better, the Lord's working on me. So I challenge you to allow him to work on you. Don't think, "I ought to pay some bills, but I think I'll throw a party for my friends." That may not be a sin, but it's not responsibly handling God's blessings. So begin to seek God in what you ought to do.

REQUESTS:

Lord, may all that we do be in your timing and your will so that our good work will not be in vain, but bring you glory. May each of these men see the depth and value of seeking you first in the decisions they need to make for themselves, their families, and their work. God, we often fail, but as we follow You, may obstacles be removed. Bless these men with your peace.

Lord, we love you and thank you for answering our prayers.
In Jesus' name. AMEN

JULY - DAILY DEVOTIONAL #31

... fixing our eyes on Jesus, the pioneer and perfecter of faith. For the joy set before him he endured the cross, scorning its shame, and sat down at the right hand of the throne of God. Consider him who endured such opposition from sinners, so that you will not grow weary and lose heart.

HEBREWS 12:2-3 NIV

REFLECTIONS:

I heard someone say the other day, the first thing they pray for is for "Jesus to take over my thoughts before I do." The Word tells us to pray consistently without ceasing; the same should be about our focus. Focus on Jesus, so our minds don't stray off into daydreams of things that will never happen. The story of David and Goliath is a perfect example. David took his brothers some supplies, but his focus was on the Lord. He knew real quick his purpose for being there because his focus was where it should be. Where's yours?

REQUESTS:

Lord, as we consider the depth of what Jesus did for us on the cross, bearing all of our sin, being declared guilty, and being crucified, may we find joy in our trials. Not what the world considers joy, but the joy Jesus found in dying for us, so that we see the depth of the victory. He's not sitting at the right hand of the throne of God, complaining and crying. He is overwhelmed with joy for those who receive him as their Lord and Savior, and he takes every relationship personally. So, Lord, may we find your joy as we go through our day. No matter the circumstances we face, help us remember we are blood-bought and paid-for children of God through Jesus!

Lord, we love you and thank you for answering our prayers.
In Jesus' name. AMEN

When you say: "I can't figure it out," God says, "I will direct your steps!"

AUGUST - DAILY DEVOTIONAL #1

Then the men went as a group to King Darius and said to him, "Remember, Your Majesty, . . . no decree or edict that the king issues can be changed." So the king gave the order, and they brought Daniel and threw him into the lions' den. The king said to Daniel, "May your God, whom you serve continually, rescue you!" A stone was brought and placed over the mouth of the den, and the king sealed it . . . so that Daniel's situation might not be changed. Then the king returned . . . without eating and without any entertainment being brought to him. And he could not sleep. At the first light of dawn, the king got up and hurried to the lions' den. When he came near the den, he called to Daniel in an anguished voice, "Daniel, servant of the living God, has your God, whom you serve continually, been able to rescue you from the lions?" Daniel answered, "May the king live forever! My God sent his angel, and he shut the mouths of the lions. They have not hurt me, because I was found innocent in his sight. Nor have I ever done any wrong before you, Your Majesty."

DANIEL 6:15-22 NIV

REFLECTIONS:

When you have a prayer life like Daniel had, actions speak louder than words. Daniel's obedience to God brought forth God's glory in the lion's den. We may never actually walk into a lion's den, but life can feel that way in many ways. So be like Daniel—don't lose focus. Stick to seeking the Lord, and he will shut the mouths that are trying to eat you up.

REQUESTS:

God, help us perceive your glory so we know your will, even in danger. Instead of panicking or running away, may we continue to seek and worship you so we may walk out of the den victorious in Jesus! God, you know the men enduring challenges right now. Bless them with victory!

Lord, we love you and thank you for answering our prayers.
In Jesus' name. AMEN

AUGUST - DAILY DEVOTIONAL #2

My brothers and sisters, if one of you should wander from the truth and someone should bring that person back, remember this: Whoever turns a sinner from the error of their way will save them from death and cover over a multitude of sins.

JAMES 5:19-20 NIV

REFLECTIONS:

We all can think of someone who has helped us turn from our wicked ways; those people are the hands and feet of Jesus. Are you willing to look beyond yourself? Do you have a deep desire for others, either coming to know Jesus as their Lord and Savior or turning back to him, as many of us have done? Then you too can be used as the hands and feet of Jesus.

Every morning, begin to ask God to use you to make a difference in someone's life today. God will surprise you with opportunities to witness, to encourage, and to pray for others. His ways aren't our ways, so hang on. It'll be a journey like you have never imagined.

REQUESTS:

Lord, may we be a witness not only in word but in deed so that all those around may see Jesus and turn from their wicked ways of this world. Lord, may we keep each other lifted up so none of us stray away from our faith and back into our old worldly ways. Bless my brothers and their families with your peace and presence, protecting them from all harm.

Lord, we love you and thank you for answering our prayers.
In Jesus' name. AMEN

AUGUST - DAILY DEVOTIONAL #3

Surely the arm of the LORD is not too short to save, nor his ear too dull to hear. But your iniquities have separated you from your God; your sins have hidden his face from you, so that he will not hear.

ISAIAH 59:1-2 NIV

REFLECTIONS:

We've prayed a lot about being the hands and feet of Jesus, so be prepared for God to use you as an arm to show just how God loves the one he's reaching out to. Each morning in your prayer time, ask the Lord to pour through you his love and glory to each person you come in contact with during the day. Whether it's at your workplace, a store, a restaurant, or just walking down the street, God can move anywhere, so be ready to be obedient when he speaks.

REQUESTS:

Lord, I know your arms are stretched out wide, waiting for the one who has separated himself from you with the things of this world. So, Lord, let us come running back to your open arms and leave those things that separate us from your presence and peace so that our walk reflects your love and goodness.

Lord, we love you and thank you for answering our prayers.
In Jesus' name. AMEN

AUGUST - DAILY DEVOTIONAL #4

Even though we speak like this, dear friends, we are convinced of better things in your case—the things that have to do with salvation. God is not unjust; he will not forget your work and the love you have shown him as you have helped his people and continue to help them. We want each of you to show this same diligence to the very end, so that what you hope for may be fully realized. We do not want you to become lazy, but to imitate those who through faith and patience inherit what has been promised.

HEBREWS 6:9-12 NIV

REFLECTIONS:

What's holding you back from being a light for Jesus in this dark world? Do you really think someone else needs to tell your children about Jesus or take them to church? If not, step up and be the man God called you to be; lead your home as Jesus leads you. When you do that, it'll flow out of you all the time, and you'll be a witness for Jesus everywhere at any time.

REQUESTS:

Lord, help us not to let all the negative things we have gone through and will go through cause us to become numb to those who need Jesus. But as we face trials, may we become all the more diligent in sharing our faith and the love of Jesus. Lord, bless these men and their families with your peace and presence today and help them with all that they need.

Lord, we love you and thank you for answering our prayers.
In Jesus' name. AMEN

AUGUST - DAILY DEVOTIONAL #5

The mind governed by the flesh is death, but the mind governed by the Spirit is life and peace. The mind governed by the flesh is hostile to God; it does not submit to God's law, nor can it do so. Those who are in the realm of the flesh cannot please God. You, however, are not in the realm of the flesh but are in the realm of the Spirit, if indeed the Spirit of God lives in you. And if anyone does not have the Spirit of Christ, they do not belong to Christ. But if Christ is in you, then even though your body is subject to death because of sin, the Spirit gives life because of righteousness.

ROMANS 8:6-10 NIV

REFLECTIONS:

Consider getting up fifteen minutes early, reading a few scriptures every morning, praying for your family, and asking God to direct your feet, hands, and mind for his service. It'll make a tremendous impact on your day and on where your thoughts go. If you do this wholeheartedly, those 15 minutes early will turn into 30 minutes, then eventually an hour to read and pray more. So take the challenge. God will not let you down. In fact, you might even get the feeling he is waiting on you.

REQUESTS:

Lord, one of our biggest battles is our minds. So I ask for your protection over our thoughts that our minds may dwell on things above and not what the flesh desires. Fill our hearts and minds with your peace so we may worship you daily, completely focused on your desires and not our own. Bless my brothers and their families with your goodness today.

Lord, we love you and thank you for answering our prayers.
In Jesus' name. AMEN

AUGUST - DAILY DEVOTIONAL #6

For in this hope we were saved. But hope that is seen is no hope at all. Who hopes for what they already have? But if we hope for what we do not yet have, we wait for it patiently. In the same way, the Spirit helps us in our weakness. We do not know what we ought to pray for, but the Spirit himself intercedes for us through wordless groans. And he who searches our hearts knows the mind of the Spirit, because the Spirit intercedes for God's people in accordance with the will of God. And we know that in all things God works for the good of those who love him, who have been called according to his purpose.

ROMANS 8:24-28 NIV

REFLECTIONS:

As a child of God, one thing is for sure: God will never let you down. That's why he sent his Spirit to live in us so we always have him with us. When this work weighs us down so heavily that we don't know what to do or say, he's already interceding for us. So never doubt if he is with you or not, and always remember: someone is always interceding on your behalf. Now go live your life for the hope you don't see but know is there.

REQUESTS:

Lord, thank you that as your children, your Spirit in us gives the hope that we need to wait patiently for you. Thank you, that when our world seems to crumble down around our feet, or we are just not sure what to pray for, your Spirit is already interceding for us, working all things out for our good. You are such a good, good Father. Lord, if one of my brothers has any doubt about your goodness, I ask you to show him in only a way you could.

Lord, we love you and thank you for answering our prayers.
In Jesus' name. AMEN

AUGUST - DAILY DEVOTIONAL #7

" . . . In the Law Moses commanded us to stone such women. Now what do you say?" They were using this question as a trap, in order to have a basis for accusing him. But Jesus bent down and started to write on the ground with his finger. When they kept on questioning him, he straightened up and said to them, "Let any one of you who is without sin be the first to throw a stone at her." Again he stooped down and wrote on the ground. At this, those who heard began to go away one at a time, the older ones first, until only Jesus was left, with the woman still standing there. Jesus straightened up and asked her, "Woman, where are they? Has no one condemned you?" "No one, sir," she said. "Then neither do I condemn you," Jesus declared. "Go now and leave your life of sin."

JOHN 8:5-11 NIV

REFLECTIONS:

When Jesus went to the cross, I believe he was saying to the world, "I didn't come to condemn you, but to be condemned for you, even unto death on the cross. If you accept me as your Lord and Savior, you can go and sin no more." Our everyday lives preach either about the things of this world, drawing more people into it, or they preach Jesus, bearing witness to the glory of God, giving hope of better things to come with Jesus. So, what are you preaching?

REQUESTS:

Lord, thank you that you hate the sin but love us sinners. With Jesus leading, you've empowered us to conquer the world. Then, our lives may bear witness to what Jesus did for us on the cross—when we accepted him as our Lord and Savior, and he washed us white as snow. Father, may we seek Your desires, not earthly pleasures. Bless my brothers with your peace and confidence, knowing they're forgiven and not condemned.

Lord, we love you and thank you for answering our prayers.
In Jesus' name. AMEN

AUGUST - DAILY DEVOTIONAL #8

"You are the salt of the earth. But if the salt loses its saltiness, how can it be made salty again? It is no longer good for anything, except to be thrown out and trampled underfoot. You are the light of the world. A town built on a hill cannot be hidden. Neither do people light a lamp and put it under a bowl. Instead they put it on its stand, and it gives light to everyone in the house. In the same way, let your light shine before others, that they may see your good deeds and glorify your Father in heaven. . . . "

MATTHEW 5:13-16 NIV

REFLECTIONS:

What is holding you back from uncovering the light that Jesus gave you when you invited him into your heart and received him as your Lord and Savior? You can't hold back the tidal wave of joy that's in you. *Let it rip, tater chip!*

Go brighten someone's life by shining the light that's in you. Show them the way to Jesus. Let your light shine the pathway, so no brother is left behind. Begin asking the Lord for one person to share your light with, and watch what happens; the number will grow.

REQUESTS:

Lord, salt in wounds burns, but it also brings healing. Please give us a deep, deep desire to dig into your Word, or better yet, into your salt pit, so we may be healed. When we do not allow your salt to heal us, we turn to the world. And although we think we're better, the world draws out our salt and dims our light. So may we continue to chase after you, keeping our salt fresh and our light fueled. Lord, bless my brothers with your presence and peace.

Lord, we love you and thank you for answering our prayers.
In Jesus' name. AMEN

AUGUST - DAILY DEVOTIONAL #9

Their visions are false and their divinations a lie. Even though the LORD has not sent them, they say, "The Lord declares," and expect him to fulfill their words. Have you not seen false visions and uttered lying divinations when you say, "The LORD declares," though I have not spoken? "'Therefore this is what the Sovereign LORD says: Because of your false words and lying visions, I am against you, declares the Sovereign LORD.. . . "

EZEKIEL 13:6-8 NIV

REFLECTIONS:

Walking with Jesus brings joy and makes you feel good at times. But Jesus is not a feel-good movement. He doesn't say everything is going to be perfect from here on out. But what he does say when times get unbearable is that he is there to strengthen you to be more than a conqueror over the bad times. So don't get caught up in the feel-good movement that denies the power of the cross and the strength we have from Jesus to be more than just a survivor. Life is hard knocks at times, but nothing can separate us from the love of Jesus and his overwhelming power to provide all that we need.

REQUESTS:

Lord, give us eyes to see the falseness of many of those sharing the gospel. Give us ears to hear the difference between the true gospel and when they are twisting Scripture for their own good. Lord, help us to only process what you have told us, so we are testifying for you and not against you. May our yes be yes and our no be no. May we be diligent in seeking your truth and will for our lives. Lord, bless each one of my brothers and their families with your goodness.

Lord, we love you and thank you for answering our prayers.
In Jesus' name. AMEN

AUGUST - DAILY DEVOTIONAL #10

" . . . I have seen their ways, but I will heal them; I will guide them and restore comfort to Israel's mourners, creating praise on their lips. Peace, peace, to those far and near," says the LORD. "And I will heal them."

ISAIAH 57:18-19 NIV

REFLECTIONS:

Sometimes we need to stop and look around and see what's happening. We can get so wrapped up in our work with kids and grandkids, it's amazing how much we live in a bubble. We need to remember, even with all the good things we have going on in our lives, we live in a dying world.

We need to be praying not just for our home and our town, but for our country to get on the right side of the cross with God leading us. So don't just sit hoping your bubble won't get popped. Get up and begin protecting it by praying and seeking the Lord for his direction.

REQUESTS:

Lord, we claim this over our churches and our country: As we wake up each day, just as Israel wakes up in a new world each day, a world where wickedness is trying to destroy the world we live in, we claim your healing. Let us have a new song on our lips and shine our light of Jesus, so the darkness will not overtake us, and so the world around us will know you are our God, and we serve no other. Lord, I ask you to bless each of my brothers and their families with all that they need, and may your glory shine upon them.

Lord, we love you and thank you for answering our prayers.
In Jesus' name. AMEN

AUGUST - DAILY DEVOTIONAL #11

Peace I leave with you; my peace I give you. I do not give to you as the world gives. Do not let your hearts be troubled and do not be afraid.

JOHN 14:27 NIV

REFLECTIONS:

If you were reading that verse in the Bible, it would be in red letter because Jesus spoke it directly to us. If he said it, I believe it, and that is enough. So when you get up every morning, the first thing you should seek is his peace. He left it for you, so pick it up. It's yours.

REQUESTS:

Lord, may your peace be like a blanket over my brothers and their families today. May your goodness shine on them and your love be poured out on them.

Lord, we love you and thank you for answering our prayers.
In Jesus' name. AMEN

AUGUST - DAILY DEVOTIONAL #12

They refused to listen and failed to remember the miracles you performed among them. They became stiff-necked and in their rebellion appointed a leader in order to return to their slavery. But you are a forgiving God, gracious and compassionate, slow to anger and abounding in love. Therefore you did not desert them, even when they cast for themselves an image of a calf and said, 'This is your god, who brought you up out of Egypt,' or when they committed awful blasphemies. "Because of your great compassion you did not abandon them in the wilderness. By day the pillar of cloud did not fail to guide them on their path, nor the pillar of fire by night to shine on the way they were to take . . .. "

NEHEMIAH 9:17-19 NIV

REFLECTIONS:

This is the God we serve. Get to know him so you can receive and feel the love he showed us through Jesus and the cross, forgiving all of our sins once and for all, so we could have a personal relationship with him. He tells us, "I will never leave you nor forsake you." That's the best deal I've heard all day. You'd better get yourself some of that.

REQUESTS:

Lord, we could very easily say that sounds like me or us as a whole. You have been very faithful, showing more grace and mercy than we have ever deserved, through Jesus our Lord and Savior. Lord, may we become a people of light, burning out all darkness within us so that our light is transparent. And as people look through it, they see Jesus and not us. Lord, may each of our lives show that Jesus did not die in vain, and his resurrection is something to celebrate and not desecrate by being a stiff-necked people.

Lord, we love you and thank you for answering our prayers.
In Jesus' name. AMEN

AUGUST - DAILY DEVOTIONAL #13

They were all trying to frighten us, thinking, "Their hands will get too weak for the work, and it will not be completed." But I prayed, "Now strengthen my hands."

NEHEMIAH 6:9 NIV

REFLECTIONS:

I don't know what page of this devotional you're on, but I hope by now you've begun not to just read the prayer, but to pray yourself. Praying out loud to the Father is a show of strength to the enemy who wants to destroy you with fear. Praying also helps you realize you have a personal relationship with the Father who will never leave your side.

REQUESTS:

Lord, the world wants Christians all over the world to be frightened by all that is going on. It wants us to stop doing the work of spreading the gospel. But Lord, you didn't give us a spirit of fear but one of faith and confidence in you, for we know where our strength comes from—you and you alone. So, Lord, as the world gets more aggressive, may your Spirit within us become bolder so we may not fear but be overcomers!

Lord, we love you and thank you for answering our prayers.
In Jesus' name. AMEN

AUGUST - DAILY DEVOTIONAL #14

At one time we too were foolish, disobedient, deceived and enslaved by all kinds of passions and pleasures. We lived in malice and envy, being hated and hating one another. But when the kindness and love of God our Savior appeared, he saved us, not because of righteous things we had done, but because of his mercy. He saved us through the washing of rebirth and renewal by the Holy Spirit, whom he poured out on us generously through Jesus Christ our Savior, so that, having been justified by his grace, we might become heirs having the hope of eternal life.

TITUS 3:3-7 NIV

REFLECTIONS:

If we ever get to where we believe we earned all that God has done for us—from the cross, to things we have in our homes, or as some think, it is owed to us—if anything like that ever happens, then we are more lost than a Christmas goose. You cannot earn salvation, you cannot buy it, and you certainly don't deserve it. What we deserve is death, hell, and the grave. So, straighten up and seek the Lord with all your heart because it's owed to him and he surely deserves it.

REQUESTS:

Lord, thank you for sending Jesus to pay a debt he didn't owe. May we as men spend our time telling others how, when we accepted Jesus as our Lord and Savior, he pulled us out of the hell we were living in. So thank you that each morning your mercies are new, and yesterday is gone. May what we do today represent who you are in us.

Lord, we love you and thank you for answering our prayers.
In Jesus' name. AMEN

AUGUST - DAILY DEVOTIONAL #15

Let the morning bring me word of your unfailing love, for I have put my trust in you. Show me the way I should go, for to you I entrust my life. Rescue me from my enemies, LORD, for I hide myself in you. Teach me to do your will, for you are my God; may your good Spirit lead me on level ground. For your name's sake, LORD, preserve my life; in your righteousness, bring me out of trouble. In your unfailing love, silence my enemies; destroy all my foes, for I am your servant.

PSALM 143:8-12 NIV

REFLECTIONS:

Find a place where you can have 10 or 15 minutes to pray, and then sit in silence. God will speak. God created you to fellowship with him so he could bless you beyond measure. If you don't already fellowship with him, may you seek him daily for all things and see what happens.

REQUESTS:

Lord, I ask for your protection and guidance for my brothers and their families. I ask that your peace wash over them and your presence surround them. Lord, as men, we need you to speak to us in the way we should go. Let us have ears to hear and eyes to see the path you're leading us down.

Lord, we love you and thank you for answering our prayers.
In Jesus' name. AMEN

AUGUST - DAILY DEVOTIONAL #16

For you were once darkness, but now you are light in the Lord. Live as children of light (for the fruit of the light consists in all goodness, righteousness and truth) and find out what pleases the Lord. Have nothing to do with the fruitless deeds of darkness, but rather expose them. It is shameful even to mention what the disobedient do in secret. But everything exposed by the light becomes visible—and everything that is illuminated becomes a light. This is why it is said: "Wake up, sleeper, rise from the dead, and Christ will shine on you."

EPHESIANS 5:8-14 NIV

REFLECTIONS:

What is it you do that darkens your world? We all have that one habit that we do, and as we do it, the light is sucked right out of the room. We fall back for hours, asking or begging God for help and saying we won't do it again. The problem with that is we've never actually turned that part of us over to him.

Every day when you wake up, give him everything until there is no more to give. I could name something that would resonate with you, but there's no need. You know what yours is. So, lay it at his feet.

REQUESTS:

Lord, help us shine the light you have given us and not let ourselves cover it with our own selfish desires. Help us remember that true character is shown in what we do when we think no one is watching. Lord, let us always remember and never forget that you're always with us.

Lord, we love you and thank you for answering our prayers.
In Jesus' name. AMEN

AUGUST - DAILY DEVOTIONAL #17

But whatever were gains to me I now consider loss for the sake of Christ. What is more, I consider everything a loss because of the surpassing worth of knowing Christ Jesus my Lord, for whose sake I have lost all things. I consider them garbage, that I may gain Christ and be found in him, not having a righteousness of my own that comes from the law, but that which is through faith in Christ—the righteousness that comes from God on the basis of faith. I want to know Christ—yes, to know the power of his resurrection and participation in his sufferings, becoming like him in his death, and so, somehow, attaining to the resurrection from the dead.

PHILIPPIANS 3:7-11 NIV

REFLECTIONS:

Have you ever cleaned out a storeroom or a closet that has accumulated stuff over the years? I bet most of you thought it was already gone. I bet you sorted through it and threw a lot of it away or carried it down to Goodwill. Then there's the stuff you kept hanging on to a little longer. It's the same way with our hearts. It's time to allow God to do a full clean out and allow him to fill it full with his goodness. It's a simple prayer, so pray it daily. "Clean my heart, O, God. Make it ever true."

REQUESTS:

God, anything within us that doesn't honor you, let us discard it, and instead, fill us with the things of heaven that do. All our possessions are yours. Whatever cannot be used for your glory is garbage. Help us draw closer to you and be more like you today than we were yesterday. Bless my brothers and their families with your peace and presence, guiding them and protecting them from all harm.

Lord, we love you and thank you for answering our prayers.
In Jesus' name. AMEN

AUGUST - DAILY DEVOTIONAL #18

The LORD will guide you always; he will satisfy your needs in a sun-scorched land and will strengthen your frame. You will be like a well-watered garden, like a spring whose waters never fail.

ISAIAH 58:11 NIV

REFLECTIONS:

One question: What are you waiting on? Be like Peter and step out of the comfort of the boat and see how God uses you. Don't let the circumstances around you dictate the amount of obedience you have to the Lord. Be fully committed despite what the world says. Be like Noah; he was dumb till it rained, and then it was too late for the rest of them.

REQUESTS:

Lord, this is my prayer for my brothers: Bless them beyond measure, help them in every way, and fill their cup today.

Lord, we love you and thank you for answering our prayers.
In Jesus' name. AMEN

AUGUST - DAILY DEVOTIONAL #19

Therefore let all the faithful pray to you while you may be found; surely the rising of the mighty waters will not reach them. You are my hiding place; you will protect me from trouble and surround me with songs of deliverance.

PSALM 32:6-7 NIV

REFLECTIONS:

Your prayer is the most powerful tool the Lord has given you, but it's used less than the household hammer. If you want peace during fearful times, pray. If you want to know how to handle any situation or problem, pray. God wants a personal relationship with you, and to be personal, you need to talk to him through prayer.

I have mentioned a 1000 times that you need to find a place in your home that you can go to daily. I prefer early morning as I drink my coffee with God, to pray. I pray for the day, my family, and yes, you. So pray daily. It'll change your life.

REQUESTS:

Lord, today give us a new song. May your goodness cover us like a blanket and your peace run over us like a deep, slow-moving river.

Lord, we love you and thank you for answering our prayers.
In Jesus' name. AMEN

AUGUST - DAILY DEVOTIONAL #20

I always thank my God as I remember you in my prayers, because I hear about your love for all his holy people and your faith in the Lord Jesus. I pray that your partnership with us in the faith may be effective in deepening your understanding of every good thing we share for the sake of Christ. Your love has given me great joy and encouragement, because you, brother, have refreshed the hearts of the Lord's people.

PHILEMON 1:4-7 NIV

REFLECTIONS:

I used to drop hundreds, if not thousands, of dollars a month on alcohol for people I didn't even know just because I wanted everyone to have a good time. So now God has delivered me from alcohol, and I pray for you. I may not know you, but because I want you to know the conditional love of Jesus, I pray. It's better than any drink I could buy you, and the effects have a more positive outcome on your life, your family, and those around you. So above all else, learn to pray.

REQUESTS:

Lord, give us an opportunity today to encourage those who know Christ but have been beaten down by the world, so that they may continue the fight in Christ. You have truly given them the victory. And for those who may have never heard the gospel of Jesus Christ, may the steps in our own lives lead them to the cross. Our daily walk should always start at the cross to remind us that without you and your glory, Lord, we are nothing. Lord, bless these men today with peace and surround them in your presence.

Lord, we love you and thank you for answering our prayers.
In Jesus' name. AMEN

AUGUST - DAILY DEVOTIONAL #21

Understand, then, that those who have faith are children of Abraham. Scripture foresaw that God would justify the Gentiles by faith, and announced the gospel in advance to Abraham: "All nations will be blessed through you." So those who rely on faith are blessed along with Abraham, the man of faith.

GALATIANS 3:7-9 NIV

REFLECTIONS:

What example of you having faith do people see? Abraham was known for his faith, and because of his faith and obedience, we are here. Do those around you see you as a man who walks by faith, or just a man who talks about faith? Abraham walked in faith more than he talked about it. So may we all seek the Lord daily, and learn to completely trust, so we are truly walking by faith rather than just talking.

REQUESTS:

Lord, thank you that it's by faith alone that we are saved, not by our own works, but by the gospel we have heard. Jesus was crucified and rose again on the third day, so all who believe and put their faith in him will be saved. So, Lord, help us not put our faith in our abilities but in Christ alone! Lord, bless these men today with peace that passes all understanding and your joy that's unspeakable.

Lord, we love you and thank you for answering our prayers.
In Jesus' name. AMEN

AUGUST - DAILY DEVOTIONAL #22

Anyone who listens to the word but does not do what it says is like someone who looks at his face in a mirror and, after looking at himself, goes away and immediately forgets what he looks like. But whoever looks intently into the perfect law that gives freedom, and continues in it—not forgetting what they have heard, but doing it—they will be blessed in what they do.

JAMES 1:23-25 NIV

REFLECTIONS:

The one thing I used to get into trouble for, and still do, is not listening. I hear, but listening is different than hearing. As my momma used to say, "I know you heard me, but if you had listened, you wouldn't have gotten into trouble or gotten hurt." So I ask God for a lot of things, but especially for the ability to listen and the wisdom to apply it. If we learn to do that, it'll solve a world of problems.

REQUESTS:

Lord, may we be hungry for your Word. As we read it, may it plant roots in our hearts, so we are ready and prepared to share the goodness of the gospel. Lord, I ask you to bless each one of these men with your goodness this week. May we have opportunities to share the good news of Jesus!

Lord, we love you and thank you for answering our prayers.
In Jesus' name. AMEN

AUGUST - DAILY DEVOTIONAL #23

You then, my son, be strong in the grace that is in Christ Jesus. And the things you have heard me say in the presence of many witnesses entrust to reliable people who will also be qualified to teach others. Join with me in suffering, like a good soldier of Christ Jesus. No one serving as a soldier gets entangled in civilian affairs, but rather tries to please his commanding officer. Similarly, anyone who competes as an athlete does not receive the victor's crown except by competing according to the rules. The hardworking farmer should be the first to receive a share of the crops. Reflect on what I am saying, for the Lord will give you insight into all this.

2 TIMOTHY 2:1-7 NIV

REFLECTIONS:

Probably the question most asked daily is, "Did you hear about ol' so and so?" My answer usually is "No, but who told you that?" And the response is usually, "Well, no one; it's all over Facebook or Twitter."

Most of the time, social media platforms are just like the *National Enquirer*, because the enquiring minds want to know. If we spent more time seeking the Lord than we do scrolling through other people's lives, we would be stronger soldiers for Christ. So next time you scroll and read about someone else, and it's not good, pray for them. Be the light.

REQUESTS:

Lord, help us not get so entangled in things of this world that we become lazy in doing the work you have called us to do. When we stand before you, let us not be ashamed but hear, "Welcome, my good and faithful servants." Lord, give us eyes to see and ears to hear, so we know what our true calling is.

Lord, we love you and thank you for answering our prayers.
In Jesus' name. AMEN

AUGUST - DAILY DEVOTIONAL #24

Who has believed our message and to whom has the arm of the LORD been revealed? He grew up before him like a tender shoot, and like a root out of dry ground. He had no beauty or majesty to attract us to him, nothing in his appearance that we should desire him. He was despised and rejected by mankind, a man of suffering, and familiar with pain. Like one from whom people hide their faces he was despised, and we held him in low esteem. Surely he took up our pain and bore our suffering, yet we considered him punished by God, stricken by him, and afflicted. But he was pierced for our transgressions, he was crushed for our iniquities; the punishment that brought us peace was on him, and by his wounds we are healed.

ISAIAH 53:1-5 NIV

REFLECTIONS:

It's my intent every day to live in such a way that Jesus never has the thought I wasn't worth dying for. But by his grace and mercy, when I fail to do so, he picks me up, dusts me off, and we continue to walk out life together. So take his hand today and begin to walk in all that he's blessed you with and all that he has for your future. Remember, just like me, he considered my stupidity before he went to the cross. So, get to work. No, you're not worthy, but He is worthy of all our praise. So go praise him in your life.

REQUESTS:

Lord, may our lives testify to what Jesus did on the cross, taking our punishment for our wicked ways, so that we may be forgiven and walk in his grace and receive his mercy every day. Lord, bless these men and their families with peace and consume them with your presence.

Lord, we love you and thank you for answering our prayers.
In Jesus' name. AMEN

AUGUST - DAILY DEVOTIONAL #25

Servants, respectfully obey your earthly masters but always with an eye to obeying the *real* master, Christ. Don't just do what you have to do to get by, but work heartily, as Christ's servants doing what God wants you to do. And work with a smile on your face, always keeping in mind that no matter who happens to be giving the orders, you're really serving God. Good work will get you good pay from the Master, regardless of whether you are slave or free. Masters, it's the same with you. No abuse, please, and no threats. You and your servants are both under the same Master in heaven. He makes no distinction between you and them.

EPHESIANS 6:5-9 MSG

REFLECTIONS:

If we live to be an example of who Jesus was, then we're certainly going to be persecuted, even in our jobs. But truthfully, if we serve as Jesus did and work as if we were working for the Lord, we may not receive the best treatment from those around us. If they were honest with themselves, they would probably never want you to leave.

So keep shining the light of Jesus. Whether you can see it or not, you're making a difference by letting Jesus use you. Handle everything with prayer first; that means stay quiet like Jesus did while he was on trial and see what God does.

REQUESTS:

Lord, I ask you to bless us with hearts of service filled with your peace. Give us tongues that honor you as well as those around us, so we may not grumble but speak of your goodness and faithfulness. Lord, may we honor and bring glory to you in all that we do. Lord, bless us with opportunities to share the good news of Jesus with the lost.

Lord, we love you and thank you for answering our prayers.
In Jesus' name. AMEN

AUGUST - DAILY DEVOTIONAL #26

Husbands, go all out in love for your wives. Don't take advantage of them.
COLOSSIANS 3:19 MSG

REFLECTIONS:

As Christians, we are the bride of Christ. Do you treat your wife like you want Jesus to treat the church, his bride? I bet not. Don't take anything from your wife or future wife for granted. And no matter how tired you are, always ask her when you get home if there is anything you can help with. You don't know what kind of day she's had. Don't take your bad day out on her.

REQUESTS:

Lord, we lift up our wives and the future wives of single men. We ask you to surround them in your peace and presence. May you give them eyes to see and ears to hear your glory all around them. Give us a heart like theirs that loves unconditionally without holding back. Lord, I know without you and my wife, I wouldn't be the man I am today. So, Lord, bless them mightily and help them with every step they take. And bless these men with your wisdom on how to help and support their wives.

Lord, we love you and thank you for answering our prayers.
In Jesus' name. AMEN

AUGUST - DAILY DEVOTIONAL #27

"'... My hand will be against the prophets who see false visions and utter lying divinations. They will not belong to the council of my people or be listed in the records of Israel, nor will they enter the land of Israel. Then you will know that I am the Sovereign LORD.

"'Because they lead my people astray, saying, "Peace," when there is no peace, and because, when a flimsy wall is built, they cover it with whitewash, therefore tell those who cover it with whitewash that it is going to fall. Rain will come in torrents, and I will send hailstones hurtling down, and violent winds will burst forth . . .. '"

EZEKIEL 13:9-11 NIV

REFLECTIONS:

The best way to see if a preacher or even your pastor is hearing the Lord is to measure everything you hear by the Word of God. Ask God to reveal the truth in the message you heard. God will show you all the truth. Pray for your pastor, asking God to guide him in his sermon preparation, and pray for the Lord's protection over him. Remember, pastors fall under attack just as we do.

REQUESTS:

Lord, mid-term elections are this year. Most of us decide by what we hear and see physically, but I ask you to give us eyes to see and ears to hear what you see and hear. I ask you, Lord, let nothing stand in the way of the one whose name is written in the Lamb's book of life and has a heart that seeks you. Lord, let us not be led off to slaughter. Lord, bless these men and their families with wisdom and peace, guiding them in their walk with you.

Lord, we love you and thank you for answering our prayers.
In Jesus' name. AMEN

AUGUST - DAILY DEVOTIONAL #28

Rejoice always, pray without ceasing, give thanks in all circumstances; for this is the will of God in Christ Jesus for you.

1 THESSALONIANS 5:16-18 ESV

REFLECTIONS:

A friend of mine recently lost his brother in a motorcycle crash. He rushed to the crash site and found the older man who had pulled out and caused the accident with his brother. My friend prayed for that gentleman, and he forgave him.

Even though his heart was broken at the loss of his brother, my friend could only do that because he knew to rejoice always and pray without ceasing. Allowing anger and unforgiveness to consume him would have prevented him from praying or rejoicing.

REQUESTS:

Lord, in all situations, may we give you glory, for no matter what, you're still on the throne and in control. Lord, I don't know what all these men are going through, but I ask you to bless them with peace and fill them with your hope. Lord, may your glory shine upon them with healing so they may have a victory!

Lord, we love you and thank you for answering our prayers.
In Jesus' name. AMEN

AUGUST - DAILY DEVOTIONAL #29

If any of you lacks wisdom, let him ask God, who gives generously to all without reproach, and it will be given him. But let him ask in faith, with no doubting, for the one who doubts is like a wave of the sea that is driven and tossed by the wind. For that person must not suppose that he will receive anything from the Lord; he is a double-minded man, unstable in all his ways.

JAMES 1:5-8 ESV

REFLECTIONS:

You have not because you ask not. God wants us as his children to have the very best he has to offer; he will equip you with all that you need for your calling in life. So don't doubt God, ask and see what happens. If you need milk, pray for it, but don't be surprised if someone gives you a milk cow. God may want you and the entire neighborhood to have milk. As you deliver it, he just might use you to lead someone to Christ. So whatever you pray for, be prepared for the unexpected. And be ready to work for the Lord.

REQUESTS:

Lord, I ask you to forgive us where we have doubted you. May our flesh get in line with your Spirit that is within us, so there is no doubt of faith. We believe that you are more than capable and willing to do more than our minds and hearts can imagine, not because of who we are, but because of who you are—our Father in heaven. Lord, I ask you to bless these men with all that they need today.

Lord, we love you and thank you for answering our prayers.
In Jesus' name. AMEN

AUGUST - DAILY DEVOTIONAL #30

The steadfast love of the LORD never ceases; his mercies never come to an end; they are new every morning; great is your faithfulness. "The LORD is my portion," says my soul, "therefore I will hope in him." The LORD is good to those who wait for him, to the soul who seeks him.

LAMENTATIONS 3:22-25 ESV

REFLECTIONS:

If you don't have time in the mornings to do anything else but thank the Lord for another day, then do it. Acknowledge him as your Father, because one day you're going to want him to acknowledge you. Remember, not all good ol' boys are going to get into heaven. In fact, they're going to be told I never knew you.

So if you have no doubt that your name is written in the Lamb's book of life, then act like it. Acknowledge him even when you don't feel like it. Someone needs it even if you don't think you do. Shine the light that's within you.

REQUESTS:

Lord, thank you for your mercies this morning. I pray for guidance through this day as we seek your direction and your answer to many prayers. May we wait in your peace and presence. May we always, without ceasing, seek you in everything we do.

Lord, we love you and thank you for answering our prayers.
In Jesus' name. AMEN

AUGUST - DAILY DEVOTIONAL #31

So I tell you this, . . . that you must no longer live as the Gentiles do, in the futility of their thinking. They are darkened in their understanding and separated from the life of God because of the ignorance that is in them due to the hardening of their hearts. Having lost all sensitivity, they have given themselves over to sensuality so as to indulge in every kind of impurity, and they are full of greed. That, however, is not the way of life you learned when you heard about Christ . . . You were taught . . . to put off your old self, which is being corrupted by its deceitful desires; to be made new in the attitude of your minds; and to put on the new self, created to be like God in true righteousness and holiness. Therefore each of you must put off falsehood and speak truthfully to your neighbor, for we are all members of one body. "In your anger do not sin": Do not let the sun go down while you are still angry, and do not give the devil a foothold.

EPHESIANS 4:17-27 NIV

REFLECTIONS:

It's ok to talk about our past and even laugh about it, but I always say, "Thank the Lord I don't live like that anymore." Thank the Lord I'm not even close to being that guy anymore because of God's mercy and grace. I don't ever want to go back to that life, and I hope you don't either. That's why it's so important to seek the Lord daily in prayer for his protection and direction over you and your family.

REQUESTS:

Lord, I ask you to forgive us where we have allowed ourselves to pick back up the stuff that you have delivered us from. Give us a heart that will chase after you daily, so we don't lose all sensitivity to the Spirit who leads us where we should go. Lord, bless each one of my brothers and their families today with your joy, peace, and presence, filling their every moment with your goodness.

Lord, we love you and thank you for answering our prayers.
In Jesus' name. AMEN

Faith is not hoping God can. It is knowing He will.

SEPTEMBER - DAILY DEVOTIONAL #1

You will keep in perfect peace those whose minds are steadfast, because they trust in you. Trust in the LORD forever, for the LORD, the LORD himself, is the Rock eternal.

ISAIAH 26:3-4 NIV

REFLECTIONS:

Do you find yourself hesitant or even dreading meetings with others when you anticipate a difficult situation and a negative result? Stop before you go in, ask God to fill the room with his peace and presence, and to bind up all tension and hostility. God does not want his children to carry anxiety or worry, so pray that prayer every time and see what God does.

REQUESTS:

Lord, today, may we be steadfast in sharing your love with others. As we go about our day, may your peace go before us, walk with us, and come behind us, so that at the end of the day we can surely say God was with us. Lord, in any and every place we go today, may we find your peace there; not because of us, but because of you.

Lord, we love you and thank you for answering our prayers.
In Jesus' name. AMEN

SEPTEMBER - DAILY DEVOTIONAL #2

'Ah, Lord GOD! It is you who have made the heavens and the earth by your great power and by your outstretched arm! Nothing is too hard for you. You show steadfast love to thousands, but you repay the guilt of fathers to their children after them, O great and mighty God, whose name is the LORD of hosts, great in counsel and mighty in deed, whose eyes are open to all the ways of the children of man, rewarding each one according to his ways and according to the fruit of his deeds. You have shown signs and wonders in the land of Egypt, and to this day in Israel and among all mankind, and have made a name for yourself, as at this day. . . . '

JEREMIAH 32:17-20 ESV

REFLECTIONS:

Teach your children to love the Lord your God and raise them to seek him in all their ways, so they may receive the Lord's blessing over their lives. Those blessings will go from generation to generation. That's how you break generational curses. Raise them to know the Lord's ways and not your sinful ways. They'll have enough of their own to deal with; they don't need yours. So, begin to pray and ask God to protect your children and to help you raise them to know him.

REQUESTS:

Lord, we thank you that through Jesus our Lord and Savior, the punishment for our parents' sins is washed away by the blood when we come to Jesus. And we can walk in your glorious riches and leave your blessings for our children from one generation to the next. Lord, I ask you to bless each of these men with peace, delivering them from any false expectation they think they have to live up to in order to be a man like their dad. May they be set free to seek you and answer the call you have for them.

Lord, we love you and thank you for answering our prayers.
In Jesus' name. AMEN

SEPTEMBER - DAILY DEVOTIONAL #3

As long as Moses held up his hands, the Israelites were winning, but whenever he lowered his hands, the Amalekites were winning.

EXODUS 17:11 NIV

REFLECTIONS:

Throughout your day, when someone's name pops into your head and you can't stop thinking about them, stop and pray for them. If nothing else, ask God to bless them with his peace and presence around them. Or say Lord, I don't know what they are going through, but you do, so help them. The more you do that, the more sensitive you'll become to the Spirit prompting you to pray. I sometimes send a prayer in a text or I call—however the Lord leads. However you choose to do it, don't wait and don't ignore the prompting of God's calling on you to fight for them.

REQUESTS:

Lord, stir in our hearts to hold up each other in prayer continually. Whether they are in a spiritual battle or a physical battle, help those in the fight not grow weary and faint. But help them stand boldly in the battle with the power of prayer, holding them up. Lord, you know what each of these men is battling, and I ask you to fill them with your strength and power to walk in victory. Lord, we love you. We thank you for all that you've done for us and for what you're still doing.

Lord, we love you and thank you for answering our prayers.
In Jesus' name. AMEN

SEPTEMBER - DAILY DEVOTIONAL #4

"'... Reform your ways and your actions, and I will let you live in this place. Do not trust in deceptive words and say, "This is the temple of the LORD . . . !" If you really change your ways and your actions and deal with each other justly, if you do not oppress the foreigner, the fatherless or the widow and do not shed innocent blood in this place, and if you do not follow other gods to your own harm, then I will let you live in this place, in the land I gave your ancestors for ever and ever. But look, you are trusting in deceptive words that are worthless. "'Will you steal and murder, commit adultery and perjury, burn incense to Baal and follow other gods you have not known, and then come and stand before me in this house, which bears my Name, and say, "We are safe"—safe to do all these detestable things? Has this house, which bears my Name, become a den of robbers to you? But I have been watching! declares the LORD . . .."'

JEREMIAH 7:3B-11 NIV

REFLECTIONS:

First, look around your home and see what worldly things you have allowed to slide. My granddad wouldn't let any of his grandsons walk around his house with a t-shirt on, especially when we sat down at the table to eat. Not once did he ever let it slide. That has nothing to do with God, but we need to be more like that, so the enemy isn't allowed in the door. What we allow in our homes eventually shows up in our workplaces and even in our churches. So, look around, and ask God to show you how to get rid of it.

REQUESTS:

Lord, your message is still the same for Christians today. Help us turn from our hateful and deceptive ways so glory will shine on our country again and revival will break out across our land. Bless each of these men and their families with all that they need.

Lord, we love you and thank you for answering our prayers.
In Jesus' name. AMEN

SEPTEMBER - DAILY DEVOTIONAL #5

Now this I know: The LORD gives victory to his anointed. He answers him from his heavenly sanctuary with the victorious power of his right hand. Some trust in chariots and some in horses, but we trust in the name of the LORD our God. They are brought to their knees and fall, but we rise up and stand firm. LORD, give victory to the king! Answer us when we call!

PSALM 20:6-9 NIV

REFLECTIONS:

Our lives in Jesus are eternal, so when we pray for healing, we think that if there is no physical healing, God didn't answer our prayers. But we don't know what healing happened spiritually for the one we were praying for. If I've been praying for healing for someone and they pass away, I am sad that they're gone, but God gave them healing as they entered heaven. I've seen many people I've prayed for who didn't receive a physical healing. But, spiritually, they became very close to the Lord. Some have passed, and some are still living a productive life for Jesus.

So today, for that person you've been saying, "What's the point in praying for them," it's not our choice how the Lord chooses to handle their healing. But it is our job to seek him in all situations and to pray for them.

REQUESTS:

Lord, thank you for the victory we have in Jesus. Many times, our victories don't even resemble what we thought a victory should look like, but the victory is yours. We must fully trust you to truly live in the victory you've given us. So, Lord, this morning we lay down any doubt we may have, and we give you all the glory for whatever our victories look like.

Lord, we love you and thank you for answering our prayers.
In Jesus' name. AMEN

SEPTEMBER - DAILY DEVOTIONAL #6

In him and through faith in him we may approach God with freedom and confidence. . . . I pray that out of his glorious riches he may strengthen you with power through his Spirit in your inner being, so that Christ may dwell in your hearts through faith. And I pray that you, being rooted and established in love, may have power, together with all the Lord's holy people, to grasp how wide and long and high and deep is the love of Christ, and to know this love that surpasses knowledge—that you may be filled to the measure of all the fullness of God.

EPHESIANS 3:12, 16-19 NIV

REFLECTIONS:

I have brothers in Christ who, before we hang up from a phone call, tell each other, "I love you, brother." Usually, if we're around each other, we hug and say, "I love you, brother." Those words from a Christian brother give me confidence that he's got my back in prayer, and if I need something, he's a phone call away. That is the love for other men Jesus intended us to have.

I don't know who is reading this, but I love you too. As I've been writing this book one day at a time, I've been praying for my brothers. So get out of your comfort zone and lay down your pride and tell your brother in Christ you love him, just as Jesus loves you.

REQUESTS:

Lord, may we men everywhere continue to pray together in your spirit with loving hearts. Let us see your Word fulfilled that we may surely grasp one day the depth and width of your love. And may we have that same love for each other. Lord, search our hearts. Make them ever true so we may be more like Jesus.

Lord, we love you and thank you for answering our prayers.
In Jesus' name. AMEN

SEPTEMBER - DAILY DEVOTIONAL #7

When you were dead in your sins and in the uncircumcision of your flesh, God made you alive with Christ. He forgave us all our sins, having canceled the charge of our legal indebtedness, which stood against us and condemned us; he has taken it away, nailing it to the cross. And having disarmed the powers and authorities, he made a public spectacle of them, triumphing over them by the cross.

COLOSSIANS 2:13-15 NIV

REFLECTIONS:

You know, every time someone accuses you of your past, remember Jesus squatted down and drew in the sand and asked the crowd who here is without sin. Much more powerful is the cross where he paid the ultimate price for our sins. You remember what can wash away my sins? Nothing but the blood of Jesus. If you know Jesus as your Lord and Savior, you're washed white as snow. So, go tell someone about Jesus today.

REQUESTS:

Lord, thank you for destroying at the cross what condemns us in the dark, so we who call upon Jesus our Lord will be saved from death, hell, and the grave! Lord, may we walk in victory and not defeat because through Jesus and the cross we stand joint heirs with Christ!

Lord, we love you and thank you for answering our prayers.
In Jesus' name. AMEN

SEPTEMBER - DAILY DEVOTIONAL #8

So then, just as you received Christ Jesus as Lord, continue to live your lives in him, rooted and built up in him, strengthened in the faith as you were taught, and overflowing with thankfulness. See to it that no one takes you captive through hollow and deceptive philosophy, which depends on human tradition and the elemental spiritual forces of this world rather than on Christ. For in Christ all the fullness of the Deity lives in bodily form, and in Christ you have been brought to fullness. He is the head over every power and authority.

COLOSSIANS 2:6-10 NIV

REFLECTIONS:

The crazier this old world gets, the more the importance of prayer abounds. Seek the Lord and his will every day. Ask him for wisdom and peace through every situation you go through. Just like a mother waits for her child to talk to her, God the Father is waiting for you to talk to him. So why not today!

REQUESTS:

Lord, the more deceptive this world becomes, may we all hold fast to Jesus and be a light in this lost world. Bless these men and their families. As this world abounds, may your glory also abound in us.

Lord, we love you and thank you for answering our prayers.
In Jesus' name. AMEN

SEPTEMBER - DAILY DEVOTIONAL #9

. . . pray continually, ...

1 THESSALONIANS 5:17 NIV

REFLECTIONS:

If you think prayer is not that important, then why did Jesus continually go off by himself to pray, seeking the Father's will? Why not start today? If you have ever played football in school, I know you know the Lord's Prayer. If you don't know how to pray, start there and ask God to grow your prayer life. Set an example for those around you—kids, wife/ girlfriend, or just friends. Start praying. Today is a great day to begin!

REQUESTS:

Lord, today in our hearts, as men, may we continue to carry our families and friends' needs to you in prayer. May we always be sensitive to those around us who need prayer. But most importantly, Lord, may we be in a constant state of prayer for ourselves, seeking you and your will.

Lord, we love you and thank you for answering our prayers.
In Jesus' name. AMEN

SEPTEMBER - DAILY DEVOTIONAL #10

". . . 'This is what the Sovereign LORD says: Woe to the women who sew magic charms . . . in order to ensnare people. Will you ensnare the lives of my people but preserve your own? You have profaned me among my people . . . By lying to my people, who listen to lies, you have killed those who should not have died and have spared those who should not live. "'Therefore this is what the Sovereign LORD says: I am against your magic charms with which you ensnare people like birds and I will tear them from your arms; I will set free the people that you ensnare like birds. I will tear off your veils and save my people from your hands, and they will no longer fall prey to your power. Then you will know that I am the LORD. . . ..'"

EZEKIEL 13:18B-21 NIV

REFLECTIONS:

The grass may look green on the other side of the fence, but it's not better than what God has blessed you with. If you treat your wife just as Jesus treats the bride of the church, you will only have eyes for her. My worst day of marriage with my wife is better than being with someone God didn't pick for me. When I think of it that way, there are no bad days, just blessed ones. So begin to ask the Lord for eyes only for your wife, and if you're not married yet, ask the Lord for a godly woman who only has eyes for you, and you for her. Those who pray together stay together. Make Jesus the center of your relationship.

REQUESTS:

God, grant these men eyes only for their spouse or future spouse if they aren't currently married. Let nothing about other women capture their thoughts and desires. Bless these men with all that they need to stand firm by putting on the full armor of God.

Lord, we love you and thank you for answering our prayers.
In Jesus' name. AMEN

SEPTEMBER - DAILY DEVOTIONAL #11

When all our enemies heard about this, all the surrounding nations were afraid and lost their self-confidence, because they realized that this work had been done with the help of our God.

NEHEMIAH 6:16 NIV

REFLECTIONS:

When the haters talk trash about you, when you get knocked down by life, remember: you know the great restorer, and he will restore you right in front of your enemies. He will prepare a meal to share with you in front of them. So as they see you being restored, pray for them to see the Lord's goodness over you. Pray that they want some of his goodness, so they, too, will come to know Jesus as their Lord and Savior.

REQUESTS:

Lord, may our relationship and our dependence on you to guide us be so evident that our enemies, those that hate us and talk trash about us, become fearful of you bringing them to salvation. Lord, may our country turn back to you. As you do great and mighty things for us, may other countries begin to fear you. Bless these men and their families with all that they need.

Lord, we love you and thank you for answering our prayers.
In Jesus' name. AMEN

SEPTEMBER - DAILY DEVOTIONAL #12

Even though we speak like this, dear friends, we are convinced of better things in your case—the things that have to do with salvation. God is not unjust; he will not forget your work and the love you have shown him as you have helped his people and continue to help them. We want each of you to show this same diligence to the very end, so that what you hope for may be fully realized. We do not want you to become lazy, but to imitate those who through faith and patience inherit what has been promised.

HEBREWS 6:9-12 NIV

REFLECTIONS:

Is the Lord calling you, or is he leading you to do his work? If he is, say, "Here I am, Lord. Use me." Those are the best words you could ever say. In fact, every one of us should have that same attitude every day, no matter how tired we are or how bad the week has been. There is always someone who has had it worse, and they may need Jesus. Be prepared to testify to his goodness, no matter what.

REQUESTS:

Lord, may we never hinder you from loving and blessing others through us. Our hope in you is never covered up but always on display to show your goodness and mercy and bring others to salvation in Christ Jesus. Lord, may we always remember, never forgetting, it's not by our actions that we were saved, but by Jesus who bore our sins and was crucified on the cross to pay our debt. He did this so we may have an unblemished relationship with you. Lord, may our daily walk with you testify to your goodness and mercy.

Lord, we love you and thank you for answering our prayers.
In Jesus' name. AMEN

SEPTEMBER - DAILY DEVOTIONAL #13

I pray that out of his glorious riches he may strengthen you with power through his Spirit in your inner being, so that Christ may dwell in your hearts through faith. And I pray that you, being rooted and established in love, may have power, together with all the Lord's holy people, to grasp how wide and long and high and deep is the love of Christ, and to know this love that surpasses knowledge—that you may be filled to the measure of all the fullness of God. Now to him who is able to do immeasurably more than all we ask or imagine, according to his power that is at work within us, to him be glory in the church and in Christ Jesus throughout all generations, for ever and ever! Amen.

EPHESIANS 3:16-21 NIV

REFLECTIONS:

If you've gotten to this point and still don't understand God's love and how he wants to have a personal relationship with you, stop what you're doing and ask God to reveal himself to you. If you know someone who has a relationship with the Lord, call them.

Jesus wants to show you his glory. Many Christians don't know the depth of the Lord's love, so we all need to ask daily for the Lord to reveal himself to us. Don't put it off till tomorrow because tomorrow is not promised.

REQUESTS:

This is my prayer for you today: May the Lord bless you mightily!

Lord, we love you and thank you for answering our prayers.
In Jesus' name. AMEN

SEPTEMBER - DAILY DEVOTIONAL #14

"Do not be afraid, little flock, for your Father has been pleased to give you the kingdom. Sell your possessions and give to the poor. Provide purses for yourselves that will not wear out, a treasure in heaven that will never fail, where no thief comes near and no moth destroys. For where your treasure is, there your heart will be also. . . ."

LUKE 12:32-34 NIV

REFLECTIONS:

It's ok to have nice things. If the Lord has blessed you materially, don't hoard it over people who you think are less fortunate. Rather, in all things, give God the glory. Ask him to show you how to use what you've been blessed with to further his kingdom by blessing others as he leads you to them. So today be a blessing.

REQUESTS:

Lord, may we give up all earthly desires we have for new cars, new houses, and things that the world thinks make us more important than others. May we share our hearts with those who need Jesus instead of our bank accounts. May we store up our inheritance in heaven. Lord, by faith we know you are a good, good Father, and when we're sold out to the kingdom and selflessness, all our earthly possessions are truly blessings from you. Bless these men and their families beyond measure.

Lord, we love you and thank you for answering our prayers.
In Jesus' name. AMEN

SEPTEMBER - DAILY DEVOTIONAL #15

For we know that our old self was crucified with him so that the body ruled by sin might be done away with, that we should no longer be slaves to sin—because anyone who has died has been set free from sin. Now if we died with Christ, we believe that we will also live with him.

ROMANS 6:6-8 NIV

REFLECTIONS:

Are you a dead man trying to live your best life, or are you made alive in Christ, walking in his way? Every day, we have a choice to walk in the path of the world or seek the Lord's will for our lives. That's why prayer is so important. It's an open conversation with the Lord with unlimited minutes, hours, and days. So every morning acknowledge to yourself and the Lord: I have died to sin and I live for Jesus and not my sinful desires.

REQUESTS:

Lord, bless these men with a desire to seek your will and your direction in Christ. Lead them away from empty ideals and philosophies of life and set them free from worldly ways so they may walk in the ways of Jesus. Bless these men beyond measure with your peace and your presence. Fill their homes with your glory.

Lord, we love you and thank you for answering our prayers.
In Jesus' name. AMEN

SEPTEMBER - DAILY DEVOTIONAL #16

Therefore, there is now no condemnation for those who are in Christ Jesus, because through Christ Jesus the law of the Spirit who gives life has set you free from the law of sin and death.

ROMANS 8:1-2 NIV

REFLECTIONS:

There is a difference between conviction and condemnation. God convicts us to bring us to repentance of our sins. The enemy condemns us, so we feel guilty and unworthy of forgiveness. So, always remember and never forget that our condemnations were put on Jesus at the cross. Conviction brings life, and condemnation brings death. So today, extend the grace and mercy that the Lord has shown you to others around you.

REQUESTS:

Lord, I ask you to bless these men. I don't know what they're facing today, but you do. Surround them with your presence and peace. Direct our steps and hearts toward your ways and not our own.

Lord, we love you and thank you for answering our prayers.
In Jesus' name. AMEN

SEPTEMBER - DAILY DEVOTIONAL #17

This is what the Lord says to me: "Go, post a lookout and have him report what he sees. When he sees chariots with teams of horses, riders on donkeys or riders on camels, let him be alert, fully alert." And the lookout shouted, "Day after day, my Lord, I stand on the watchtower; every night I stay at my post. Look, here comes a man in a chariot with a team of horses. And he gives back the answer: 'Babylon has fallen, has fallen! All the images of its gods lie shattered on the ground!'" My people who are crushed on the threshing floor, I tell you what I have heard from the LORD Almighty, from the God of Israel.

ISAIAH 21:6-10 NIV

REFLECTIONS:

God's victory for your battles is found in Jesus when we earnestly seek him in prayer. Stay steadfast in prayer mode so the enemy will not get a foothold, but will turn tail and run as far away from you as he possibly can. Remember and never forget that most of the time our victories are the way we wanted them to be, so don't be discouraged, for the Lord knows better than we do what we need. Today, as you pray, pray expecting the Lord to move on your behalf.

REQUESTS:

Lord, when we are seeking a victory, no matter what it is, help us to be steadfastly looking out for it, longing for it to come. Many pray seeking victory, but some are always hanging their head low, saying, "Woe is me." To truly seek the Lord for a victory, we need to have our head up—looking—not sulking, but filled with joy, knowing victory comes in the morning. Lord, bless each of these men this morning with victory and not defeat!

Lord, we love you and thank you for answering our prayers.
In Jesus' name. AMEN

SEPTEMBER - DAILY DEVOTIONAL #18

With the tongue we praise our Lord and Father, and with it we curse human beings, who have been made in God's likeness. Out of the same mouth come praise and cursing. My brothers and sisters, this should not be. Can both fresh water and salt water flow from the same spring? My brothers and sisters, can a fig tree bear olives, or a grapevine bear figs? Neither can a salt spring produce fresh water.

JAMES 3:9-12 NIV

REFLECTIONS:

For out of the heart a man speaks, so you yourself can see what your heart looks like by listening to the words you speak. My grandmother used to tell me to think before I speak, because our words either bring life or death. So may we speak life even to those who have hurt us and upset us, so we both may be built up in Jesus. Today, concentrate on speaking life into those around you, even those who are against you.

REQUESTS:

Good morning, Lord. Today we're asking for a tongue that only speaks of your goodness to others—whether we're in a long, slow line in the store or driving down the road behind a slow, out-of-control car. No matter the circumstances, may your goodness roll off our tongue with great joy! Lord, one day we could be in the same shape as the person we're speaking ill of, so let us sow your goodness into them. Bless these men and their families with your presence and peace.

Lord, we love you and thank you for answering our prayers.
In Jesus' name. AMEN

SEPTEMBER - DAILY DEVOTIONAL #19

"'Because they lead my people astray, saying, "Peace," when there is no peace, and because, when a flimsy wall is built, they cover it with whitewash, therefore tell those who cover it with whitewash that it is going to fall. Rain will come in torrents, and I will send hailstones hurtling down, and violent winds will burst forth. When the wall collapses, will people not ask you, "Where is the whitewash you covered it with?"

EZEKIEL 13:10-12 NIV

REFLECTIONS:

That's why it's so important to read the Word and stay in prayer, asking for discernment, so we may know the difference between the truth and what sounds like the truth. God will bless you with wisdom that reaches beyond your earthly understanding. You just have to ask for it. So don't wait. Ask for it today, for your and your family's sake.

REQUESTS:

Lord, now more than ever, we need to be plugged into you, seeking your truth and your direction for the body of Christ, direction for our families, and for our country. May we be sensitive to your Spirit that's in us to direct our steps in all that we do. May we have eyes to see and ears to hear you beyond the whitewash. Lord, bless each of these men with all that they need!

Lord, we love you and thank you for answering our prayers.
In Jesus' name. AMEN

SEPTEMBER - DAILY DEVOTIONAL #20

And he said to me, "Son of man, eat what is before you, eat this scroll; then go and speak to the people of Israel." So I opened my mouth, and he gave me the scroll to eat. Then he said to me, "Son of man, eat this scroll I am giving you and fill your stomach with it." So I ate it, and it tasted as sweet as honey in my mouth. He then said to me: "Son of man, go now to the people of Israel and speak my words to them. . .."

EZEKIEL 3:1-4 NIV

REFLECTIONS:

The news and all the doctors say that obesity or being overweight is because of a lack of exercise. But honestly, it could very well be because people don't know the difference between spiritual hunger and physical hunger. Therefore, they just eat food when their spirit is actually craving the Word of God. So the next time you're hungry an hour after you eat, don't grab a snack, grab your Bible and ask the Lord to fill you up.

REQUESTS:

Lord, may we study your Word as if we are eating it so we may also go out and speak it to those around us who are lost and hardhearted. May we speak your words that bring life and not speak as the world speaks—with words that bring death. Lord, bless these men with all that they need to be successful in your kingdom.

Lord, we love you and thank you for answering our prayers.
In Jesus' name. AMEN

SEPTEMBER - DAILY DEVOTIONAL #21

"My people, what have I done to you? How have I burdened you? Answer me. I brought you up out of Egypt and redeemed you from the land of slavery. I sent Moses to lead you, also Aaron and Miriam. My people, remember what Balak king of Moab plotted and what Balaam son of Beor answered. Remember your journey from Shittim to Gilgal, that you may know the righteous acts of the LORD."

MICAH 6:3-5 NIV

REFLECTIONS:

May the Lord and his love for us forever be on our hearts and minds so we are always prepared to tell of his goodness to us.

REQUESTS:

Lord, may we also remember and never forget what Jesus did on the cross for us. May we also remember and never forget the valleys you have brought us through and continue to bring us through. Lord, may you be a light through us in this dark world.

Lord, we love you and thank you for answering our prayers.
In Jesus' name. AMEN

SEPTEMBER - DAILY DEVOTIONAL #22

Then I said, "Listen, you leaders of Jacob, you rulers of Israel. Should you not embrace justice, you who hate good and love evil; . . . ?" Then they will cry out to the LORD, but he will not answer them. . . . he will hide his face from them because of the evil they have done. This is what the LORD says: "As for the prophets who lead my people astray, . . . night will come over you, without visions, and darkness, without divination. The sun will set for the prophets, and the day will go dark for them. The seers will be ashamed . . . because there is no answer from God." But as for me, I am filled with power, with the Spirit of the LORD, and with justice and might, to declare to Jacob his transgression, to Israel his sin. Hear this, you . . . who despise justice and distort all that is right; who build Zion with bloodshed, and Jerusalem with wickedness. . . . Yet they look for the LORD's support and say, "Is not the LORD among us? No disaster will come upon us." Therefore because of you, Zion will be plowed like a field, Jerusalem will become a heap of rubble, the temple hill a mound overgrown with thickets.

MICAH 3:1-2, 4-12 NIV

REFLECTIONS:

Even if you're walking with the Lord, you can allow yourself to be conformed to the things that are not of God. Stay in constant prayer, asking the Lord in every situation to show his truth; whether it is public politics or things in the church or our homes, may his truth reign in our lives, and may we always seek after it in prayer.

REQUESTS:

Lord, may our leaders turn from their wicked ways. May your Spirit rise up in all believers and push out the evil. Let our yes be yes and our no be no in this country again. Lord, let news begin to show and tell of true and not fabricated stories to cover up the truth. Bless each of these men and their families.

Lord, we love you and thank you for answering our prayers.
In Jesus' name. AMEN

SEPTEMBER - DAILY DEVOTIONAL #23

On the twenty-fourth day of the same month, the Israelites gathered together, fasting and wearing sackcloth and putting dust on their heads. Those of Israelite descent had separated themselves from all foreigners. They stood in their places and confessed their sins and the sins of their ancestors. They stood where they were and read from the Book of the Law of the LORD their God for a quarter of the day, and spent another quarter in confession and in worshiping the LORD their God. Standing on the stairs of the Levites were Jeshua, Bani, Kadmiel, Shebaniah, Bunni, Sherebiah, Bani and Kenani. They cried out with loud voices to the LORD their God. And the Levites—Jeshua, Kadmiel, Bani, Hashabneiah, Sherebiah, Hodiah, Shebaniah and Pethahiah—said: "Stand up and praise the LORD your God, who is from everlasting to everlasting." "Blessed be your glorious name, and may it be exalted above all blessing and praise...."

NEHEMIAH 9:1-5 NIV

REFLECTIONS:

We as men need to stand up and repent of our sins and begin to lead where God has called us to lead. The Lord called us to be the leaders of our homes, being the example of Jesus to our wives and our children first. Then we need to stand firm in our faith along with other brothers in the faith of Jesus. So we, as men, can influence a change across our country.

REQUESTS:

May every family, beginning with the men, turn from their wicked desires and confess from the rooftops that you are Lord over their homes. Help men see your blessings over them and their families as they give more of themselves to you. May our desire for you surpass our worldly, selfish desires!

> Lord, we love you and thank you for answering our prayers.
> In Jesus' name. AMEN

SEPTEMBER - DAILY DEVOTIONAL #24

When word came to Sanballat, Tobiah, Geshem the Arab and the rest of our enemies that I had rebuilt the wall and not a gap was left in it—though up to that time I had not set the doors in the gates—Sanballat and Geshem sent me this message: "Come, let us meet together in one of the villages on the plain of Ono." But they were scheming to harm me; so I sent messengers to them with this reply: "I am carrying on a great project and cannot go down. Why should the work stop while I leave it and go down to you?" Four times they sent me the same message, and each time I gave them the same answer.

NEHEMIAH 6:1-4 NIV

REFLECTIONS:

Every day, we need to ask God for eyes to see and ears to hear what the enemy is doing in their planning and scheming. We also need to be asking the Lord for wisdom on how to pray for our families and friends to defend them from the attacks of the enemy.

REQUESTS:

Lord, may we have guidance and understanding of the purpose or intent of people when we are trying to do your good work, but they want us to do this or that. Lord, no matter how hard the enemy tries to stop us, may we stand on your Word so we may never be shaken. Lord, you know who and how each of these men is being attacked, so I ask you to cover them with the blood of Jesus. Protect them and their families from any attack, no matter how sneaky or direct the enemy is. We ask that they not be harmed.

Lord, we love you and thank you for answering our prayers.
In Jesus' name. AMEN

SEPTEMBER - DAILY DEVOTIONAL #25

You will eat but not be satisfied; your stomach will still be empty. You will store up but save nothing, because what you save I will give to the sword. You will plant but not harvest; you will press olives but not use the oil, you will crush grapes but not drink the wine.

MICAH 6:14-15 NIV

REFLECTIONS:

Many people wake up hungry and go to bed hungry, not because they haven't eaten, but because they haven't fed their souls the Word of the Lord. So let's ask him for a hunger for his Word that they can't go one day without. Let us be satisfied daily as we seek him in the Word.

REQUESTS:

Lord, thank you that through Jesus, even when we seem empty, we are full, unlike those of the world. Even when they have too much and are envious, they are still not satisfied. They are always searching and never finding anything that will fill the empty hole in their soul. Again, Lord, thank you, whether our barns are running over or there's not a speck of dust on the floor. We are rich in your goodness. Lord, may our daily walk with you reflect Jesus and his goodness!

Lord, we love you and thank you for answering our prayers.
In Jesus' name. AMEN

SEPTEMBER - DAILY DEVOTIONAL #26

This is what the LORD says: "Maintain justice and do what is right, for my salvation is close at hand and my righteousness will soon be revealed. Blessed is the one who does this—the person who holds it fast, who keeps the Sabbath without desecrating it, and keeps their hands from doing any evil."

ISAIAH 56:1-2 NIV

REFLECTIONS:

Jesus is that salvation. He sets us free from death, hell, and the grave. So if you're feeling bound by life's troubles, take them to the foot of the cross and lay them at Jesus' feet. Do not look back or pick them back up again, so you may be free and free indeed. May we all learn to hang on to the Lord's Word with a death grip so it may always be with us.

REQUESTS:

Lord, help us be steadfast in our faith, never wavering to suit the world, but sharing the gospel of Jesus and the salvation we receive through him. Let us not get caught up in worldly things that will desecrate our witness to the lost. But when you come back, may we be found sharing the love of Jesus and his righteousness. Lord, I know not everything is peachy in each of these men's lives, but you are the way when we think there is no way out; you are always there in our time of need. Grant these men peace as they place their trust in you during the difficult valleys of life.

Lord, we love you and thank you for answering our prayers.
In Jesus' name. AMEN

SEPTEMBER - DAILY DEVOTIONAL #27

"Son of man, prophesy against the prophets of Israel, who are prophesying, and say to those who prophesy from their own hearts: 'Hear the word of the LORD!' Thus says the LORD GOD, Woe to the foolish prophets who follow their own spirit, and have seen nothing! Your prophets have been like jackals among ruins, O Israel. You have not gone up into the breaches, or built up a wall for the house of Israel, that it might stand in battle in the day of the LORD. They have seen false visions and lying divinations. They say, 'Declares the LORD,' when the LORD has not sent them, and yet they expect him to fulfill their word . . .."

EZEKIEL 13:2-6 ESV

REFLECTIONS:

Beware of false teachings by digging into the Word and seeking the truth. Men, let me encourage you to be bold in preaching the truth to others.

REQUESTS:

Lord, guard our hearts and minds against false teaching. As we open your Word each day, Lord, may we begin to see the depth of your Word. May we not entertain the teachings of those who preach a "feel good" message, but give us the boldness to preach the true death, hell, and grave message out of love. Lord, bless these men and their families with a deep yearning to know you more.

Lord, we love you and thank you for answering our prayers.
In Jesus' name. AMEN

SEPTEMBER - DAILY DEVOTIONAL #28

" . . . Though the mountains be shaken and the hills be removed, yet my unfailing love for you will not be shaken nor my covenant of peace be removed," says the LORD, who has compassion on you.

ISAIAH 54:10 NIV

REFLECTIONS:

Have you ever had a day, week, a month, a year where your entire world was rocked in a way that you couldn't catch your breath, much less see straight? Here is our hope in those times of uncertainty: nothing shakes our Father in heaven, and he is with you, pouring his love out over you. So today, ask the Lord how you can pour out his love over someone who is hurting emotionally and physically.

REQUESTS:

Lord, there is nothing we can do that'll ever compare with what you have done for us through Jesus. So we thank you for the peace we have through Jesus, and may we share that peace with others. Lord, open doors where we can tell those who are lost and hurting where our help comes from. Bless these men wherever they're going and whatever they're doing. May the opportunities to tell others about you be all around them today!

Lord, we love you and thank you for answering our prayers.
In Jesus' name. AMEN

SEPTEMBER - DAILY DEVOTIONAL #29

Do not be anxious about anything, but in every situation, by prayer and petition, with thanksgiving, present your requests to God.

PHILIPPIANS 4:6 NIV

And pray in the Spirit on all occasions with all kinds of prayers and requests. With this in mind, be alert and always keep on praying for all the Lord's people.

EPHESIANS 6:18 NIV

REFLECTIONS:

One of the most irritating comments or sayings I hear a lot, and I have probably said more than once, is, "That's just life." I don't like it because I usually hear it when someone is told to keep praying that the situation will get better.

Another one: "Well, I guess that's just the way it is supposed to be." Jesus never said you should accept it because that's just life, or that's just the way it's supposed to be. No, Jesus prayed about everything in all situations. So don't just accept things as they are. Pray until you know the Father's will. Jesus prayed until the very last moment for God not to send him to the cross.

There is an old saying that the dumbest question in the world is the one not asked. The same could be said about prayer. The world's most foolish prayer is the unspoken one.

REQUESTS:

Lord, may we never quit seeking you in prayer daily. May we never think you don't want to be bothered with certain situations that we call life. Bless my brothers today with your peace and presence. Walk with them as they venture through their day.

Lord, we love you and thank you for answering our prayers.
In Jesus' name. AMEN

SEPTEMBER - DAILY DEVOTIONAL #30

Jesus looked at them and said, "With man this is impossible, but with God all things are possible."

MATTHEW 19:26 NIV

REFLECTIONS:

I'm not sure what you're needing to have happen today—a new job, a physical healing, and/or a spiritual healing—but you're doubting God can do it. First, don't mistake *can t* and *won t* as the same thing. God can do anything, but sometimes he doesn't for our own good. If he can raise a valley of dry bones, he can raise a dead relationship to flourish again.

Never think God doesn't love you enough or that you're not good enough. He has already proven those statements wrong when He sent his son to the cross. He loves you enough, and we certainly didn't deserve it. So go out and live like all things are possible for God today, but they just may not be beneficial.

REQUESTS:

Lord, I ask you to bless my brothers today with the same amount of joy and peace, whether you answer their prayers the way they want or not. We know you want the very best for us. Help us truly mean it when we remember the hymn, "It is Well With My Soul." Lord, fill our homes with your presence today.

Lord, we love you and thank you for answering our prayers.
In Jesus' name. AMEN

OCTOBER - DAILY DEVOTIONAL #1

For the living know that they will die, but the dead know nothing; they have no further reward, and even their name is forgotten. Their love, their hate and their jealousy have long since vanished; never again will they have a part in anything that happens under the sun.

ECCLESIASTES 9:5-6 NIV

REFLECTIONS:

Does this make you think of someone you know who has no other reward when they're dead? If it does, begin to pray for God to open the door for someone to witness Jesus to them. Also, pray that they will be quick to receive Jesus as their Lord and Savior, so there is no doubt in your mind and theirs where they're going when they suck in their last breath. So go out and be a witness for Christ.

REQUESTS:

Lord, may we live our lives in a way that is pleasing to you. Let our steps be directed by you, so the memories of us are the things you did through us. Lord, without you directing our steps and using us for your kingdom, the memories of us and our lives are soon forgotten by those who come after us. So today, if any of these men have never accepted Jesus as their Lord and Savior, may they do so today, so their legacy of being used by you affects generation to generation. Lord, bless these men and their families today with your love and grace!

Lord, we love you and thank you for answering our prayers.
In Jesus' name. AMEN

OCTOBER - DAILY DEVOTIONAL #2

"I am the good shepherd. The good shepherd lays down his life for the sheep. The hired hand is not the shepherd and does not own the sheep. So when he sees the wolf coming, he abandons the sheep and runs away. Then the wolf attacks the flock and scatters it. The man runs away because he is a hired hand and cares nothing for the sheep.
"I am the good shepherd; I know my sheep and my sheep know me—just as the Father knows me and I know the Father—and I lay down my life for the sheep. . . . "

JOHN 10:11-15 NIV

REFLECTIONS:

David had no fear of any animal, so he fought for his father's flock—first for his earthly father, and then his Heavenly Father—because he knew where his victories came from: his Good Shepherd, God himself. So, if you know that you know God is with you, you may be filled with his peace even in the midst of the battle because he's already won it for you.

REQUESTS:

Lord, as men of God, let us not be like the hired hand and run from danger, but may we hit our knees seeking your victory over our attacker. Lord, you are our Good Shepard. May we seek your will daily so we can be a light in a dark world, never wavering but always seeking more of you. Lord, bless these men today with your presence and peace all around them.

Lord, we love you and thank you for answering our prayers.
In Jesus' name. AMEN

OCTOBER - DAILY DEVOTIONAL #3

" . . . As long as it is day, we must do the works of him who sent me. Night is coming, when no one can work. While I am in the world, I am the light of the world."

JOHN 9:4-5 NIV

REFLECTIONS:

If you measure your life like a day, with morning being the time you were born and the sun going down being the time you pass away, you will see we just don't have that much time here on earth to do the Lord's will. And unfortunately, some have less time than others.

So, value today more than you did yesterday because today may be your sunset. Do not wait to tell someone about Jesus. We don't know if we have plenty of time for that or not. So don't look for the joy the world offers, but find your joy and peace in God's calling to spread the gospel of Jesus.

REQUESTS:

Lord, because you have given us another day, we should do the work you have called us to do. We only have a short time before our last breath, and we will no longer be able to work. So while we are still here, may we shine your light that is within us. Lord, you know what each of these men needs, and I ask you to bless them beyond measure!

Lord, we love you and thank you for answering our prayers.
In Jesus' name. AMEN

OCTOBER - DAILY DEVOTIONAL #4

For everything God created is good, and nothing is to be rejected if it is received with thanksgiving, because it is consecrated by the word of God and prayer. If you point these things out to the brothers and sisters, you will be a good minister of Christ Jesus, nourished on the truths of the faith and of the good teaching that you have followed. Have nothing to do with godless myths and old wives' tales; rather, train yourself to be godly.

1 TIMOTHY 4:4-7 NIV

REFLECTIONS:

As long as we have breath in our lungs, may our lives demonstrate Jesus' truth. That should be our prayer every day so that we walk in true freedom of his love and grace. Be straightforward in your speech, so you will not damage the message of Jesus. Let your "Yes" be yes and your "No" be no! Go be a helping hand and not a stumbling block for others.

REQUESTS:

Lord, may we have eyes to see, ears to hear, and discernment, so we know exactly what or who has been sent from you, so we do not get caught up in something or someone that's not from you, thereby ruining our testimony of your goodness. Lord, we do rejoice in all that you've done and will do for us. May hearts all show our thankfulness to you.

Lord, we love you and thank you for answering our prayers.
In Jesus' name. AMEN

OCTOBER - DAILY DEVOTIONAL #5

May the God of hope fill you with all joy and peace as you trust in him, so that you may overflow with hope by the power of the Holy Spirit.

ROMANS 15:13 NIV

REFLECTIONS:

We are always getting filled up, so we must choose, as much as possible, what we are filled up with. If you're constantly watching the news or scrolling through Facebook, allowing yourself to be filled with all the negativity that the world posts, then your attitude is soon to be just as negative.

So, choose what you scroll through. Not all news and not all social media are negative. So choose what fills your spirit with the Lord's joy and peace. Who knows. Your smile may change someone's view of the world, from being negative to believing there is good out there.

REQUESTS:

Lord, may we be filled up and overflowing onto others, bringing them to Jesus, who is the author and finisher of our faith! Lord, you know what each man is struggling with, and I ask you to bless them with victory—not a moment of victory, but an everlasting victory.

Lord, we love you and thank you for answering our prayers.
In Jesus' name. AMEN

OCTOBER - DAILY DEVOTIONAL #6

For the LORD your God is God of gods and Lord of lords, the great God, mighty and awesome, who shows no partiality and accepts no bribes.

DEUTERONOMY 10:17 NIV

REFLECTIONS:

God is and needs to always be our constant. So no matter where we go or what we are doing, God is our purpose. And that purpose is to show the world around us that we will not have any other gods before us. We also need to show the world that just as God loves without partiality, we too can love that way. No matter color, creed, or stature, rich or poor, we love the same with all of our hearts. So go and tell the world there is but one God, and he is worthy to be praised.

REQUESTS:

Lord, may our walk with you be out of obedience to your Word and not one of thinking of ourselves higher than we ought. Not one of trying to gain our way in by gaining more favor or trying to convince you we deserve to get in heaven through what we can do for you. Lord, let the truth pierce our hearts. Without Jesus and his death and resurrection, we couldn't even see heaven, much less get in. May our hearts be truly humbled and grateful for Jesus!

Lord, we love you and thank you for answering our prayers.
In Jesus' name. AMEN

OCTOBER - DAILY DEVOTIONAL #7

When Moses finished setting up the tabernacle, he anointed and consecrated it and all its furnishings. He also anointed and consecrated the altar and all its utensils.

NUMBERS 7:1 NIV

REFLECTIONS:

Praise the Lord, our worship is not ceremonial! We don't have to be anointed with the blood of animals anymore for the atonement of our sins, but now, through the blood of Jesus, our sin debt is paid in full. We are washed clean when we accept Jesus as Lord and Savior. May we always remember and never forget that the curtain was torn completely in two, so we may come with confidence and a humbled heart before the Lord's throne.

REQUESTS:

Lord, Moses anointed people with animals' blood; you anoint with the blood of Jesus. Show us how important we are, anointed with the blood of Jesus, the one and only sacrifice that washed us clean of sin and death. May the power of the blood move us deeper into the relationship we have with you. Lord, bless these men with your presence and peace today.

Lord, we love you and thank you for answering our prayers.
In Jesus' name. AMEN

OCTOBER - DAILY DEVOTIONAL #8

. . . Jesus sent two of his disciples, saying to them, "Go to the village ahead of you, and just as you enter it, you will find a colt tied there, which no one has ever ridden. Untie it and bring it here. If anyone asks you, 'Why are you doing this?' say, 'The Lord needs it and will send it back here shortly.'" . . . When they brought the colt to Jesus and threw their cloaks over it, he sat on it.

MARK 11:1B-3, 7 NIV

REFLECTIONS:

This passage gives us hope. God uses anyone at any time, and for whatever reason he chooses. But we have to be present. So, if you're asked to speak or begin to teach and you know the Lord is asking you to do something, you have an opportunity and a choice to make. Either you can be an obedient donkey or pitch a fit like a stubborn donkey. Look for opportunities today to carry the gospel to someone.

REQUESTS:

Lord, thank you that you can take the wildest of hearts and tame them, and they can be used to carry the gospel. Lord, bless these men with your peace and presence all around them, just as you used this never-before-ridden donkey to carry you. Humble our hearts so we can be used to carry the gospel.

Lord, we love you and thank you for answering our prayers.
In Jesus' name. AMEN

OCTOBER - DAILY DEVOTIONAL #9

For I am the LORD your God who takes hold of your right hand and says to you, Do not fear; I will help you.

ISAIAH 41:13 NIV

REFLECTIONS:

There is no age at which holding onto your mom or dad's hand doesn't give you confidence that you're not alone. So it's the same with the Lord. Holding onto our hand, he is filling us up with trust and confidence in him. So take hold of him because he's already holding onto you. When someone asks where your confidence comes from, you can confidently say, "From my God, who is my strength. In him I have no fear."

REQUESTS:

Lord, thank you that we can lay our fears down and you will guide our steps no matter what. If we fear what other people think, you've taken away that fear by making us joint heirs to the King of kings. If we fear losing something, you'll guide us to something better, because in following you, blessings come. Lord, thank you for always being there when our hearts break over losing someone. You comfort us, and we can leave the fear of being alone at your feet. So, today, pour your love into these men and lead us through our fears so we overcome them in our daily walk with you.

Lord, we love you and thank you for answering our prayers.
In Jesus' name. AMEN

OCTOBER - DAILY DEVOTIONAL #10

. . . you who call yourselves citizens of the holy city and claim to rely on the God of Israel—the LORD Almighty is his name: I foretold the former things long ago, my mouth announced them and I made them known; then suddenly I acted, and they came to pass. For I knew how stubborn you were . . . Therefore, I told you these things long ago; before they happened I announced them to you so that you could not say, 'My images brought them about; my wooden image and metal god ordained them.' You have heard these things; look at them all. Will you not admit them? From now on I will tell you of new things, of hidden things unknown to you . . ..

ISAIAH 48:2-6 NIV

REFLECTIONS:

Guys, there is no better time than now to seek the Lord. We must ask God to help us, as one body, to live in unity. At one time, our churches looked like a plat map with property lines and with *No Trespassing* signs up.

But God has pulled those lines up, burned the maps, and put up signs saying all are welcome. The Lord is telling each of us, if we can't walk, talk, and worship as one body, stay on the porch. It doesn't mean we have to have one big building, but we do have to allow our one big God in to guide us.

REQUESTS:

Lord, this morning may our hearts be turned to you, and may we see each other as brothers in Christ. May we love and serve each other without boundaries, just as you're a father without boundaries. Lord, rest your peace on each of these men and their families. Fill their homes with your presence and hope.

Lord, we love you and thank you for answering our prayers.
In Jesus' name. AMEN

OCTOBER - DAILY DEVOTIONAL #11

This is what the LORD says: "Cursed is the one who trusts in man, who draws strength from mere flesh and whose heart turns away from the LORD . . . ."

JEREMIAH 17:5 NIV

REFLECTIONS:

"I can do it, I don't need any help, and I am fine." As men, we all say these words one time or another. It's almost a crushing blow to our egos by worldly standards to ask for help. The Lord wants to help us in all that he is leading us to do. Many folks say, "Well, if the Lord is leading me, why am I struggling so hard?"

Let's put it this way. If I didn't have struggles walking through something with the Lord leading me, I would be worried I was going the wrong way. So, the stronger the storm, the stronger the trust. So let him strengthen you so you may carry the light into someone's storm.

REQUESTS:

Lord, I ask you to be a light, a beacon of hope through us, for all men who trust in their own earthly wisdom and strength and not in you. You are our hope and strength in our time of need, and we give you all the glory for the blessing in our lives.

Lord, we love you and thank you for answering our prayers.
In Jesus' name. AMEN

OCTOBER - DAILY DEVOTIONAL #12

For God is not a God of disorder but of peace—as in all the congregations of the Lord's people.

1 CORINTHIANS 14:33 NIV

REFLECTIONS:

Just as in marriage, a couple who prays together, and seeks the Lord's direction together, stays together. A church congregation that prays together and seeks the Lord's direction together will stay together. So if there's not a prayer time already established, suggest a time to come together in prayer.

REQUESTS:

Lord, may all your people be of one heart, one mind, and one voice praising and giving you all the glory. May we seek your direction, and may your Spirit sweep across our nation, changing hearts to follow Jesus, healing our land. Lord, I ask you to fill these men's homes with your peace and your presence.

Lord, we love you and thank you for answering our prayers.
In Jesus' name. AMEN

OCTOBER - DAILY DEVOTIONAL #13

Give us each day our daily bread.

LUKE 11:3 NIV

REFLECTIONS:

Men, take your daily portion of Jesus and share him with others so they, too, may come to know Jesus as their Lord and Savior. We try, but we cannot even come close to manufacturing our own bread. So today, grab your portion of Jesus and go out and share him with the lost and hurting.

REQUESTS:

Lord, I ask you to forgive us for making or at least trying to make the bread of life look like the grocery store bread shelf, where you can get different sizes, shapes, flavors, and colors of bread. Lord, just like store-bought bread, we try to color up and mold the bread from heaven to where it fits our lifestyle, and it seems more inviting to others. Lord, fill our hearts today with the untainted bread from heaven—Jesus. Lord, bless these men with your peace and surround them in your presence today.

Lord, we love you and thank you for answering our prayers.
In Jesus' name. AMEN

OCTOBER - DAILY DEVOTIONAL #14

However, as it is written: "What no eye has seen, what no ear has heard, and what no human mind has conceived"—the things God has prepared for those who love him—these are the things God has revealed to us by his Spirit. The Spirit searches all things, even the deep things of God.

1 CORINTHIANS 2:9-10A NIV

REFLECTIONS:

When we seek the Lord in prayer and ask him for wisdom and direction, he will direct our steps and our ways toward his ways. May we have eyes to see, and ears to hear him calling us to his goodness. So open yourself up today so he can search you deeply, removing the clutter and filling you back up with the good things he has prepared for you.

REQUESTS:

Lord, you are our hope and strength, no matter what we're going through or facing—good, bad, or ugly. You still have more for us, so let us not lose hope, but draw strength from you and be filled with unspeakable, unexplainable joy that you give to those who are seeking you.

Lord, we love you and thank you for answering our prayers.
In Jesus' name. AMEN

OCTOBER - DAILY DEVOTIONAL #15

"For my thoughts are not your thoughts, neither are your ways my ways," declares the LORD. "As the heavens are higher than the earth, so are my ways higher than your ways and my thoughts than your thoughts. As the rain and the snow come down from heaven, and do not return to it without watering the earth and making it bud and flourish, so that it yields seed for the sower and bread for the eater, so is my word that goes out from my mouth: It will not return to me empty, but will accomplish what I desire and achieve the purpose for which I sent it . . .. "

ISAIAH 55:8-11 NIV

REFLECTIONS:

I was once told you cannot out-give God, and you certainly can't out-think him. His ways are so much higher; we burn the tires off just trying to start thinking the way he thinks. So, ask for wisdom and understanding. Do we see what he sees and hear what he hears so we may be used by him most productively? Start today. The Lord is waiting on you.

REQUESTS:

Lord, this morning we come asking that our thoughts and our ways line up with your thoughts and your ways so our lives reflect who you are to the dying world around us.

Lord, we love you and thank you for answering our prayers.
In Jesus' name. AMEN

OCTOBER - DAILY DEVOTIONAL #16

"See, it is I who created the blacksmith who fans the coals into flame and forges a weapon fit for its work. And it is I who have created the destroyer to wreak havoc; no weapon forged against you will prevail, and you will refute every tongue that accuses you. This is the heritage of the servants of the LORD, and this is their vindication from me," declares the LORD.

ISAIAH 54:16-17 NIV

REFLECTIONS:

Don't ever give up on your fight, but let the Lord lead the way, for he is the foundation of our faith, and he sent his son to die for you and me so we might have victory over death, hell, and the grave. If he can give us victory over those things, there's nothing he can't defeat. So when the fight comes, hit your knees in prayer seeking the commander-in-chief's direction.

REQUESTS:

Lord, thank you, no matter how big or small the attack from the enemy is. You are just and faithful to protect us from all harm. Lord, we may not see the battle here, but we know the victory comes from heaven, where the victory is won. Lord, bless these men with peace today, knowing you have our backs!

Lord, we love you and thank you for answering our prayers.
In Jesus' name. AMEN

OCTOBER - DAILY DEVOTIONAL #17

And God said, "Let there be light," and there was light. God saw that the light was good, and he separated the light from the darkness.

GENESIS 1:3-4 NIV

REFLECTIONS:

Another way to look at this scripture would be to say: "And God said, 'Let there be man,' and there was man. God saw that man was good, and he separated the man from darkness."

When we ask Jesus to come into our hearts and save us, he puts a light in us that cannot be overtaken by the darkness we were living in. So always remember and never forget that you bring the light of Jesus into every dark situation.

REQUESTS:

Lord, thank you for separating us from the darkness on our day of salvation. May we be the men you called us to be, the light in a dark world, so others will be separated from the darkness. Lord, bless us this week with opportunities to share Jesus with others.

Lord, we love you and thank you for answering our prayers.
In Jesus' name. AMEN

OCTOBER - DAILY DEVOTIONAL #18

Then he said to me, "Prophesy to the breath; prophesy, son of man, and say to it, 'This is what the Sovereign LORD says: Come, breath, from the four winds and breathe into these slain, that they may live.'"

EZEKIEL 37:9 NIV

REFLECTIONS:

We were just like the valley of dry bones before we accepted Jesus into our hearts. So as you breathe today, remember it's the Lord's breath in your lungs. That's why even when we breathe, we say his name. So when we tell the lost about Jesus, it is like performing CPR on them, blowing God's breath into them.

REQUESTS:

Lord, thank you that when Jesus went to the cross, died, and rose again for all who are slain by sin, the four winds began to blow once again. For those who believe in Jesus, you give eternal life. Lord, I ask you to bless these men as they face the day. No matter what, nothing can take that breath away that is given through Jesus.

Lord, we love you and thank you for answering our prayers.
In Jesus' name. AMEN

OCTOBER - DAILY DEVOTIONAL #19

Blessed is the one who perseveres under trial because, having stood the test, that person will receive the crown of life that the Lord has promised to those who love him.

JAMES 1:12 NIV

REFLECTIONS:

You're not done with the calling the Lord has on your life, so don't give up yet. Instead, give the Lord the reins. He will lead your persevering drive to victory. So keep up the good fight, for the Lord our God is with you.

REQUESTS:

Lord, many of these men are struggling. I ask you to fill them with your confidence and peace, which comes with knowing you've gone ahead of them, clearing a path through the struggle of life. Lord, may they receive the crown you have promised them. May the power of the cross always light their path and give them strength.

Lord, we love you and thank you for answering our prayers.
In Jesus' name. AMEN

OCTOBER - DAILY DEVOTIONAL #20

"He himself bore our sins" in his body on the cross, so that we might die to sins and live for righteousness; "by his wounds you have been healed."

1 PETER 2:24 NIV

REFLECTIONS:

If you do not feel bad for doing the things that you asked God to deliver you from, but you still want to quit, you need to spend more time in God's Word and in prayer, so you get delivered and not just sit in the pigpen, telling all those who will listen that you're saved and the Lord delivered you.

You may be saved, but you haven't given up your free will to him, because you're still sitting in the pigpen he was supposed to deliver you from. So today, try asking him for a hand to get you up and out.

REQUESTS:

Lord, strengthen us in our spirits so we do not continue to wake up or raise the dead part of us to chase our sins that are dead. But may that strength help us to walk out our righteousness in you through serving others as Jesus did and still does. Lord, I ask you to walk with us today, guiding us in every detail of our day.

Lord, we love you and thank you for answering our prayers.
In Jesus' name. AMEN

OCTOBER - DAILY DEVOTIONAL #21

When they had finished eating, Jesus said to Simon Peter, "Simon son of John, do you love me more than these?" "Yes, Lord," he said, "you know that I love you." Jesus said, "Feed my lambs." Again Jesus said, "Simon son of John, do you love me?" He answered, "Yes, Lord, you know that I love you." Jesus said, "Take care of my sheep." The third time he said to him, "Simon son of John, do you love me?" Peter was hurt because Jesus asked him the third time, "Do you love me?" He said, "Lord, you know all things; you know that I love you." Jesus said, "Feed my sheep . . .. "

JOHN 21:15-17 NIV

REFLECTIONS:

Who are you taking care of, other than yourself? God has called us to be caretakers by serving others just the way he came to serve us. I'm pretty sure you know at least one family that could use some help. If you don't want to give them money, buy a few sacks of groceries, but don't do it just once.

Feed them in different ways until they're on their feet. Every time we serve someone the way Jesus asks us to, we are washing their feet, letting them know they are worthy, and our Lord is hearing their prayers. So today, go serve!

REQUESTS:

Lord, help us answer the call to feed your sheep by sharing your love at every opportunity we have during our day. Lord, may we have eyes to see and ears to hear these opportunities and not be so focused on what we're doing that we have tunnel vision and miss out on your goodness.

Lord, we love you and thank you for answering our prayers.
In Jesus' name. AMEN

OCTOBER - DAILY DEVOTIONAL #22

Now this I know: The LORD gives victory to his anointed. He answers him from his heavenly sanctuary with the victorious power of his right hand. Some trust in chariots and some in horses, but we trust in the name of the LORD our God.

PSALM 20:6-7 NIV

REFLECTIONS:

Many would say, "Well, I am not anointed, so the Lord doesn't have a victory for me." That is a bold-faced lie from the devil. When you invited Jesus into your heart, you became just as anointed as anyone in the Bible. So, trust the Lord with all that you have, so you may serve just as he did with all of your heart.

REQUESTS:

Lord, whatever these men are facing this week, I pray for your victory over them. Pour into them your peace, as you give them the victory. Lord, may we trust nothing or anyone more than we trust in you.

Lord, we love you and thank you for answering our prayers.
In Jesus' name. AMEN

OCTOBER - DAILY DEVOTIONAL #23

Now all has been heard; here is the conclusion of the matter: Fear God and keep his commandments, for this is the duty of all mankind. For God will bring every deed into judgment, including every hidden thing, whether it is good or evil.

ECCLESIASTES 12:13-14 NIV

REFLECTIONS:

Make sure more of your words and actions point to Jesus, rather than to the things of this world. If you don't already have a steady prayer life, I would begin one today; it's not hard. Just set apart a time during the day to read the Word and to pray. If you do that daily, in a year, your life will be so much better and so different, it will make you cry.

REQUESTS:

Lord, search our hearts now, clearing out all the misdeeds or desires of the flesh. As things do come to an end, may all that's in us, seen and unseen, point to Jesus. May our actions resemble what's in our hearts. Lord, bless these men with your presence and peace, and guide them through the day.

Lord, we love you and thank you for answering our prayers.
In Jesus' name. AMEN

OCTOBER - DAILY DEVOTIONAL #24

"Be careful," Jesus said to them. "Be on your guard against the yeast of the Pharisees and Sadducees." They discussed this among themselves and said, "It is because we didn't bring any bread." Aware of their discussion, Jesus asked, "You of little faith, why are you talking among yourselves about having no bread? Do you still not understand? Don't you remember the five loaves for the five thousand, and how many basketfuls you gathered? Or the seven loaves for the four thousand, and how many basketfuls you gathered? How is it you don't understand that I was not talking to you about bread? But be on your guard against the yeast of the Pharisees and Sadducees." Then they understood that he was not telling them to guard against the yeast used in bread, but against the teaching of the Pharisees and Sadducees.

MATTHEW 16:6-12 NIV

REFLECTIONS:

Do you know what spreads quicker than anything in the world and hurts worse than anything in the world? Gossip. Gossip is like yeast: if you don't know how to handle it, it will swell up bigger than Dallas, and you won't be able to control it.

So, don't get caught up in gossip or rumors. You don't want to be caught in a web of lies through gossip. Set your eyes and mind on Jesus.

REQUESTS:

Lord, help us guard our hearts against the teachings of this world, but may our yes be yes and no be no in you. May we be used to influence those around us for the kingdom. Lord, may your goodness and peace wash over these men and their families, keeping them in you.

Lord, we love you and thank you for answering our prayers.
In Jesus' name. AMEN

OCTOBER - DAILY DEVOTIONAL #25

If you fully obey the LORD your God and carefully follow all his commands I give you today, the LORD your God will set you high above all the nations on earth. All these blessings will come on you and accompany you if you obey the LORD your God: You will be blessed in the city and blessed in the country. The fruit of your womb will be blessed, and the crops of your land and the young of your livestock—the calves of your herds and the lambs of your flocks. Your basket and your kneading trough will be blessed. You will be blessed when you come in and blessed when you go out.

DEUTERONOMY 28:1-6 NIV

REFLECTIONS:

Do you see Jesus with the eyes of your heart and hear him with the ears of your heart? Do we work earnestly to follow his commands, so the blessings pour out over us and fall on those all around us? His blessings are meant to be shared. So, may we be eager to share with others our blessings. May we be a light of hope in this dark world.

REQUESTS:

Lord, I claim these blessings over these men. As we love on others as Jesus loves us, may these blessings be poured out over them, and all that the enemy has stolen from them be replaced with a greater blessing. Lord, you know what each of these men and their families needs, so bless them beyond measure.

Lord, we love you and thank you for answering our prayers.
In Jesus' name. AMEN

OCTOBER - DAILY DEVOTIONAL #26

For his anger lasts only a moment, but his favor lasts a lifetime; weeping may stay for the night, but rejoicing comes in the morning.

PSALM 30:5 NIV

REFLECTIONS:

IF God didn't show you any more favor than Jesus dying on the cross for our sins, it would be more than all the favor this world has to offer. So quit wanting everybody you work with to pat you on the back, and start seeking after the Lord and his favor. When we do that (unlike the world, which continues to want more and more from us), God will bless you more than you could ever imagine with favor among your peers.

So, start with a prayer every morning seeking God and his steps for you today. And in your obedience, God's favor will be shown to you.

REQUESTS:

Lord, may our hearts chase after your joy that's everlasting. It's not an external joy, but the internal one knowing, regardless of our lives, we're your children, and we'll reunite soon. Lord, bless my brothers with your joy today.

Lord, we love you and thank you for answering our prayers.
In Jesus' name. AMEN

OCTOBER - DAILY DEVOTIONAL #27

"... When you pass through the waters, I will be with you; and when you pass through the rivers, they will not sweep over you. When you walk through the fire, you will not be burned; the flames will not set you ablaze. For I am the LORD your God, the Holy One of Israel, your Savior; I give Egypt for your ransom, Cush and Seba in your stead. Since you are precious and honored in my sight, and because I love you, I will give people in exchange for you, nations in exchange for your life. Do not be afraid, for I am with you; I will bring your children from the east and gather you from the west. I will say to the north, 'Give them up!' and to the south, 'Do not hold them back.' Bring my sons from afar and my daughters from the ends of the earth—everyone who is called by my name, whom I created for my glory, whom I formed and made."

ISAIAH 43:2-7 NIV

REFLECTIONS:

I have heard so many opinions about our President protecting Israel, but here's the reason we all should protect them: whether they know it or believe it, they are God's chosen people. And by the grace and mercy of God, we've been adopted into the family. So, as things unfold in the Middle East, keep them lifted up in prayer, because those that are against them are not just fighting Israel—they are against God himself.

REQUESTS:

Lord, may we be a people who support your people in prayer. We thank you for the hand of protection that's over them and over us through Jesus, our Lord and Savior. Bless my brothers with your favor today, and may your goodness shine on them as it shines on Israel. Lord, fill my brother's homes with your peace and presence.

Lord, we love you and thank you for answering our prayers.
In Jesus' name. AMEN

OCTOBER - DAILY DEVOTIONAL #28

So the wall was finished on the twenty-fifth day of the month Elul, in fifty-two days. And when all our enemies heard of it, all the nations around us were afraid and fell greatly in their own esteem, for they perceived that this work had been accomplished with the help of our God.

NEHEMIAH 6:15-16 ESV

REFLECTIONS:

If enemies tremble when God helps a nation rebuild a wall, how much more do they tremble when we accept Jesus? God knows we can't be destroyed by the enemy, who steals, kills, and destroys. The enemy can no longer wreak havoc because we have the victory in Christ. He has placed a wall of protection around us; this has been accomplished with the help of God.

REQUESTS:

Lord, if any of these men are struggling, give them a peace that passes all understanding and fill them with confidence that you have their back. You are their wall of protection. And as we abide in you, we have been given the victory!

Lord, we love you and thank you for answering our prayers.
In Jesus' name. AMEN

OCTOBER - DAILY DEVOTIONAL #29

"Be strong and courageous. Do not be afraid or discouraged because of the king of Assyria and the vast army with him, for there is a greater power with us than with him. With him is only the arm of flesh, but with us is the LORD our God to help us and to fight our battles." And the people gained confidence from what Hezekiah the king of Judah said.

2 CHRONICLES 32:7-8 NIV

REFLECTIONS:

Someone I know well taught me a new saying recently. I asked him about a situation he was going through, and he said he was "unbothered" by it. The best thing we can do in the midst of a battle is to be unbothered by it and not get in the Lord's way as he fights the battle for us.

So, mostly when we allow ourselves to be so bothered by a situation, we react instead of praying about it. Reactions can dig us into a bigger hole than it started out to be. So before you are so bothered by something you can't see straight, take it to the Lord in prayer and watch him work.

REQUESTS:

Lord, whatever we're battling today, may you fill us with your power and courage, pushing out all fear, so we are standing in your peace and presence in the midst of the battle. Lord bless my brothers and their families beyond measure. May we always remember and never forget you're not just our God, you are our Father, and the victory is yours if we will put our eyes on the cross where the battle was won!

Lord, we love you and thank you for answering our prayers.
In Jesus' name. AMEN

OCTOBER - DAILY DEVOTIONAL #30

There was a man sent from God whose name was John. He came as a witness to testify concerning that light, so that through him all might believe. He himself was not the light; he came only as a witness to the light.

JOHN 1:6-8 NIV

REFLECTIONS:

Light is used to dispel the darkness. But as the Bible teaches, sometimes we hide our light from the world. We don't want our friends to think we are too holy or better than them. Can you honestly replace John's name with your own in the scripture above? Do you believe God sent you to testify concerning the light?

Does it shine through you all the time or only at certain times? It isn't our light that shines; it is the light of Christ. As with John, we are only witnesses to the light and examples of how Christ can change people who live in darkness for the better.

REQUESTS:

Lord, may our lives be a testimony of Jesus, the true light, so that all whom we meet may come to know Jesus as their Lord and Savior. Lord, may you use us just as you used John to testify to your goodness and salvation through Jesus. Bless us and our families beyond measure.

Lord, we love you and thank you for answering our prayers.
In Jesus' name. AMEN

OCTOBER - DAILY DEVOTIONAL #31

One day, Jesus was praying in a certain place. When he finished, one of his disciples said to him, "Lord, teach us to pray, just as John taught his disciples."

LUKE 11:1 NIV

REFLECTIONS:

Other than the power of the blood of Jesus, prayer is the most powerful tool God put in our tool belt. And yet many of us look at it just like a leaf blower, used only occasionally. We think *I live in an apartment. Why do I need that?*

Well, it's my prayer that when I die, anyone who comes to the house finds that the most worn-out piece in the carpet is not near the doorway where I walked every day. But it is where my knees were every day, praying. Without prayer, I am lost. So, how important is prayer to you?

REQUESTS:

Lord, bless the men and their generations to come with a life of intentional prayer so we are all in continuous contact with the Father. Lord, you know the needs of these men and also each of their family's needs, so I ask you to bless them beyond measure, pouring over them your grace and mercy.

Lord, we love you and thank you for answering our prayers.
In Jesus' name. AMEN

When we work, we work.

When we pray, God works.

Hudson Taylor

NOVEMBER - DAILY DEVOTIONAL #1

As a father has compassion on his children, so the LORD has compassion on those who fear him; for he knows how we are formed, he remembers that we are dust. The life of mortals is like grass, they flourish like a flower of the field; the wind blows over it and it is gone, and its place remembers it no more. But from everlasting to everlasting the LORD's love is with those who fear him, and his righteousness with their children's children—with those who keep his covenant and remember to obey his precepts.

PSALM 103:13-18 NIV

REFLECTIONS:

I know people who spend their whole lives building a sizable bank account for their children. That is awesome, because they need all the help they can get. But wealth can be gone in just a short amount of time, while the fear and love for Jesus can last forever.

Remember, the only thing here on earth you can make sure gets into heaven is not your golf clubs or your Cadillac, but your children and their children. So, as you build your fortune or work until midnight to provide a meal, make sure you're teaching them to seek the Lord and his righteousness first.

REQUESTS:

Lord, we may only have a speck of time here on earth, and we may not be remembered. But let our love, honor, and obedience to you be passed from one generation to another, so that only your glory will be seen and heard. Lord, you know each one of my brothers and their families. You know exactly the things they need, so I ask you to fulfill those needs.

Lord, we love you and thank you for answering our prayers.
In Jesus' name. AMEN

NOVEMBER - DAILY DEVOTIONAL #2

A sluggard's appetite is never filled, but the desires of the diligent are fully satisfied.

PROVERBS 13:4 NIV

REFLECTIONS:

John Wayne once said in the movie *Jake* that he started eating peaches as a child, and he could never get his fill. That's how we need to be about Jesus. Get into the Word and in prayer and chase after him as if we will never get our fill. Going a moment without Jesus watching over us is like missing a meal or two. The hunger will drive you nuts. So get up and feast on the Word daily.

REQUESTS:

Lord help us not be lazy in seeking your will and desire for our lives, so we are not caught up in chasing things of the world. The world is only filling to the flesh, but leaves our spirit yearning and hungry for you. So may we be adamant in seeking and listening for you daily so we may be filled with your goodness.

Lord, we love you and thank you for answering our prayers.
In Jesus' name. AMEN

NOVEMBER - DAILY DEVOTIONAL #3

As for you, if you redirect your heart and spread out your hands to him in prayer—if there is iniquity in your hand, remove it, and don't allow injustice to dwell in your tents—then you will hold your head high, free from fault. You will be firmly established and unafraid. For you will forget your suffering, recalling it only as water that has flowed by. Your life will be brighter than noonday; its darkness will be like the morning. You will be confident, because there is hope. You will look carefully about and lie down in safety.

JOB 11:13-18 CSB

REFLECTIONS:

Jesus is the light, and if he lives in us and through us, his light will outshine our own. So are you full of Jesus, or are you just full of the *knowledge* of Jesus? There is a difference. If you don't know what the difference is, I suggest you ask him to show you. As we seek and grow in Jesus, his light in us gets brighter. I'm praying for his light to be so bright that no one sees me or my light, but they see all of Jesus.

REQUESTS:

Lord, help us turn our hearts to prayer and seek you in all that we do so we may walk in your will and favor. You know each one of our weaknesses, so as we seek you, may we have victory over them.

Lord, we love you and thank you for answering our prayers.
In Jesus' name. AMEN

NOVEMBER - DAILY DEVOTIONAL #4

. . . revere Christ as Lord. Always be prepared to give an answer to everyone who asks you to give the reason for the hope that you have. But do this with gentleness and respect, keeping a clear conscience, so that those who speak maliciously against your good behavior in Christ may be ashamed of their slander. For it is better, if it is God's will, to suffer for doing good than for doing evil. For Christ also suffered once for sins, the righteous for the unrighteous, to bring you to God. He was put to death in the body but made alive in the Spirit. After being made alive, he went and made proclamation to the imprisoned spirits—to those who were disobedient long ago when God waited patiently in the days of Noah while the ark was being built. In it only a few people, eight in all, were saved through water, and this water symbolizes baptism that now saves you also—not the removal of dirt from the body but the pledge of a clear conscience toward God. It saves you by the resurrection of Jesus Christ, who has gone into heaven and is at God's right hand . . ..

1 PETER 3:15-22 NIV

REFLECTIONS:

The people in Noah's time got a second chance, even after death, to get into heaven through Jesus and the resurrection. But there won't be another trip for Him to hell to set anyone free. So today, our conscience is clear in doing what God called us to do. We must spread the good news of Jesus, not just by word of mouth, but in our actions. We are showing the world who Jesus is, what he's done for us, and what he will do for them.

REQUESTS:

Lord, be the light in us. Let your light shine through us so that others may see Jesus and not us. May they come to know Him through what they see in us.

Lord, we love you and thank you for answering our prayers.
In Jesus' name. AMEN

NOVEMBER - DAILY DEVOTIONAL #5

The end of all things is near. Therefore be alert and of sober mind so that you may pray. Above all, love each other deeply, because love covers over a multitude of sins. Offer hospitality to one another without grumbling. Each of you should use whatever gift you have received to serve others, as faithful stewards of God's grace in its various forms. If anyone speaks, they should do so as one who speaks the very words of God. If anyone serves, they should do so with the strength God provides, so that in all things God may be praised through Jesus Christ. To him be the glory and the power forever and ever. Amen.

1 PETER 4:7-11 NIV

REFLECTIONS:

Every day should start with prayer, inviting the Lord to lead you to those you can serve. Sometimes they may come to you, and sometimes you may run into them in random places, so be prepared. It's ok to pray in the middle of a store if the Lord presents the opportunity. Never, ever, think it's not the time or place to share the love of Jesus with someone God has put before you to serve. The last thing of the day should be a prayer of thanking the Lord for another day of opportunities to share Jesus.

REQUESTS:

Lord, we are all called to serve, so I ask you to put us in situations or the right places to strengthen our gift of service. Lord, grow us so we may be used fully so all that we do glorifies you. Today, open our eyes so we may see the doors that are open for us to serve others.

Lord, we love you and thank you for answering our prayers.
In Jesus' name. AMEN

NOVEMBER - DAILY DEVOTIONAL #6

Husbands, love your wives, just as Christ loved the church and gave himself up for her to make her holy, cleansing her by the washing with water through the word, and to present her to himself . . . holy and blameless. In this same way, husbands ought to love their wives as their own bodies. He who loves his wife loves himself. . . . they feed and care for their body, just as Christ does the church—for we are members of his body.

EPHESIANS 5:25-30 NIV

REFLECTIONS:

I have been told all my life that a man is the head of the house and he is to lead as an authoritative figure. I call that a bold-faced lie. The best way to lead is to serve as Jesus did. With us as his bride, the church, he left his authoritative position to come to earth to serve. Through his service, we were saved, and he became the Lord of our lives as we trusted him.

So men, if you want to gain the trust of your family, serve them in a way that only you can. Try to meet your wife and kids' every need. That means being present heart, soul, mind, and body. The greatest difficulty is learning not only to hear, but to listen.

REQUESTS:

Lord, give us eyes to see our wives as you see the church. May we be as diligent in taking care of them as you have in taking care of the church. Help us be honest and spend more time admiring our wives than we do ourselves. May God bless these men and their wives with the love for each other that Jesus has for the church.

Lord, we love you and thank you for answering our prayers.
In Jesus' name. AMEN

NOVEMBER - DAILY DEVOTIONAL #7

If the ax is dull and its edge unsharpened, more strength is needed, but skill will bring success.

ECCLESIASTES 10:10 NIV

REFLECTIONS:

Lifting each other up in prayer and holding each other accountable for our actions takes more than our own knowledge and strength. We need to seek the strength and skill from the Holy Spirit that lives within us. If we try to do it ourselves, we will fail. So, never forget that family and friends who pray together, stay together. Today, seek the Lord and his righteousness.

REQUESTS:

Lord, as men, may we sharpen each other by praying for each other and holding each other up so your Spirit may strengthen us. May we not lean on our own abilities, but on you. Lead us on our daily journey so we may be successful in your kingdom. Bless my brothers with your peace and your presence. Surround them with your goodness.

Lord, we love you and thank you for answering our prayers.
In Jesus' name. AMEN

NOVEMBER - DAILY DEVOTIONAL #8

The LORD says, "The women of Zion are haughty, walking along with outstretched necks, flirting with their eyes, strutting along with swaying hips, with ornaments jingling on their ankles . . .. "

ISAIAH 3:16 NIV

REFLECTIONS:

Any livestock that has ever jumped the fence for greener pastures will tell you the grass wasn't worth the loss they took from jumping the fence. The same is true in life. Jumping the fence to chase after what you think will be better, will it seem better only for a moment. Remember, every jump comes with a cost. So today, be grateful for what you have, and seek the Lord's will in all circumstances.

REQUESTS:

Lord, may the married men commit their eyes and hearts to their wives. May the single men commit to praying for the wife you have prepared for them, so that at the time of their meeting, they'll know she is from you. Lord, let none of us get caught up in the temptations of this world that lead to destruction. Bless each of my brothers with peace and surround them with your presence, guiding them in the way they should go.

Lord, we love you and thank you for answering our prayers.
In Jesus' name. AMEN

NOVEMBER - DAILY DEVOTIONAL #9

The Spirit of the LORD will rest on him—the Spirit of wisdom and of understanding, the Spirit of counsel and of might, the Spirit of the knowledge and fear of the LORD—

ISAIAH 11:2 NIV

REFLECTIONS:

If Jesus lives in you, then you have all these things working inside of you. So draw near to the Father and ask him to give understanding and to guide you on how to allow him to work through you. Without the Lord working through you and in you, none of us has a chance. Make God the reason you breathe and desire more than anything to serve as Jesus served. If you will do that with all your heart, you will be blessed beyond your wildest imagination.

REQUESTS:

Lord, let your Spirit rest on us, so we may have the spirit of wisdom and of understanding of your will and direction for our lives and for our families. Lord, may we have the spirit of counsel and of might so we may counsel others in wisdom, and have the might to walk in victory. Last, give us the Spirit of knowledge and fear of you, Lord, so we may have a deep understanding of who you are and the love you have for us. The fear of the Lord is not for us to literally be afraid of you, but for you to be the only God we seek after and worship. Bless each one of my brothers and their families with your peace and presence.

Lord, we love you and thank you for answering our prayers.
In Jesus' name. AMEN

NOVEMBER - DAILY DEVOTIONAL #10

A man may have a hundred children and live many years; yet no matter how long he lives, if he cannot enjoy his prosperity and does not receive proper burial, I say that a stillborn child is better off than he.

ECCLESIASTES 6:3 NIV

REFLECTIONS:

As men, we all need to stop and enjoy life with our families, even if it's just going out in the backyard and making mud pies or sliding down a slip and slide on our bellies. If you don't enjoy it now, one day the thought will be there, but the ability will be gone. Instead of working your fingers off trying to leave your children something materialistic, get out and leave them memories that will last forever.

REQUESTS:

Lord, may all that we have be committed to you, so we find your unspeakable joy in the blessing of prosperity that we have received from you. May the burial of our physical body be as joyful as our lives committed to you. For just as the stillborn, we will be in your presence. A life without you is a life short-lived.

Lord, we love you and thank you for answering our prayers.
In Jesus' name. AMEN

NOVEMBER - DAILY DEVOTIONAL #11

"'How can you say, "We are wise, for we have the law of the LORD," when actually the lying pen of the scribes has handled it falsely? The wise will be put to shame; they will be dismayed and trapped. Since they have rejected the word of the LORD, what kind of wisdom do they have? . . . '"

JEREMIAH 8:8-9 NIV

REFLECTIONS:

Many people are like a child playing a game. They change the rules as they go, so they'll win every time. It's not just pastors. Many folks can't say, "If you don't know Jesus as your personal savior, then you're going to hell." This life is a two-way street. You are either headed to heaven or going straight to hell.

Those who preach or teach that there's an alternate route have no wisdom at all. But those who teach and preach that Jesus loves you enough to die for you, and by inviting him into your heart as your Lord and Savior, you will spend eternity with him in heaven, now *that's* wisdom only God can give. Which way are you headed?

REQUESTS:

Lord, help us not tweak your Word to fit our agenda or to justify our way of doing things. May the wisdom of your Word burn in our hearts, transforming us to your good work every day. Bless my brothers today with peace, and may your glory shine upon them.

Lord, we love you and thank you for answering our prayers.
In Jesus' name. AMEN

NOVEMBER - DAILY DEVOTIONAL #12

Do not quench the Spirit. Do not treat prophecies with contempt but test them all; hold on to what is good, reject every kind of evil.

1 THESSALONIANS 5:19-22 NIV

REFLECTIONS:

When we hear from God asking us to accomplish something for glory, and we are not obedient, then we quench the Spirit, and God will find someone to carry out the task that we have been asked to do. Unfortunately, when we do that, we allow someone else to have our blessing.

But don't let that scare you. When you hear from the Lord, it's ok to test or ask God to show you in a clearer way that it is him speaking. That's why I encourage you to pray daily for his direction and wisdom in all things.

REQUESTS:

Good morning, Lord. Thank you for another day to do your good work. This morning, we ask for eyes to see and ears to hear that which is truly from you. Fill us with your power and authority so we run off anything that's not from you. Lord, cover each one of my brothers and their families with the blood of Jesus, protecting them from the enemies' attacks. Bless my brothers with all that they need in their walk with you.

Lord, we love you and thank you for answering our prayers.
In Jesus' name. AMEN

NOVEMBER - DAILY DEVOTIONAL #13

"Then those who feared the LORD talked with each other, and the LORD listened and heard. A scroll of remembrance was written in his presence concerning those who feared the LORD and honored his name. "On the day when I act," says the LORD Almighty, "they will be my treasured possession. I will spare them, just as a father has compassion and spares his son who serves him. And you will again see the distinction between the righteous and the wicked, between those who serve God and those who do not . . . . "

MALACHI 3:16-18 NIV

REFLECTIONS:

You are set apart, and when you receive Jesus as your Lord and Savior, your name is instantly written in the Lamb's book of life, or the book of remembrance. In other words, God has got you written down and you're his child for eternity. Whether this world likes you, or if you feel worthless, remember God calls you his "most treasured possession." So today, go live like you're a child of God.

REQUESTS:

Lord, this morning, may your children remember their name is on a scroll in heaven, and it's called the Lamb's book of life. May there be such a distinction in us that those without Jesus can see plainly that they need him. Bless my brothers today with a deeper understanding of who we are in Christ, and that we are set apart for your good work.

Lord, we love you and thank you for answering our prayers.
In Jesus' name. AMEN

NOVEMBER - DAILY DEVOTIONAL #14

Each one should test their own actions. Then they can take pride in themselves alone, without comparing themselves to someone else, for each one should carry their own load. Nevertheless, the one who receives instruction in the Word should share all good things with their instructor. Do not be deceived: God cannot be mocked. A man reaps what he sows.

GALATIANS 6:4-7 NIV

REFLECTIONS:

Have you ever wondered why someone was being particularly nice to you, or have you ever asked yourself what their intention is behind their kindness? We should always make our intentions about Jesus and share his love with no wrong intentions or plans.

As the Scripture says, God will not be mocked. Using being a Christian to bring about results from bad intentions will cause you more problems than you ever had. So, to stay out of trouble, be real and honest in sharing the love of Jesus.

REQUESTS:

Lord, may our actions be pleasing to you, and may we not glow with selfish pride, but may we glow just as Moses did from being in your presence, seeking your will. May our actions sow seed for a harvest in your kingdom! Lord, you know where each one of us is off track in being in your will for ourselves and our families. So, I ask you to guide us back on track so we may not miss an opportunity to do your good work.

Lord, we love you and thank you for answering our prayers.
In Jesus' name. AMEN

NOVEMBER - DAILY DEVOTIONAL #15

"I have the right to do anything," you say—but not everything is beneficial. "I have the right to do anything"—but I will not be mastered by anything. You say, "Food for the stomach and the stomach for food, and God will destroy them both." The body, however, is not meant for sexual immorality but for the Lord, and the Lord for the body. By his power God raised the Lord from the dead, and he will raise us also. Do you not know that your bodies are members of Christ himself? Shall I then take the members of Christ and unite them with a prostitute? Never!

1 CORINTHIANS 6:12-15 NIV

REFLECTIONS:

I've lost a lot of things because I didn't consider the cost of what I was doing. The ultimate choice we have to make will cost us everything. If you choose to live without Jesus, it will cost you spending the rest of your life in hell. If you choose to live with Jesus in your heart and with him directing your footsteps, the cost may not be doing all the earthly things you'd do without him, but you gain a seat at his table, which he has prepared for you. Everything involves a choice, so seek the Lord for what choices are right for you.

REQUESTS:

Lord, may our bodies be as committed to you as our hearts. May we commit our bodies to your good work as we have our hearts. May our minds, hearts, and bodies be in one accord with you and not be split with the perversions of this world. Help each one of us who struggles against the flesh and its desires. You know what each of my brothers needs help with. Help them find that help in you.

Lord, we love you and thank you for answering our prayers.
In Jesus' name. AMEN

NOVEMBER - DAILY DEVOTIONAL #16

After this the Lord appointed seventy-two others and sent them two by two ahead of him to every town and place where he was about to go. He told them, "The harvest is plentiful, but the workers are few. Ask the Lord of the harvest, therefore, to send out workers into his harvest field. Go! I am sending you out like lambs among wolves.

LUKE 10:1-3 NIV

REFLECTIONS:

Don't be scared to share the gospel anywhere, if David, as a shepherd boy, killed a lion and a bear to protect the sheep he was looking after. How much will Jesus, our heavenly shepherd, protect us as we go out into the world spreading the gospel? Don't be afraid to speak about Jesus anywhere at any time!

REQUESTS:

Lord, every time we go on a trip, whether it's vacation, business, or especially a trip to the doctor, may we see and act upon the opportunities you give us to share Jesus. No matter how difficult or hateful the world is, may we never hide our faith in you. Bless my brothers today with all that they need to be a light to a dark world.

Lord, we love you and thank you for answering our prayers.
In Jesus' name. AMEN

NOVEMBER - DAILY DEVOTIONAL #17

"I myself will gather the remnant of my flock out of all the countries where I have driven them and will bring them back to their pasture, where they will be fruitful and increase in number. I will place shepherds over them who will tend them, and they will no longer be afraid or terrified, nor will any be missing," declares the LORD."

JEREMIAH 23:3-4 NIV

REFLECTIONS:

Where is your identity? Is what identifies you your job, the name of the church you go to, or the name of the bar you go to? Or is it your good or bad actions that identify you? I want to be identified as a Christ follower.

As we all begin to assume Christ's identity and quit separating ourselves according to our denomination, God's presence will be overwhelming and all around us. If you want to see a revival breakout, let's let him gather us all together with purpose and with one goal: to glorify him.

REQUESTS:

Lord, just as you scattered the Jews because of sin and disobedience, many of our families are torn apart by sin. So I ask you for forgiveness and for you to draw our families back together. May we all come to the Good Shepherd and allow him to make all things new. May our relationships be made new, and may our families prosper in your kingdom. Lord, you know each of my brothers' needs. I ask you to bless them mightily in their walk with you today.

Lord, we love you and thank you for answering our prayers.
In Jesus' name. AMEN

NOVEMBER - DAILY DEVOTIONAL #18

Let us behave decently, as in the daytime, not in carousing and drunkenness, not in sexual immorality and debauchery, not in dissension and jealousy. Rather, clothe yourselves with the Lord Jesus Christ, and do not think about how to gratify the desires of the flesh.

ROMANS 13:13-14 NIV

REFLECTIONS:

My grandmother used to quote the scripture that says, "Idle hands are the devil's workshop." So, to prevent my brothers and me from having idle hands when we were young, we worked most of the time. I would shell black-eyed peas for her to can, other times we cleaned flower beds or raked leaves and pecans.

If we commit our hearts and hands to God's service, just like my grandmother, he will keep us busy. Our minds and hands will not have time to be idle, getting us into worldly things. Follow God and his directions for serving others every day.

REQUESTS:

Lord, may the Spirit in us give us a kingdom heart and mind: a mind that focuses on what you would have us do today to further the kingdom, and not a mind that seeks ways that will satisfy our fleshly desires. Lord, may our hearts find joy in showing the love of Jesus and not a heart that doesn't care who it hurts or hates to gain all that it desires from the world. Bless my brothers with your peace and presence, blessing them and their families with all that they need.

Lord, we love you and thank you for answering our prayers.
In Jesus' name. AMEN

NOVEMBER - DAILY DEVOTIONAL #19

And the LORD said, "I will cause all my goodness to pass in front of you, and I will proclaim my name, the LORD, in your presence. I will have mercy on whom I will have mercy, and I will have compassion on whom I will have compassion. But," he said, "you cannot see my face, for no one may see me and live." Then the LORD said, "There is a place near me where you may stand on a rock. When my glory passes by, I will put you in a cleft in the rock and cover you with my hand until I have passed by. Then I will remove my hand and you will see my back; but my face must not be seen."

EXODUS 33:19-23 NIV

REFLECTIONS:

Can you imagine the anticipation Moses had to see the back of God? What an awesome time that would have been. We have something that Moses did not, but we don't have that anticipation or excitement that Moses had. We have God's glory living inside of us, and we get up like it's just another day, complaining and worrying about everything. But we ought to be waking up every day, anticipating God's glory to work through us, bringing someone to salvation. This morning and throughout today, look for God's glory. It's in us and all around us, so take a second and look up.

REQUESTS:

God, we thank you that through Jesus and the cross, we don't need to climb a mountain to be in your presence and hear from you. We can feel your presence when we look for you. Thank you that our eyes are not covered with your hand. We can see your goodness and glory all around us if we are seeking you with our whole hearts. Bless my brothers with eyes to see your glory and give them ears and hearts to hear you speaking.

Lord, we love you and thank you for answering our prayers.
In Jesus' name. AMEN

NOVEMBER - DAILY DEVOTIONAL #20

The life appeared; we have seen it and testify to it, and we proclaim to you the eternal life, which was with the Father and has appeared to us. We proclaim to you what we have seen and heard, so that you also may have fellowship with us. And our fellowship is with the Father and with his Son, Jesus Christ. We write this to make our joy complete.

1 JOHN 1:2-4 NIV

REFLECTIONS:

Jesus is the bread of life, so don't withhold that bread when people are hungry. Share this with those who feel physical hunger, but are actually spiritually hungry. God gave you a gift that continues to be uncontainable if we will let him run free, and that gift is the Holy Spirit that lives within us. But he's not confined to just us, so let him use you to spread and share the good news of Jesus.

REQUESTS:

Lord, let us not keep hidden what we have seen and heard, but may we proclaim salvation through Jesus Christ our Lord and Savior, so others may join in the fellowship of believers and proclaim the good news. Lord, I ask for forgiveness for where we fall short. Bless each of my brothers with the opportunities to look beyond themselves and proclaim the gospel to someone.

Lord, we love you and thank you for answering our prayers.
In Jesus' name. AMEN

NOVEMBER - DAILY DEVOTIONAL #21

I consider that our present sufferings are not worth comparing with the glory that will be revealed in us. For the creation waits in eager expectation for the children of God to be revealed. . . . We know that the whole creation has been groaning as in the pains of childbirth right up to the present time. Not only so, but we ourselves, who have the first fruits of the Spirit, groan inwardly as we wait eagerly for our adoption to sonship, the redemption of our bodies. For in this hope we were saved. But hope that is seen is no hope at all. Who hopes for what they already have? But if we hope for what we do not yet have, we wait for it patiently. In the same way, the Spirit helps us in our weakness. We do not know what we ought to pray for, but the Spirit himself intercedes for us through wordless groans. And he who searches our hearts knows the mind of the Spirit, because the Spirit intercedes for God's people in accordance with the will of God.

ROMANS 8:18-27 NIV

REFLECTIONS:

When we don't know what to pray, it is okay to say. "Lord, I don't even know how or where to start. So, I'm going to sit in your presence and wait for you." That's probably the most powerful thing you can ever say to the Lord, because you have surrendered everything to him and now you're waiting for him to move or speak. He will move and speak on your behalf, so be prepared because his answer is coming, and it'll be clear. Learn to sit in silence and listen.

REQUESTS:

Lord, we thank you for the Holy Spirit, our advocate in times of difficulty. Firm up the ground for those who are struggling so they may not lose hope, but be strengthened in their hope. Lord, give peace to my brothers.

Lord, we love you and thank you for answering our prayers.
In Jesus' name. AMEN

NOVEMBER - DAILY DEVOTIONAL #22

Serve wholeheartedly, as if you were serving the Lord, not people, because you know that the Lord will reward each one for whatever good they do, whether they are slave or free.

EPHESIANS 6:7-8 NIV

REFLECTIONS:

When we think of serving, many think of serving food like a server does at a restaurant. True Christian service comes in many ways, but with one purpose: to share the love of Jesus. Many ways you can serve are probably not what most people would say is serving. For instance, paying for a single mom's groceries or paying for someone's gas, many would say, is just being kind. Serving others is when you see a need and fulfill that need, because you love that person just as Jesus loves you.

So if you're standing in line at the store and someone says, "I need five dollars' worth of gas," and God moves on your heart, don't be afraid to speak up and say, "Here, fill it up, and I'll take care of it." The same applies at the grocery store, or sitting in line at McDonald's, and paying for the car behind you. Maybe go mow someone's lawn who can't do it for themselves. Serving others can come in many forms, so get up, get out, and find your form.

REQUESTS:

Lord, this morning, give us a servant's heart. May we serve others selflessly, just as Christ selflessly went to the cross for us. Let us not shy away from serving even our enemies, but may they see the love of Jesus through our actions. Lord, bless us with opportunities to serve.

Lord, we love you and thank you for answering our prayers.
In Jesus' name. AMEN

NOVEMBER - DAILY DEVOTIONAL #23

Keep on loving one another as brothers and sisters. Do not forget to show hospitality to strangers, for by so doing some people have shown hospitality to angels without knowing it. Continue to remember those in prison as if you were together with them in prison, and those who are mistreated as if you yourselves were suffering.

HEBREWS 13:1-3 NIV

REFLECTIONS:

It's crazy, but I know many folks who have told stories of talking to someone outside a store or restaurant, and they go back to give them some food or money, but they've vanished. I've even turned around to pick up a stranger walking by, and by the time I got back to them, they were gone.

So, don't take everyone for granted. It's really true—you might entertain or merely see an angel that looks like a normal person. Now you probably think I'm crazy, but ask God to show you and see what happens.

REQUESTS:

Lord, may the love of Christ continue to shine through us and help us always remember, not all angels are big and beautiful, dressed in white like the world thinks they should be. Most of the time, they look like everyday folks or are even homeless. Let us not be fooled by appearance. Lord, we've all been locked up, maybe not behind bars but within ourselves, so may we always be ready to share Jesus, who sets the captives free. Bless each one of my brothers and their families with all that they need.

Lord, we love you and thank you for answering our prayers.
In Jesus' name. AMEN

NOVEMBER - DAILY DEVOTIONAL #24

Whoever has ears, let them hear what the Spirit says to the churches. To the one who is victorious, I will give some of the hidden manna. I will also give that person a white stone with a new name written on it, known only to the one who receives it.

REVELATION 2:17 NIV

REFLECTIONS:

Can you imagine sitting down at a table with Jesus, and he serves you some of the hidden manna? When you're done eating, he hands you a white stone with your new name. If that doesn't set your excitement gauge off past its limits, I don't know what will. What a day that will be!

REQUESTS:

Lord, may we be victorious over our struggles not only against the world, but also against our flesh by seeking you. May we not only hear what you speak, but also be obedient. Lord, you know the struggles and worries my brothers have today. I ask you to speak into them victory, so they may look forward to seeing Jesus and receiving their new name in glory.

Lord, we love you and thank you for answering our prayers.
In Jesus' name. AMEN

NOVEMBER - DAILY DEVOTIONAL #25

When Jesus looked up and saw a great crowd coming toward him, he said to Philip, "Where shall we buy bread for these people to eat?" He asked this only to test him, for he already had in mind what he was going to do. Philip answered him, "It would take more than half a year's wages to buy enough bread for each one to have a bite!" Another of his disciples, Andrew, Simon Peter's brother, spoke up, "Here is a boy with five small barley loaves and two small fish, but how far will they go among so many?" Jesus said, "Have the people sit down." There was plenty of grass in that place, and they sat down (about five thousand men were there). Jesus then took the loaves, gave thanks, and distributed to those who were seated as much as they wanted. He did the same with the fish.

JOHN 6:5-11 NIV

REFLECTIONS:

Never doubt how God can stretch your finances to bless you with enough. You may be struggling with more than you think you can handle, but give it all to Jesus and see how he fills your cup each day with exactly what you need. As the song says, "He is a Good, Good Father!"

REQUESTS:

Lord, thank you for what we have—even though we may feel we have very little you can use to further the kingdom. The obedience is what counts. If we give in complete obedience, you can move in more lives than we can count. Lord, today pour your goodness into my brothers and their families. Bless them beyond measure with all that they need.

Lord, we love you and thank you for answering our prayers.
In Jesus' name. AMEN

NOVEMBER - DAILY DEVOTIONAL #26

My brothers and sisters, believers in our glorious Lord Jesus Christ must not show favoritism. Suppose a man comes into your meeting wearing a gold ring and fine clothes, and a poor man in filthy old clothes also comes in. If you show special attention to the man wearing fine clothes and say, "Here's a good seat for you," but say to the poor man, "You stand there" or "Sit on the floor by my feet," have you not discriminated among yourselves and become judges with evil thoughts? Listen, my dear brothers and sisters: Has not God chosen those who are poor in the eyes of the world to be rich in faith and to inherit the kingdom he promised those who love him?

JAMES 2:1-5 NIV

REFLECTIONS:

Remember that Jesus always entertained strangers. You may be feeding an angel. God doesn't send angels down to us in their heavenly splendor. They usually look like what we call a homeless beggar. Be kind and generous to anyone whom God puts in your path, because you never know who they truly are.

REQUESTS:

Lord, forgive us when we act or think, because of the things we own or the clothes we wear, that we deserve a better seat at the table than the man who has less. Lord, humble our hearts so we would offer our seat at the table to the one standing at the window looking in. Let us always remember and never forget that all that we have is not ours, it's yours. So, as we are blessed, may we bless others.

Lord, we love you and thank you for answering our prayers.
In Jesus' name. AMEN

NOVEMBER - DAILY DEVOTIONAL #27

Each of you should use whatever gift you have received to serve others, as faithful stewards of God's grace in its various forms. If anyone speaks, they should do so as one who speaks the very words of God. If anyone serves, they should do so with the strength God provides, so that in all things God may be praised through Jesus Christ. To him be the glory and the power forever and ever. Amen.

1 PETER 4:10-11 NIV

REFLECTIONS:

Think about what serving others truly means. We get sentimental during the holidays, even those who don't know Jesus. We pray on Thanksgiving Day, and everyone has a warm meal. We give a little here and there to help the needy on Thanksgiving Day and Christmas. But what do we do the rest of the year? Do we still want to help others? Two days a year don't meet the needs for an entire year!

REQUESTS:

Lord, may we have eyes to see the needs of others. Give us wisdom to understand how to fulfill those needs all year, not just two days a year. You know each of these men's needs. I ask you to fill them. As they are served on these special days, may they have a deep desire to serve in return.

Lord, we love you and thank you for answering our prayers.
In Jesus' name. AMEN

NOVEMBER - DAILY DEVOTIONAL #28

So Christ himself gave the apostles, the prophets, the evangelists, the pastors and teachers, to equip his people for works of service, so that the body of Christ may be built up until we all reach unity in the faith and in the knowledge of the Son of God and become mature, attaining to the whole measure of the fullness of Christ.

EPHESIANS 4:11-13 NIV

REFLECTIONS:

God has called all of us to serve. Whatever that looks like for you, he has prepared you for the job and will continue to grow you in your calling. So continue to answer the call, whatever that is. Who knows? You might be preparing one, or many, for their calling. Also, remember God did not give you a spirit of fear or timidity, but a spirit of boldness. So answer the phone; the Lord's calling.

REQUESTS:

Good morning, Lord. First, thank you for another beautiful day. Lord, I ask you to open the eyes of our hearts, and may we see that a pew filler is not all we're called to do. May we have eyes to see what you are equipping us for in the kingdom, and may we have a deep desire to answer that call to serve so we may truly see the fullness of Christ. Lord, you know everyone who is on our hearts and who needs your healing touch. So we ask you to lay your hand upon them and bless them with all that they need.

Lord, we love you and thank you for answering our prayers.
In Jesus' name. AMEN

NOVEMBER - DAILY DEVOTIONAL #29

Do to others as you would have them do to you. "If you love those who love you, what credit is that to you? Even sinners love those who love them. And if you do good to those who are good to you, what credit is that to you? Even sinners do that. And if you lend to those from whom you expect repayment, what credit is that to you? Even sinners lend to sinners, expecting to be repaid in full. But love your enemies, do good to them, and lend to them without expecting to get anything back. Then your reward will be great, and you will be children of the Most High, because he is kind to the ungrateful and wicked. Be merciful, just as your Father is merciful. . .. "

LUKE 6:31-36 NIV

REFLECTIONS:

Obedience brings blessings, and disobedience costs more than you may know. So when God moves on you to bless someone, no matter whether they have less than or more than you, be obedient to the Father's call to serve. If you learn to do that, then no matter if you call the bank and you're a thousand dollars overdrawn or you have a thousand dollars more than you thought, your attitude is the same—to serve others. Look for ways to serve and ask God to show you where to serve, and watch what he does.

REQUESTS:

Lord, I ask you to forgive us where we have failed to treat others or respect others, as we expect ourselves to be treated. May we share the love of Jesus with the homeless as well as the rich and everyone in between. Lord, may we always place them higher than we place ourselves. Bless each of my brothers and their families with peace. Surround them with your presence.

Lord, we love you and thank you for answering our prayers.
In Jesus' name. AMEN

NOVEMBER - DAILY DEVOTIONAL #30

For this reason, since the day we heard about you, we have not stopped praying for you. We continually ask God to fill you with the knowledge of his will through all the wisdom and understanding that the Spirit gives, so that you may live a life worthy of the Lord and please him in every way: bearing fruit in every good work, growing in the knowledge of God, being strengthened with all power according to his glorious might so that you may have great endurance and patience, and giving joyful thanks to the Father, who has qualified you to share in the inheritance of his holy people in the kingdom of light. For he has rescued us from the dominion of darkness and brought us into the kingdom of the Son he loves, in whom we have redemption, the forgiveness of sins.

COLOSSIANS 1:9-14 NIV

REFLECTIONS:

I have no idea what you're up against today. But I can promise you that you were made for more. God has never told you that you are a failure. Stop the tears, stop kicking yourself, and quit letting the devil have a seat at the table. Get up, look in the mirror, and tell yourself, "I am a child of the king who came and died for me, so that I may live for him." So quit telling people and God how big your problems are. Start telling your problems how big your God is and how big the people of God are. Go be the light!

REQUESTS:

Lord, I ask you to continue to grow and strengthen us in our walk with you so we may be prepared in all seasons to do your good work of sharing Jesus with others. Bless each of my brothers and their families today with peace and surround them in your presence.

Lord, we love you and thank you for answering our prayers.
In Jesus' name. AMEN

DECEMBER - DAILY DEVOTIONAL #1

Search me, God, and know my heart; test me and know my anxious thoughts. See if there is any offensive way in me, and lead me in the way everlasting.

PSALM 139:23-24 NIV

REFLECTIONS:

Is there something the enemy has you afraid of the Lord finding in your heart? Spoiler alert. He already knows it's there. But he is such a loving, merciful Father that he is just waiting for you to say, "Lord, you can have it." That's what his grace is all about. So today, say it, and I promise you will feel the weight of the world lift off your shoulders.

REQUESTS:

Lord, fill our hearts. Make it your resting place so we are not led astray by its deceitfulness, but may we be led by the Holy Spirit, always seeking to do your will. You know every need today, so I ask you to fill the needs of my brothers. At the end of this day, may we be closer to you than when it started.

Lord, we love you and thank you for answering our prayers.
In Jesus' name. AMEN

DECEMBER - DAILY DEVOTIONAL #2

Love the LORD your God with all your heart and with all your soul and with all your strength. These commandments that I give you today are to be on your hearts. Impress them on your children. Talk about them when you sit at home and when you walk along the road, when you lie down and when you get up. Tie them as symbols on your hands and bind them on your foreheads.

DEUTERONOMY 6:5-8 NIV

REFLECTIONS:

I remember going to the Senior Citizens' Center every year to visit my grandparents. Within five minutes of getting there, I heard the words, "We've heard so much about you. They talk about you all the time." I hope that's what at least one person I have been around for a while tells Jesus when they meet him for the first time: "I have heard so much about you, Jesus! I'm so glad to finally meet you."

REQUESTS:

Lord, if we're uncomfortable talking about Jesus anywhere, then make us uncomfortable until we are as comfortable sharing Jesus as we are talking about our truck, our job, or any other subject men talk about. Help us get the gospel out to unbelievers, but more importantly, to our children from generation to generation, carrying Jesus through our families. Lord, you know what each of my brothers is struggling with, and I ask you to send help to strengthen them in you.

Lord, we love you and thank you for answering our prayers.
In Jesus' name. AMEN

DECEMBER - DAILY DEVOTIONAL #3

The fear of the LORD is the beginning of wisdom, and knowledge of the Holy One is understanding. For through wisdom your days will be many, and years will be added to your life. If you are wise, your wisdom will reward you; if you are a mocker, you alone will suffer.

PROVERBS 9:10-12 NIV

REFLECTIONS:

Godly wisdom adds years to your life. I can't explain that one, but what I can say is the wisdom of the Father will fill your life with more peace and more joy than you can find anywhere on earth. So go out today and live your best life with Jesus walking with you.

REQUESTS:

God, grant us wisdom and let our wisdom in You grow daily. Let us not be like many who seek after the world's wisdom yet lose their lives. But may all that we do honor you. Lord, only you know what each of us is struggling with in our hearts. We ask for your direction.

Lord, we love you and thank you for answering our prayers.
In Jesus' name. AMEN

DECEMBER - DAILY DEVOTIONAL #4

. . . one Lord, one faith, one baptism; one God and Father of all, who is over all and through all and in all. But to each one of us grace has been given as Christ apportioned it. This is why it says: "When he ascended on high, he took many captives and gave gifts to his people." (What does "he ascended" mean except that he also descended to the lower, earthly regions? . . ..)

EPHESIANS 4:5-9 NIV

REFLECTIONS:

There have been many arguments over where Jesus actually descended, but it doesn't matter. I know he descended to the pits of hell on earth to get me, as he did for all of us. The problem is that few have opened the gift they were given; they just put it up on a shelf and think, "I'm good where I'm at."

REQUESTS:

Lord, I ask you to give us all a desire to dig into the gift you have given us—whether it's a gift to sing, preach, teach, or to serve others in whatever matter they need. Lord, for my brothers who are not sure what their gift is, I ask you to begin to open their eyes so they may see what's in the box. Lord, again we ask you to bless those who are struggling with difficult situations with your peace. Bless those who are helping and serving for your glory.

Lord, we love you and thank you for answering our prayers.
In Jesus' name. AMEN

DECEMBER - DAILY DEVOTIONAL #5

I looked for someone among them who would build up the wall and stand before me in the gap on behalf of the land so I would not have to destroy it, but I found no one.

EZEKIEL 22:30 NIV

REFLECTIONS:

God gave us a gift to communicate with him—it's called prayer. It's an open line that never has a busy signal, and you never get sent to voicemail. So if God lays someone on your heart, hit the pause button, and pray for them, because they may be fighting for their life. GOD put that burden on your heart to stand in the gap for them in prayer.

I can't tell you how many ambulances I've prayed for. It's simple—you say, "I don't know the situation, but you do, Lord, so I speak life into that ambulance and I ask for your healing on that person so they may be healed and live life abundantly." Look for ways to lift someone up in prayer today and fill the gap for them.

REQUESTS:

Lord, this morning, I stand in the gap with prayer for my brothers. No matter the need, it's not too big for you. Bless them right where they're at. Lord, give them peace, comfort, and your strength as you guide them free of their situation, no matter what that looks like.

Lord, we love you and thank you for answering our prayers.
In Jesus' name. AMEN

DECEMBER - DAILY DEVOTIONAL #6

I have seen the burden God has laid on the human race. He has made everything beautiful in its time. He has also set eternity in the human heart; yet no one can fathom what God has done from beginning to end. I know that there is nothing better for people than to be happy and to do good while they live. That each of them may eat and drink, and find satisfaction in all their toil—this is the gift of God.

ECCLESIASTES 3:10-13 NIV

REFLECTIONS:

In your busiest moments of the day, and you're feeling overwhelmed by it all, pause for a moment, take a deep breath, and tell Jesus all that you are thankful for. I will guarantee you will feel a peace come over you like you have never felt before. Whatever stress you're under, it will be gone because you have changed your focus from worldly things to your heavenly Father.

So today, when it gets overwhelming, make a personal decision to pause and make time to give God glory for what he has done for you.

REQUESTS:

Lord, today and every day, may we see your beauty and splendor in what we do in our earthly work and our heavenly work for you. Lord, may all that we see give a deeper yearning to tell of your goodness. You know the struggles each one of us has, and I ask for your beautiful light to shine through those struggles so we may walk through them in peace.

Lord, we love you and thank you for answering our prayers.
In Jesus' name. AMEN

DECEMBER - DAILY DEVOTIONAL #7

For to us a child is born, to us a son is given, and the government will be on his shoulders. And he will be called Wonderful Counselor, Mighty God, Everlasting Father, Prince of Peace.

ISAIAH 9:6 NIV

REFLECTIONS:

Today, we observe the anniversary of Pearl Harbor being bombed. Many sons died that day. In every war or battle, sons and now daughters give their lives for our freedom and peace.

During this time of Advent, we hear the message of peace. Let's not just go through the motions of celebrating the season, but spend some time praying. Ask Jesus to give you eyes to see, ears to hear, and a heart to receive his true, unexplainable peace that he is freely giving to those who will receive it.

REQUESTS:

Lord, bless these men with your love and grace today. May they seek your peace, not just today, but every day, in every situation.

Lord, we love you and thank you for answering our prayers.
In Jesus' name. AMEN

DECEMBER - DAILY DEVOTIONAL #8

Keep on loving one another as brothers and sisters. Do not forget to show hospitality to strangers, for by so doing some people have shown hospitality to angels without knowing it. Continue to remember those in prison as if you were together with them in prison, and those who are mistreated as if you yourselves were suffering.

HEBREWS 13:1-3 NIV

REFLECTIONS:

Let the love of Christ continue to shine through us and help us to always remember, not all angels are big and beautiful, dressed in white like the world thinks they should be. Most of the time, they look like everyday folks or even homeless. So let us not be fooled by appearance.

REQUESTS:

Lord, we've all been locked up, maybe not behind bars but within ourselves, so may we always be ready to share Jesus, who sets the captives free. Lord, bless each one of these men and their families with all that they need.

Lord, we love you and thank you for answering our prayers.
In Jesus' name. AMEN

DECEMBER - DAILY DEVOTIONAL #9

But if you harbor bitter envy and selfish ambition in your hearts, do not boast about it or deny the truth. Such "wisdom" does not come down from heaven but is earthly, unspiritual, demonic. For where you have envy and selfish ambition, there you find disorder and every evil practice. But the wisdom that comes from heaven is first of all pure; then peace-loving, considerate, submissive, full of mercy and good fruit, impartial and sincere. Peacemakers who sow in peace reap a harvest of righteousness.

JAMES 3:14-18 NIV

REFLECTIONS:

Jesus could have envied all his ancestors. After all, Abraham had more than he could ever want, and David was a king who ruled mightily. But Jesus knew his purpose was to serve as a servant does and to serve as a sacrifice for all, even his ancestors. While he walked this earth, he considered himself a man without a home; that's the example we should be. He did not consider any earthly possession something to boast about. Instead, he boasted about spending eternity with him. Remember, he left his throne to come serve. So, when you leave your home, are you going out to boast about yourself or to serve others as Jesus served?

REQUESTS:

Lord, may our ambition be to serve people and bring peace, so we may not stir up trouble but further your kingdom. Help us not to see others as having more, but to strive to grow together in unity in Christ. Bless my brothers today. You know the things they are battling through, so today I ask for victory for them.

Lord, we love you and thank you for answering our prayers.
In Jesus' name. AMEN

DECEMBER - DAILY DEVOTIONAL #10

We put no stumbling block in anyone's path, so that our ministry will not be discredited. Rather, as servants of God we commend ourselves in every way: in great endurance; in troubles, hardships and distresses; . . ..
2 CORINTHIANS 6:3-4 NIV

REFLECTIONS:

One time when I was ten years old, my dad had fallen asleep. I tied his feet together just enough so that when he woke up and took a step, he would bust his rear end. I think about that day often when I think about being a stumbling block for others in their faith.

Before I figured out the best way not to be a stumbling block, I caused a lot of folks to stumble in their walk with the Lord. Now all I want to do is serve well enough so there are no stumbling blocks to be stumbled over; period. When we serve as Jesus served, we are actually lifting people out of what they've stumbled into.

REQUESTS:

Lord, may we grow and be strengthened in you every day, so people who are watching for mistakes in our testimony see more of Jesus than they do us. May we not cause someone to stumble, but be there to help those who are down by showing your love, grace, and mercy. No matter what we're going through, may your light always shine through us.

Lord, we love you and thank you for answering our prayers.
In Jesus' name. AMEN

DECEMBER - DAILY DEVOTIONAL #11

Consider it pure joy, my brothers and sisters, whenever you face trials of many kinds, because you know that the testing of your faith produces perseverance. Let perseverance finish its work so that you may be mature and complete, not lacking anything.

JAMES 1:2-4 NIV

REFLECTIONS:

A cow or bull will run from a storm and put its backside to it so it endures all the storm. But a buffalo will head straight into it because it knows the quickest way out of the storm is to go through it headfirst. So today, are you going to turn away from the storm, or are you going to be a buffalo and head straight through it with Jesus?

REQUESTS:

Lord, as we approach our trials, help us always to remember you are with us to help us and to lean on you so we may grow in faith and in wisdom. May your good work be completed in us. Lord, teach us in our pain and struggles that we can still find joy in the fact that we are going to get through it. Even if it doesn't seem like it, you are with us. Lord, even in our weakness and fears, may you be glorified. Bless each one of my brothers with your presence and your goodness.

Lord, we love you and thank you for answering our prayers.
In Jesus' name. AMEN

DECEMBER - DAILY DEVOTIONAL #12

And he told them this parable: "The ground of a certain rich man yielded an abundant harvest. He thought to himself, 'What shall I do? I have no place to store my crops.' Then he said, 'This is what I'll do. I will tear down my barns and build bigger ones, and there I will store my surplus grain.' And I'll say to myself, 'You have plenty of grain laid up for many years. Take life easy; eat, drink and be merry.' But God said to him, 'You fool! This very night your life will be demanded from you. Then who will get what you have prepared for yourself?' This is how it will be with whoever stores up things for themselves but is not rich toward God."

LUKE 12:16-21 NIV

REFLECTIONS:

God never said we couldn't live a good life with what we have, but when Jesus gets put in the shadows of our blessings and not in front of our blessings, then we have a problem. When we put Jesus first, we open ourselves and all that we have to be used by Jesus to bless others. And guys, that's where the real blessing is. To bless others the way we've been blessed. Man! What a way to serve!

REQUESTS:

Lord, may we remember that all that we have comes from you; therefore, guide us to be good stewards with all you have blessed us with to further the kingdom. May you use what we have in abundance to help those who are in need, and Lord, that does not exclude the gospel that's within us. Please allow it to flow like a river through us, giving all who are lost a drink. Give us eyes to see and ears to hear where we may serve.

Lord, we love you and thank you for answering our prayers.
In Jesus' name. AMEN

DECEMBER - DAILY DEVOTIONAL #13

They [the Israelites] assembled at Jerusalem in the third month of the fifteenth year of Asa's reign. At that time, they sacrificed to the LORD seven hundred head of cattle and seven thousand sheep and goats from the plunder they had brought back. They entered into a covenant to seek the LORD, the God of their ancestors, with all their heart and soul. All who would not seek the LORD, the God of Israel, were to be put to death, whether small or great, man or woman. They took an oath to the LORD . . . All Judah rejoiced about the oath because they had sworn it wholeheartedly. They sought God eagerly, and he was found by them. So the LORD gave them rest on every side.

2 CHRONICLES 15:10-15 NIV [EMPHASIS ADDED]

REFLECTIONS:

The only difference between then and now is that we don't have to sacrifice all those animals, but we *do have* to seek after the Lord with all our hearts. I can't imagine smelling like a dead animal all the time, but our sin, when not given to the Lord and washed off by the blood of Jesus, smells that bad to the Lord. That's the purpose of seeking him daily—when we fail, we can run back to him and be cleansed of all unrighteousness. Wake up early and spend that time with the Lord. It'll make your day go so much better.

REQUESTS:

Through Jesus, we don't need to strive to find you as the Israelites did, Lord. Give us a heart to seek you together in our homes, in our churches, in our town, and in our country. The Israelites took oaths and made a covenant to seek you earnestly with all their hearts, and they found you. And you, Lord, gave them peace! Bless my brothers and their families with that same peace, and instill in us a heart that yearns to seek you daily!

Lord, we love you and thank you for answering our prayers.
In Jesus' name. AMEN

DECEMBER - DAILY DEVOTIONAL #14

He said to them, "Go into all the world and preach the gospel to all creation. Whoever believes and is baptized will be saved, but whoever does not believe will be condemned . . .. "

MARK 16:15-16 NIV

REFLECTIONS:

These days, the world comes to you through many different avenues. Almost every day, there is a new social media app. It's crazy. So, literally, the world is at your fingertips.

What are you sharing with the world? Do your Facebook, Twitter, TikTok, and Instagram pages show who Jesus is and how much you love him? Or do you use those to search out the worldly things you're interested in?

REQUESTS:

Lord, we always stop at the resurrection and the freedom we have because of Jesus, but Jesus didn't stop there. He gave us a command to go tell of God's love, grace, mercy, and salvation through Jesus. I ask you to give us eyes to see opportunities to share the gospel of Jesus. Protect my brothers and their families. Surround them with your peace and presence so they know they're not alone in whatever they are going through.

Lord, we love you and thank you for answering our prayers.
In Jesus' name. AMEN

DECEMBER - DAILY DEVOTIONAL #15

Who is wise and understanding among you? Let them show it by their good life, by deeds done in the humility that comes from wisdom. But if you harbor bitter envy and selfish ambition in your hearts, do not boast about it or deny the truth. Such "wisdom" does not come down from heaven but is earthly, unspiritual, demonic. For where you have envy and selfish ambition, there you find disorder and every evil practice.

JAMES 3:13-16 NIV

REFLECTIONS:

When I see people do things I don't understand, I shake my head and think, "How dumb can you be?"

I did that until I heard Jesus say, "You know how many times I've thought the same about your actions?"

So may your actions represent Jesus and not yourself. Jesus will be there to remind you just how human you really are. Serve others so they may see Jesus, perhaps in a way they've never seen before.

REQUESTS:

Lord, pour into us your wisdom so we may be humble and thankful for all you have blessed us with. Keep envy and jealousy from settling in our hearts, making us bitter. But, Lord, with humbled and grateful hearts, may we share what we have with those who are in need.

Lord, we love you and thank you for answering our prayers.
In Jesus' name. AMEN

DECEMBER - DAILY DEVOTIONAL #16

The Spirit of the Sovereign LORD is on me, because the LORD has anointed me to proclaim good news to the poor. He has sent me to bind up the brokenhearted, to proclaim freedom for the captives and release from darkness for the prisoners, to proclaim the year of the LORD's favor and the day of vengeance of our God, to comfort all who mourn, and provide for those who grieve in Zion—to bestow on them a crown of beauty instead of ashes, the oil of joy instead of mourning, and a garment of praise instead of a spirit of despair. They will be called oaks of righteousness, a planting of the LORD for the display of his splendor.

ISAIAH 61:1-3 NIV

REFLECTIONS:

Are you as solid as an oak in your faith and in your walk with the Lord? Probably not as much as you would like to be. I know I'm not. But I'm a lot closer than I used to be. How do we get to be an oak? Jesus did it by spending as much time in prayer as the crowds would allow. To be solid, we need to know what the Lord's will is for our lives. When we know where we're headed with the Lord, it's like driving to a specific place; sometimes we have hiccups, but we still get there. Seek the Lord and find your path!

REQUESTS:

Lord, meet our needs today. It doesn't matter if it's about a broken heart or something doctors can't fix. May our faith be sturdy, so your healing glory can shine on us. May grieving, broken hearts turn to pure joy in you. Give us eyes to see and ears to hear your glory, in things we think are little, but especially the things that keep us up at night. Today is a good day to share Jesus with someone who may not know him yet, so give us an opportunity, not for our sake, but for theirs and your glory.

Lord, we love you and thank you for answering our prayers.
In Jesus' name. AMEN

DECEMBER - DAILY DEVOTIONAL #17

We do not want you to be uninformed, brothers and sisters, about the troubles we experienced in the province of Asia. We were under great pressure, far beyond our ability to endure, so that we despaired of life itself. Indeed, we felt we had received the sentence of death. But this happened so that we might not rely on ourselves but on God, who raises the dead. He has delivered us from such a deadly peril, and he will deliver us again. On him we have set our hope that he will continue to deliver us, as you help us by your prayers. Then many will give thanks on our behalf for the gracious favor granted us in answer to the prayers of many.

2 CORINTHIANS 1:8-11 NIV

REFLECTIONS:

You may never know who was praying for you when you went through something dramatic. God moves on prayer warriors around the world to pray. Most of the time, you get a name or a strong feeling to pray. When it happens to me, I ask God to breathe life into whoever is on my heart and ask God to surround them with his peace and presence. So when God moves you to pray, stop and pray; don't wait. It's probably urgent and needs your immediate attention.

REQUESTS:

Lord, thank you for Paul, who shows us why we should continually pray for others. We may or may not know all the details of what they are going through, but just as Paul says in this scripture, we couldn't have made it without your prayers, and now we all get to give thanks and praise the Lord. So, Lord, I want to lift up each of my brothers and their families, asking you to strengthen them in their struggles, so they may walk through them in victory.

Lord, we love you and thank you for answering our prayers.
In Jesus' name. AMEN

DECEMBER - DAILY DEVOTIONAL #18

Those who want to impress people by means of the flesh are trying to compel you to be circumcised. The only reason they do this is to avoid being persecuted for the cross of Christ. Not even those who are circumcised keep the law, yet they want you to be circumcised that they may boast about your circumcision in the flesh. May I never boast except in the cross of our Lord Jesus Christ, through which the world has been crucified to me, and I to the world. Neither circumcision nor uncircumcision means anything; what counts is the new creation. Peace and mercy to all who follow this rule—to the Israel of God. From now on, let no one cause me trouble, for I bear on my body the marks of Jesus. The grace of our Lord Jesus Christ be with your spirit, brothers and sisters. Amen.

GALATIANS 6:12-18 NIV

REFLECTIONS:

The only thing you can take to heaven or make sure is in heaven, is people. There is nothing you could ever possess materially that you can take with you. But many people spend more time playing the "Look at me and what I have" game than saying "Look to Jesus and see what he has for you." So instead of worrying about the next best and greatest thing, spend more time sharing Jesus, and make sure the things that really matter will be in heaven with you.

REQUESTS:

Lord, even after you've purified our hearts, the world still tempts us with fleshly pleasures. Lord, may our minds and hearts be set on heavenly things and not the worldly things our flesh desires. Bless each of my brothers today, and may we all understand it's not the marks on our flesh that make us who we are, but it's the condition of the heart that shows whose we are!

Lord, we love you and thank you for answering our prayers.
In Jesus' name. AMEN

DECEMBER - DAILY DEVOTIONAL #19

For where you have envy and selfish ambition, there you find disorder and every evil practice. But the wisdom that comes from heaven is first of all pure; then peace-loving, considerate, submissive, full of mercy and good fruit, impartial and sincere. Peacemakers who sow in peace reap a harvest of righteousness.

JAMES 3:16-18 NIV

REFLECTIONS:

Especially this time of year, be willing to share God's peace and love with others you may come across in your daily lives. And rejoice for others as you see them being blessed; then your joy and peace will be even greater.

REQUESTS:

Lord, may our hearts be full of your peace and love for others. May we rejoice in your goodness as we see others blessed, just as if we are the ones receiving the blessing. Lord, may our hearts not seek more physical things but be focused more on a deeper, more intimate relationship with you that we can freely share with others. Lord, bless this gentleman beyond his wildest dreams with your amazing peace and pour into him your overwhelming grace and mercy.

Lord, we love you and thank you for answering our prayers.
In Jesus' name. AMEN

DECEMBER - DAILY DEVOTIONAL #20

So God created mankind in his own image, in the image of God he created them; male and female he created them.

GENESIS 1:27 NIV

REFLECTIONS:

Some people are handsome or beautiful on the outside, but when they show you what's on the inside, they are ugly as sin. Those who are beautiful shine the light of Jesus from the inside out. So if you aspire to be handsome, allow God to clean you from the inside out so Jesus can be seen through you. Now that's beautiful—when people see more of Jesus than they see you.

REQUESTS:

Lord, I ask you to forgive us where we have tried to create an earthly image of ourselves. Give us a hunger to chase after Jesus, take our pride away, and give us a humbled heart. Take the thought away that I should be served and give us a desire to serve others. May Jesus be more visible to people than we are. Lord, you know every need each one of my brothers has, and I ask you to fill those needs according to your will.

Lord, we love you and thank you for answering our prayers.
In Jesus' name. AMEN

DECEMBER - DAILY DEVOTIONAL #21

Finally, brothers and sisters, rejoice! Strive for full restoration, encourage one another, be of one mind, live in peace. And the God of love and peace will be with you.

2 CORINTHIANS 13:11 NIV

REFLECTIONS:

When you accepted Jesus as your Lord and Savior, your heart was filled with his peace. Not a peace to hang on to but to share with others, because life sometimes hits us hard—so hard it not only knocks the air out of our sails, but steals our joy and peace.

That's why it's so important to be prepared to share the peace and joy the Lord has given us with the brokenhearted, so their peace and joy will be restored. So, each day, ask the Lord for a double portion to share with all those who need it.

REQUESTS:

Lord, only you can restore relationships, hope, peace, and so much more. Lord, there are brothers out there who have lost all hope, and that brings no peace. So Lord, I ask you to bring those brothers in front of us today so you may pour into the hurting and the lost. Use us for your glory. Lord, may our purpose or goal be to strive after your goodness and mercy together. Bless my brothers with your peace and presence in their homes and over their families.

Lord, we love you and thank you for answering our prayers.
In Jesus' name. AMEN

DECEMBER - DAILY DEVOTIONAL #22

Let us hold unswervingly to the hope we profess, for he who promised is faithful. And let us consider how we may spur one another on toward love and good deeds, not giving up meeting together, as some are in the habit of doing, but encouraging one another—and all the more as you see the Day approaching.

HEBREWS 10:23-25 NIV

REFLECTIONS:

The way we can spur one another along is when God lays someone on your heart. Call or text them, ask if they need anything, and pray for them. Nothing makes us feel better than knowing someone actually cares for us. When we know someone cares, it puts a pep in our step to continue towards the day Jesus comes back. So, pick up the phone and call someone.

REQUESTS:

Lord, may your presence and peace fill our conversation today. Let our focus be on you and encouraging each other when we have the opportunity, bonding together as brothers in Christ. Thank you for my brothers who have answered your call to serve. Bless them and their families beyond measure today.

Lord, we love you and thank you for answering our prayers.
In Jesus' name. AMEN

DECEMBER - DAILY DEVOTIONAL #23

A woman giving birth to a child has pain because her time has come; but when her baby is born she forgets the anguish because of her joy that a child is born into the world. So with you: Now is your time of grief, but I will see you again and you will rejoice, and no one will take away your joy.

JOHN 16:21-22 NIV

REFLECTIONS:

The joy of knowing we will see Jesus should fill our hearts every day. It doesn't make the hardships any easier, but it does give a deeper reason to keep fighting through them. The joy we have cannot be taken away from us because it's not an in-the-moment joy that fades away. It's an eternal joy that will last forever. So as the hard hits of life come, smile and know you're one day closer to being in the presence of Jesus.

REQUESTS:

Lord, just like our mothers, as they endured the hardship of birth to have us, and are filled with joy afterward, may we also endure the hardships as they come in life and not give up, so we may be filled with your joy when it's over. Lord, not every mother is perfect, and not every mother was around for whatever reason, so thank you for the lady who filled her shoes as a mom. Lord, bless each of my brothers with eyes to see you and ears to hear you.

Lord, we love you and thank you for answering our prayers.
In Jesus' name. AMEN

DECEMBER - DAILY DEVOTIONAL #24

And so we know and rely on the love God has for us. God is love. Whoever lives in love lives in God, and God in them.

1 JOHN 4:16 NIV

REFLECTIONS:

Remember, a true gift is a gift given out of love. Don't just give a gift because someone asked for something or because you know they bought you one. If you truly want to show the love of Jesus, take the time to figure out something you think or know they need, but they might not know that they do. You ask why? That's what God did. He gave us Jesus, a gift we needed, but didn't realize that we needed as much as we do. He is the difference between life and death.

REQUESTS:

Lord, the Christmas season has arrived, and as we celebrate the birth of Jesus, the Savior of the world, let us also remember the depth of Jesus's love for us. He loved us so much that he died for us so that we may die to self and be raised to life in him. This season, may we show this kind of love not only to family but to those we don't even know. May they feel and see the love of Jesus through us by the way we serve them, just as Jesus came to serve us. May my brothers know that you truly love them.

Lord, we love you and thank you for answering our prayers.
In Jesus' name. AMEN

DECEMBER - DAILY DEVOTIONAL #25

But when you ask, you must believe and not doubt, because the one who doubts is like a wave of the sea, blown and tossed by the wind. That person should not expect to receive anything from the Lord.

JAMES 1:6-7 NIV

REFLECTIONS:

When my wife and I were dating, it was Christmas Eve, and we were in Toys R Us. I was looking for a hula hoop for my niece, and there were none on the shelves. I asked the Lord to help the guys find at least one hula hoop in the back, and after about 15 minutes, they brought 12 hula hoops.

So don't ever not ask God for something big or small, and don't set limitations for how he can answer it, because it might be more than you expected. So today, don't be afraid to ask and certainly don't doubt that he will answer it, because he might just surprise you.

REQUESTS:

Lord, may the hope we received from Jesus and the cross overcome any and all doubt, that you, Lord, will fulfill all that you have promised. I lift up these men to you. Where there is doubt, fill their hearts with pure joy and hope, pushing out all fear and doubt.

Lord, we love you and thank you for answering our prayers.
In Jesus' name. AMEN

DECEMBER - DAILY DEVOTIONAL #26

Today in the town of David a Savior has been born to you; he is the Messiah, the Lord.

LUKE 2:11 NIV

REFLECTIONS:

Growing up in my home, Christmas was pretty rough. My dad didn't believe in buying gifts for us. He said the same thing every year—it's just a waste of money. Praise God, though. My mom taught me God didn't hold back on the greatest gift of all—Jesus. So, if you're an old Scrooge or an overdoer of gifts, make sure no matter what is or isn't under the tree, Jesus is and always will be the greatest Christmas gift of all!

REQUESTS:

Lord, may we not be the reason our children do not grow up knowing Jesus as the best gift we could ever get for Christmas. May we teach them why Jesus is so important. Today, on Christmas Day, may we pause and wish Jesus a happy birthday and thank him for all the many blessings we have received throughout the year. Lord, bless my brothers and their families with your peace and presence.

Lord, we love you and thank you for answering our prayers.
In Jesus' name. AMEN

DECEMBER - DAILY DEVOTIONAL #27

Now about your love for one another we do not need to write to you, for you yourselves have been taught by God to love each other. And in fact, you do love all of God's family throughout Macedonia. Yet we urge you, brothers and sisters, to do so more and more . . ..

1 THESSALONIANS 4:9-10 NIV

REFLECTIONS:

As children of God, we have the love of Jesus in our hearts; therefore, we should love even our brothers and sisters in Jesus, whom we haven't met yet. When we can do that, it becomes easier and easier to minister to strangers. Some may already know Christ, and others you may lead to Christ. But no matter whether we know them or not, we should always strive to give the love we've been given from Jesus.

REQUESTS:

Lord, may your love pour through us so we may love as you love. Bless my brothers with your peace, and may your presence go before them, walk with them, and come behind them, protecting them from attacks of the enemy.

Lord, we love you and thank you for answering our prayers.
In Jesus' name. AMEN

DECEMBER - DAILY DEVOTIONAL #28

Jesus answered, "If you want to be perfect, go, sell your possessions and give to the poor, and you will have treasure in heaven. Then come, follow me." When the young man heard this, he went away sad, because he had great wealth. Then Jesus said to his disciples, "Truly I tell you, it is hard for someone who is rich to enter the kingdom of heaven. Again I tell you, it is easier for a camel to go through the eye of a needle than for someone who is rich to enter the kingdom of God."

MATTHEW 19:21-24 NIV

REFLECTIONS:

Rich—that's a word that when it's said, everyone immediately thinks of money and lots of possessions. Money is mentioned in this story, but someone can also be dirt poor at the bank and be rich in selfishness, pridefulness, and in love with themselves more than anyone else.

So, to follow Jesus, he's saying give up all those things, so you'll be filled with love, grace, and mercy for others. Think more highly of others than yourself and love your neighbor as much, or more, than you do yourself.

REQUESTS:

Lord, may we never ever think more highly of ourselves than we do serving others, just as you serve us. Bless each of my brothers and me with all that we need to bless others as you have blessed us. Lord, I ask you to fill my brothers' day with your peace and presence all around them.

Lord, we love you and thank you for answering our prayers.
In Jesus' name. AMEN

DECEMBER - DAILY DEVOTIONAL #29

For the pagans run after all these things, and your heavenly Father knows that you need them. But seek first his kingdom and his righteousness, and all these things will be given to you as well. Therefore do not worry about tomorrow, for tomorrow will worry about itself. Each day has enough trouble of its own.

MATTHEW 6:32-34 NIV

REFLECTIONS:

Never forget and always remember, we serve and follow the one who took almost nothing and fed thousands, not once, but twice. So, there's no need to worry. Jesus will provide if we are willing to pour all of ourselves into serving others. Wait for your fish and bread, your blessing is coming—just keep pouring into your serving.

REQUESTS:

Lord, forgive us when we only seek you in our comfortable places—places like our homes, our churches, and our jobs. Teach us to seek you in the grocery stores, or any store, or places we eat. You may have a blessing for us we may not see, whether it's someone in need or a special item on sale that we need but could not afford otherwise. Lord, I know you want to be in every aspect of our lives, so may our desires become more and more about seeking you than doing our own thing. Lord, bless my brothers beyond measure today with your peace and presence.

Lord, we love you and thank you for answering our prayers.
In Jesus' name. AMEN

DECEMBER - DAILY DEVOTIONAL #30

But you, man of God, flee from all this, and pursue righteousness, godliness, faith, love, endurance and gentleness. Fight the good fight of the faith. Take hold of the eternal life to which you were called when you made your good confession in the presence of many witnesses.

1 TIMOTHY 6:11-12 NIV

REFLECTIONS:

We'll soon start hearing about resolutions as the new year gets closer. Here is a resolution everyone should make: Pursue God more than we ever have before! How is that accomplished?

- Spending one more minute in prayer and in his presence than you did last year.
- Waiting a little longer for the answers you've prayed for instead of getting impatient and going your own way.

REQUESTS:

Lord, as the new year approaches, may you guide us to a year that is more about you and your desires for our lives than it is about ourselves and our selfish desires. May your light shine brighter through us as we seek you more. Just as more wood makes a bigger fire, more of your presence in our lives fuels a brighter light in us. Bless each of these men and their families with your glory shining upon them, and may your goodness be all around them.

Lord, we love you and thank you for answering our prayers.
In Jesus' name. AMEN

DECEMBER - DAILY DEVOTIONAL #31

When he had received the drink, Jesus said, "It is finished." With that, he bowed his head and gave up his spirit."

JOHN 19:30 NIV

REFLECTIONS:

Just as Jesus said, "It is finished," this year is finished. But we have an opportunity to take what we have learned this past year and use it to glorify God in the new year. Remember, God can use even the bad stuff for his good. So tomorrow, get up a little earlier and begin the year off right by seeking the Lord and his directions for the first day of the year, and then hit repeat every day afterward.

REQUESTS:

Lord, may we commit to seeking you more than we ever have this year, so we may grow in you more and more each day. Give my brothers eyes that look forward to even better days and not look back to remember the bad days from this year. May we be the hands and feet of Jesus and serve others more than we ever have.

Lord, we love you and thank you for answering our prayers.
In Jesus' name. AMEN

ABOUT THE AUTHOR

Timothy Sherrill was born in Brownwood, Texas. His family moved shortly after to Odessa, where his father worked in the oil fields. When Tim was five years old, he was diagnosed with dyslexia, and by age seven, he had repeated first grade, and his parents had gone through their first divorce.

His mother remarried, and Tim accepted Jesus as his Lord and Savior. And through the strength of the Holy Spirit, Tim told his mother about some abuse happening by the man who watched them whenever his mother and stepfather were out on dates. Tim's life changed again at age nine when the oil company that his father worked for bought a ranch down in Marathon, TX. His father threatened to take the boys away from their mother unless she divorced Tim's stepdad. And so they all moved as one big happy family to the ranch in Marathon, 30 miles from town.

Living on a ranch was just what Tim needed. Still, it wasn't all fabulous over the next six years. Tim faced probation for underage drinking and saw his parents break up repeatedly.

Still, God had a plan that became clear when Tim started junior

ABOUT THE AUTHOR

football. Before each football game, the team prayed *The Lord's Prayer*, reminding Tim of Jesus' sacrifice. And after each game, once again, the team recited *The Lord's Prayer*.

That's when Tim began to talk directly to God. When circumstances became really difficult, he would walk and cry out to God. Who could have guessed that the Lord heard him and worked in Tim's life!

At age 17, Tim's father left for good, and by age 19, his mom had remarried yet again. Their family also moved back to Odessa. For the first couple of years, Tim attended church and had even gone on some mission trips. Life was finally getting better. In fact, it was really great.

However, God asked Tim to do something unexpected one day, and at the time, it didn't make sense—God told Tim to forgive his dad. So, Tim began doing what he had witnessed while being raised: for the next six and a half years, he drank and was the "life of the party." Every day, after work, and even on his days off, Tim drank by himself or with his cowboy buddies. But the funny thing was, he never quit crying, and the drinking didn't ease his pain.

He prayed for safety and protection. And by this time, his mom and second stepdad had moved to Lamesa, Texas. His mom was added to their church's email, and so Tim would get the same prayer requests everyone else received. And he would pray for those requests.

God is a merciful and grateful Father, and He allowed Tim to stew a little bit in his drunkenness. Tim is living proof that God had heard Tim's prayers for protection even during his struggle with alcohol.

Eventually, Tim was led to a Jonah-like place where he had only one choice: to forgive his father! Since that day, along with his

ABOUT THE AUTHOR

wife, Tim has grown into a deeper relationship with the Lord. It has taken a lot of prayer, forgiveness toward others, and much forgiveness from his wife and children.

God started the prayer text with just a couple of friends texting scripture to each other. But now every morning it's like new manna: sharing scriptures and prayers with over 200 men. And the list continues to grow!

This book is only one year's worth of prayers sent via text messaging. Tim hopes that by reading the devotions, men will develop their own personal prayer time.

As Tim puts it in his own words: *"There is nothing special about me or my story. Everyone has a story, and maybe it's time to go tell yours! Even if I don't know you and you don't know me, we are brothers in Christ and I love you."*

Sincerely,
Tim Sherrill

www.ingramcontent.com/pod-product-compliance
Lightning Source LLC
Chambersburg PA
CBHW072001150426
43194CB00008B/958